LAUGHTER

SHORT CIRCUITS
Slavoj Žižek, Mladen Dolar, and Alenka Zupančič, editors

LAUGHTER
NOTES ON A PASSION

Anca Parvulescu

THE MIT PRESS CAMBRIDGE, MASSACHUSETTS LONDON, ENGLAND

MIT Press books may be purchased at special quantity discounts for business or sales promotional use. For information, please email special_sales@mitpress .mit.edu or write to Special Sales Department, The MIT Press, 55 Hayward Street, Cambridge, MA 02142.

This book was set in Joanna MT by Graphic Composition, Inc., Bogart, Georgia. Printed and bound in the United States of America.

Library of Congress Cataloging-in-Publication Data

Parvulescu, Anca.
    Laughter : notes on a passion / Anca Parvulescu.
      p.   cm. — (Short circuits)
    Includes bibliographical references and index.
    ISBN 978-0-262-51474-3 (pbk. : alk. paper) 1. Laughter—Social aspects.
2. Laughter—Psychological aspects. 3. Laughter in literature. I. Title.
BF575.L3P37 2010
152.4'3—dc22

                                  2009054314

10 9 8 7 6 5 4 3 2 1

For Laura

It is the past—the longest, deepest, hardest of pasts—that seems to surge up whenever we turn serious.

Friedrich Nietzsche

Contents

A short circuit occurs when there is a faulty connection in the network—faulty, of course, from the standpoint of the network's smooth functioning. Is not the shock of short-circuiting, therefore, one of the best metaphors for a critical reading? Is not one of the most effective critical procedures to cross wires that do not usually touch: to take a major classic (text, author, notion) and read it in a short-circuiting way, through the lens of a "minor" author, text, or conceptual apparatus ("minor" should be understood here in Deleuze's sense: not "of lesser quality," but marginalized, disavowed by the hegemonic ideology, or dealing with a "lower," less dignified topic)? If the minor reference is well chosen, such a procedure can lead to insights which completely shatter and undermine our common perceptions. This is what Marx, among others, did with philosophy and religion (short-circuiting philosophical speculation through the lens of political economy, that is to say, economic speculation); this is what Freud and Nietzsche did with morality (short-circuiting the highest ethical notions through the lens of the unconscious libidinal economy). What such a reading achieves is not a simple "desublimation," a reduction of the higher intellectual content to its lower economic or libidinal cause; the aim of such an approach is, rather, the inherent decentering of the interpreted text, which brings to light its "unthought," its disavowed presuppositions and consequences.

And this is what "Short Circuits" wants to do, again and again. The underlying premise of the series is that Lacanian psychoanalysis is a privileged instrument of such an approach, whose purpose is to illuminate a standard text or ideological formation, making it readable in a totally new way—the long history of Lacanian interventions in philosophy, religion, the arts (from the visual arts to the cinema, music, and literature), ideology, and politics justifies this premise. This, then, is not a new series of books on psychoanalysis, but a series of "connections in the Freudian field"—of short Lacanian interventions in art, philosophy, theology, and ideology. "Short Circuits" intends to revive a practice of reading which confronts a classic text, author, or notion with its own hidden presuppositions, and thus reveals its disavowed truth. The basic criterion for the texts that will be published is that they effectuate such a theoretical short circuit. After reading a book in this series, the reader should not simply have learned something new: the point is, rather, to make him or her aware of another—disturbing—side of something he or she knew all the time.

Slavoj Žižek

ACKNOWLEDGMENTS

In its first stages and well beyond that, this book benefited from the guidance of Paula Rabinowitz, John Mowitt, and Jani Scandura. Gratitude comes as an acutely inadequate response to the gift of their teaching.

I would like to acknowledge the help of those who read various drafts and otherwise helped move the project along: Derek Attridge, Étienne Balibar, J. Dillon Brown, Tili Boon Cuillé, Diane Davis, Mladen Dolar, Jan Golinski, Eleanor Kaufman, David Lawton, Joe Lowenstein, Steven Meyer, Eric Oberle, Jessica Rosenfeld, Vincent Sherry, Julia Walker, as well as SCAG. Little could have been done without the help of my most faithful and tough reader, Constantin (Tinu) Parvulescu.

My students have been generous interlocutors. I especially would like to thank the members of my Spring 2008 graduate seminar: James Deusterberg, Sandra Dinter, Katherine Fama, Steven Hoffmann, Dustin Iler, Nicholas Miller, May Peckham, and Aileen Waters. My undergraduate research assistants, Katherine Gaertner and Eric Rosenbaum, have done invaluable work.

The project benefited from the financial help of a number of fellowships. At University of Minnesota, I received a Thomas F. Wallace Fellowship, a Harold Leonard Memorial Fellowship in Film Study, and a Doctoral Dissertation Fellowship. A Norbert Elias Graduate Stipend in Marbach, Germany, allowed me to read Elias's unpublished work on laughter. A Barbara Thom Postdoctoral Fellowship at the Huntington Library helped me finish the writing. A short-term fellowship at the William Andrews Clark Memorial Library offered further time for research. Support from the Interdisciplinary Project in the Humanities and the Dean of Arts and Sciences office at Washington University helped with the illustrations.

Various short parts appeared in a different format in "To Die Laughing and to Laugh at Dying: Revisiting The Awakening" (New Literary History 36, no.

3 [2005], 477–495); "'So We Will Go Bad': Laughter, Women, Film" (*Camera Obscura* 21, no. 62 [2006], 144–167); and "The Professor's Desire: On Roland Barthes's *The Neutral*" (*Diacritics* 37, no. 1 [2007], 32–39).

Most importantly, there are those who share the laughter: Mulţumesc.

Introduction

Laughter is the only way out.

Georges Bataille

INCANTATION   It is 1909, the year when a remarkable statement sees the light of day. Velimir Khlebnikov, emerging but still unknown Russian futurist poet, publishes "Incantation by Laughter":

> O, laugh, laughers!
> O, laugh out, laughers!
> You who laugh with laughs, you who laugh it up laughishly
> O, laugh out laugheringly
> O, belaughable laughterhood—the laughter of laughering laughers!
> O, unlaugh it outlaughingly, belaughering laughists!
> Laughily, laughily,
> Uplaugh, enlaugh, laughlings, laughlings
> Laughlets, laughlets.
> O, laugh, laughers!
> O, laugh out, laughers![1]

It is the beginning of a century in which many laughing voices respond to Khlebnikov's insistent call, "Laugh, laughers!" Retrospectively, the poem appears as an aesthetic event, one of the documents through which an emerging twentieth century announces its investment in laughter, if somewhat belatedly.

Khlebnikov's poem starts from language, it makes use of language, but it gradually disposes of it, to retain only a sound. The poem is improvising on *smekh*, the Russian word for "laughter." The word as such appears only in the title, when it is "invoked." The rest of the poem is a variation on *smekh*, stretching, bending, twisting it in unpredictable ways. It could be said that Khlebnikov's experiment results in a new familial idiom of laughter (a new *zaum*), which includes "laughers," "laughists," and a "laughterhood," who "enlaugh" and "uplaugh," all "laugheringly."[2] What is at stake here, however, is precisely not the new, extravagant idiom, but an imagined beyond. The word *smekh* is a threshold toward this beyond.

The *kh* sounds in *smekh* are onomatopoeic. Something of the very sound of laughter has seeped into the word, which is only partially arbitrary or unmotivated, having been remotivated through an affective correlation between the sound of the signifier and that of its elusive signified. Khlebnikov's poem exploits the idea that if one repeats the word enough times—thirty-one times, to be exact—every time with a small difference, laugh upon laugh, on the model of a painting playing with nuances of the same color, one summons "the real thing," its realness a function of a barely perceptible minimal difference. It is as if the poet is striving to capture a forgotten secret, remnants of which, he intuits, persist in the magic sound of laughter. The poem is trying to enchant its readers into laughter by touching them with the ticklish feather of the word "laughter." The occlusive, guttural *khs* of *smekh* (also of *hlæhhan* and *hlahhen*, ancestors of the English *laugh* and the German *Lachen*, respectively) blow a breath of laughter over a reader whom they hope to instantaneously enliven.

As an incantation, Klebnikov's poem is witness and participant in a trend that hopes to find the real of laughter in an imagined "before" of folk traditions and sacred rituals. It is a movement backward toward a less civilized laughter that, ideally, laughs laughingly. One incants laughter, in the same way one incants the name of a god, in the hope that, through repetition, laughter can magically be brought into the present of the incantator. One repeats the word *smekh*, each time with a small difference, the very insistence of the repetition touching on something like the word's sacred kernel, imagined to be safely lodged in its sound, in the fabric of its onomatopoeic sound combinations.[3] For Khlebnikov, the incantation is at the same time a means of avoiding the "I" of the poet, as the incantator (usually a child) speaks magical words that do not belong to her. The poet effaces himself behind the incantation, whose words have lost all originality and seem to repeat themselves magically.

Importantly, the incantation is also an imperative: "Laugh, laughers!" The time of the poem is that of an imperative, a radical present. The exclamation point of "laugh!" marks a "now." The poem acquires qualities of a manifesto, conjuring a laughterhood of laughers. Coming in 1909, it is an appeal to the laughers of the world, a fictive collective it itself creates. But even as it fashions itself on the genre of the manifesto, the poem does not become a program. No "we" utterances follow the constitutive appeal to laughers, who in fact never become a "we." The laughers of the laughterhood are called upon to laugh but not project an identity beyond the minimal bond of the word "laughers," even less a future or a cause. The response to the call "Laugh, laughers!"—the laughers' *yes*—is imagined by the poem as a laugh, a *yes-laugh*. The poem creates a collective of laughers loyal to the *yes* of laughter, their first sound (a multiple first: there is never a single burst in laughter).

An important dimension of the century Khlebnikov's poem can be said to inaugurate—the laughing twentieth century—will have been that of a preoccupation with listening. The new century took it upon itself to listen to a secret Khlebnikov's poem glimpsed in echoes of a laugh. If, following Alain Badiou's recent encounter with it, the century is to be imagined as a beast, subjectivized as "the century," the question is: What kind of beast has it been? What passions have tormented it? In 1909, Khlebnikov's poem came to announce that one of the century's passions will have been the passion of laughter. In Khlebnikov's poem, laughter is a variation on what Badiou calls "the passion for the real," which brings forth the real's own passion for the present, with its joys and horrors. Badiou writes: "Is there or is there not within the century a will aimed at forcing art to extract from the mines of reality, by means of willful artifice, a real mineral, hard as diamond?"[4] In the twentieth century, art would indeed take up the task of extracting, through a range of artifices, bits of the real (or fantasies thereof) out of the mines of reality. Laughter, its very sound, is such a bit. In Khlebnikov's poem, the poet, imagining himself as an exceptional guardian of the secrets of the real, incants it (this is his artifice) in the hope of actually reaching it.

LAUGHING AT Khlebnikov's poem may draw a few laughs from its reader, but it is not necessarily funny. Khlebnikov is interested in laughter, which he locates in its sound; the laughing subject, the laugher; and a possible collective formed around laughter, a laughterhood. He does not, however, ask why laughers laugh or what the object of their laughter might be. They simply laugh, repeatedly and in bursts.

Taking its cue from Khlebnikov, this book leaves the old question of what makes us laugh behind. Instead, the focus here is the burst of laughter itself. Most "theories of laughter" are not concerned with laughter.[5] They conceive of it as a response to something else, and it is this something else that they are after—the comic, jokes, humor, the grotesque, the ridiculous, the ludicrous, etc. The turn or, rather, return to laughter is invested in questions of a different sort: What does the body in laughter look like? How does laughter sound? What is the time of laughter? Where, in what places, is it likely to burst? What does it mean for two or more people to laugh together? What work (or unwork) does laughter do? Most importantly, what kind of subjects are we when we laugh? What does it mean to be a laugher, to anchor one's subjectivity, however provisionally, in "I laugh, therefore I am (or am not)"? This, of course, is not to divorce laughter from any potential trigger. Jokes make us laugh, but in many of the contexts explored here, as in Khlebnikov's poem, there is no joke and the question of laughter's cause or origin is beside the point.

What we call "theories of laughter" share a focus on the object of laughter. Laughter is laughter *at*, and critical attention has concentrated on what follows the preposition. Crucial here is the Aristotelian premise that laughter is a reaction to something ugly or improper yet not producing pain. We laugh at such objects ("funny," we call them today), on condition that they are harmless. Aristotle's paradigmatic example: "The mask, for instance, that excites laughter is something ugly and distorted without causing pain."[6] Laughing within the comic situation, we laugh at masks and masklike objects which do not arouse our pity. Aristotle's definition is the most important point of reference for writing on comedy in classic and modern times. In the wake of this definition, critics have conceived of their task in terms of unpacking the range of the "ugly" and the "harmless" in the laughable object.

Aristotle started from a strong premise: no animal laughs, except man.[7] This statement has led to a long tradition in which man becomes a laughing animal, such that what laughs is human and what is human can laugh. Laughter is proper to man, marking the minimal threshold between the human and the animal. We *are* animals—with a small yet crucial difference. Laughter is one in a series of properties invoked as this minimal difference, a catalog that offers something to hold on to whenever the human risks contamination with the nonhuman. The list of such markers includes rationality, speech, emotion, work, dress, verticality, relation to temporality, death, the impossible, or our very bestiality. As an element in this series, laughter differentiates the human from its nonhuman other, whether the animal (the question of whether some animals, like the dog, can laugh needs to be understood in this context),[8] the child (the debate as to at what stage the child laughs a "true laughter" is framed around this issue),[9] the divine (the theological question of whether Christ laughed belongs here),[10] or the technological (can robots laugh?).

Henri Bergson gave us the modern version of Aristotle's premise in his well-known 1900 essay, *Laughter*. Aristotle meets industrialization here such that, when Bergson attempts to explain laughter in relation to a laughable object, he argues that we laugh at the mechanical inelasticity of our fellow human beings, at what has come to pass for human. Bergson proposes that we reverse the Aristotelian premise and say not that man is a laughing animal but that he is a laughable animal.[11] We describe a landscape as beautiful or charming or insignificant, but not as laughable. Likewise, we do not laugh at animals, except when we identify a human trait in them. Only man is laughable. The proper object of laughter is man.

Within Bergson's sociological exercise, laughter is the gesture of a group, necessarily a closed group, responding to an exigency of life in common. Laughter acquires a very precise social function and utility. Faced with the mechanized, clocklike rigidity of the human, defined by Bergson as the pliable and adaptable animal, we respond with a forceful gesture. Laughter is this gesture. Its role is to correct the assembly-line behavior of our neighbor, which Bergson perceives as an eccentricity. According to Bergson, the deployment of this corrective laugh is necessarily accompanied by a momentary "anesthesia of the heart," laughter appealing strictly to the intelligence.[12]

If the passionate, objectless laughter of Khlebnikov's poem could be said to be a response, it would be a laughing response to Bergson's essay. Closer to Bergson, it was, however, Georges Bataille who laughed passionately upon reading Bergson's essay. It is an important burst for the story we will be tracing here, because, as we will see, it is through Bataille that the twentieth century laughed its most distinct laugh. If the question is "How did the twentieth century laugh?" any attempt to answer this question has to listen to Bataille's laughter and its range of echoes. Bataille confirms Khlebnikov's intuition that laughter is to be considered in terms of who or what laughs and not in terms of the object laughed at. Laughter is not a response, at least not an unproblematic response, certainly not a mere effect. With Bataille, it becomes clear that thinking about the laughing subject tells us about laughter, but also that thinking about laughter tells us about subjectivity more generally.[13] Laughter is an opening in which a self unfolds.

If an "enemy" is to be found here, it is a certain kind of seriousness. After all, guardians of the prohibition on certain laughs are the *agelasts* (from *a-gelos*, non-laughers), heralds of a heavy seriousness.[14] They do not laugh, and do their best to muffle the laughs of those around them. Historically, seriousness, in its official tone and respectable dress, has intimidated, demanded, prohibited, oppressed. It has established values and rules of appropriate behavior. Slowly, they would become flesh, habits of a sedentary body. The serious man (*homo seriosus*) displays a dogmatic solemnity in language, gesture, face, and tone. He has made the slogan "Thou shall not laugh" his aegis. His mouth is closed, the very mark of seriousness. Think, Bataille invites us, of "the narrow constipation of a strictly human attitude, the magisterial look of a face with a *closed mouth*, as beautiful as a safe."[15] This closed mouth, safeguarding its precious gains, often covered in a subtle smile, accompanies seriousness in its pursuit of its projects. The opening of the mouth into loud, passional laughter is a revolt against seriousness. If laughter could be called a project, it would be a project against deep, heavy, oppressive seriousness.[16] For to live seriously, the society of the friends of laughter will have decreed, is to live in bad faith. Seriousness is a function of gravity (*gravitas*), a matter of oppressive weight, a lead-effect, pulling one down when, like the proverbial witch, one wants to fly.

PASSION In the company of twentieth-century laughers like Khlebnikov and Bataille, this book takes us back to the context in which the early modern world talked about laughter: the passions. Most of the laughs in this book are extravagant, loud, insolent; laughs that explode suddenly, shatter the normality of the face, convulsively shake the body, confuse, embarrass, and produce a loud, discordant sound. They are passional laughs, to be reconnected to a tradition of writing on the passions.

Despite the association of "passion" with, on the one hand, "the passion of Christ," and therefore with suffering and martyrdom, and, on the other, with erotic passion (love, jealousy, etc.), the passions are the ancestors of all our emotions, feelings, and sentiments. Historians of the passions tend to restrict the use of the term to the seventeenth and eighteenth centuries, but the passions do not simply die out to make room for our more delicate and more social inner states. Rather, the passions haunt our emotions and their specter comes to haunt the twentieth century. What Badiou makes visible at the very heart of the century is, after all, "the *passion* for the real."

Today it might feel somewhat counterintuitive to think about laughter as a passion, but most early modern theorists of the passions—La Chambre, Descartes, Hobbes, Spinoza, Malebranche—included a discussion of laughter in their treatises on the passions. Significantly, for Hobbes, laughter is not a passion in itself, although it is thought worthy of a separate entry on his list of passions. Laughter is only the sign of a passion (a passion without a name, as Hobbes puts it initially). It nonetheless acquires passional qualities negatively, through the perceived need to soften or diffuse the excessive nature of its burst. For both Descartes and Spinoza, on the other hand, laughter is a passion in itself even as it is also explained as a sign of other passions. The two positions are symptomatic here, as laughter in fact oscillates between being a passion in its own right and the outward manifestation ("expression") of other passions.

What is lost in the historical passage from passions to emotions and then further to feelings, sentiments, and moods is not only the class-determined coarseness and violence of the passions, but also the event-like quality of a passion like laughter. Importantly, when the list of passions is sifted into a list of emotions, although most names of passions are retained, laughter is left behind (there is an "emotion of" anger but no "emotion of" laughter). Laughter does not become an emotion and its surviving, civilized forms need to be explained as signs of other passions-turned-emotions, whether fear, cruelty, nervousness, or benevolence.

In the realm of emotions, the passional burst of laughter is out of place. This does not mean that laughter disappears as such, or that it ceases to be the object of intense discussion. It means only that from now on it is in different contexts that it is discussed. One such context is the discourse on manners and its attendant, ever-growing conduct book market. In the eighteenth and nineteenth centuries, conduct books continue some of the work done by the discourse on passions in the name of the untouchable self-control imperative. Excessive, passional, uncontrollable laughter is a *faux pas* in the discourse on manners. The counterpoint to this position is offered by another important context for the discussion of laughter, the debate on satire and caricature and their political potential. Here, the critical focus is on the rhetorical uses of laughter.[17] Acknowledging that the ability to make one's political opponent the butt of laughter is a key political weapon, the debate focuses on the ethical concerns raised by this realization.

As for the discourse on passions, it moves on to the refinement of emotions, sentiments, and feelings. We speak of these inner states, however, only once we have ostracized the passions.[18] The story traced here is that of the ostracizing of the passions as the prohibition on certain kinds of laughs. What emerges from laughter's archive is a distinction between legitimate and illegitimate laughs and a prohibition on excessive, extravagant, open-mouthed, loud forms of laughter. And, since the passions and their "expression" (the movement of passion on the face and the body) go hand in hand, inappropriate passional laughs translate into inappropriate configurations of the body and the face, which are ostracized alongside certain laughs.

The "falling into disrepute" of laughter, as Nietzsche calls it, is anchored at the point where the history of noise meets the history of the grimacing face.[19] Here, the noisy, contorted face in laughter is slowly corrected into a calm, silent smile, imagined as the sign of a range of commingled, sophisticated, soft, social emotions. This book traces the process whereby conduct books, in dialog with philosophical treatises, literary texts, and visual culture, produce a normative aesthetics of the smiling face. One of its main arguments is that smiling and laughing do not occur on a continuum. We most often smile when we cannot laugh; and a smile rarely develops into a genuine laugh. In fact, the "civilizing of laughter" is simultaneous with the production of the modern smile.

It is not an accident that Norbert Elias worked on an unfinished "Essay on Laughter."[20] Elias knew that a focus on laughter does not simply repeat or strengthen the argument of *The Civilizing Process*, but rather twists it in important ways. Despite a clear prohibition against certain kinds of laughs, and in part because of it, the passion of laughter "returns" repeatedly, such that, in the twentieth century, one can find a range of passional laughs, remnants of passion in a world of emotion. Bataille and Michel Foucault make it clear that prohibitions are in a dialectical relation with their transgression. Not only do they posit—indeed, induce—transgression, but this transgression remains in the horizon of the prohibition. And yet, as Bataille shows, there is a point, a limit point, where the passional burst of laughter exceeds and displaces the vicious circle of prohibition and transgression.

Elias's draft for his "Essay on Laughter" sheds new light on "the civilizing process," while also proposing a "change of problem" in the scholarship on laughter. Elias studied the "theories of laughter," from Hobbes to Kant to Darwin to Freud, but found that they reach an impasse. The question asked, essentially that of the interior "feeling" that causes the external "expression of laughter," coupled with a search for the stimulus leading to that feeling, is misconceived. Laughter is not simply the "accessory of an internal event." In other words, laughter is a passion in itself, not only a sign of other passions. It is time, Elias's essay argues, to ask the question of laughter differently. If laughter can be said to be anything, it is a specific facial and respiratory configuration. This is its only peculiar specificity. Elias puts aside the respiratory dimension of laughter, to focus on the face: "The problem of laughter is inextricably bound up with the problem of the human face." If man is a laughing animal, his specificity as a laugher is bound up with his specificity as an animal with a face.[21]

This is not, as it might appear, a simple return to a physiological definition of laughter. Elias enlists anatomy in what he calls his "voyage of detection," but only as one of the discourses at work here. Elias proposes an exercise in defamiliarization: "if one stands back for a moment and looks at the human face as if for the first time, several rather surprising things seem to happen to our perception." It is not the face at rest we are invited to study, but "the face in action." What we will then be able to see is "the strangeness of the human face," a function of the strangeness of the human more generally. And this strange man does not *have* a face; man *is* a face. The civilizing process turns out to have been a "machine of faciality." The phrase has become associated with the names of Gilles Deleuze and Félix Guattari, but it was in the sociological milieu of the early to mid-twentieth century that the face became visible as such.[22] Elias entered into a conversation with Georg Simmel and Erving Goffman on the social, political, and aesthetic dimensions of the face.[23] Coupled with the evidence of the "civilizing of laughter," Elias's focus on the face draws attention to the fact that the dialectic of smiling and laughing offers a key to the understanding of processes of facialization and defacialization.

MOUTH To begin again: A mouth opens. Not to speak, which is what a mouth does for the most part when it opens. Not to breathe, although air will be passing vehemently through it. A certain sound becomes perceptible, apparently the sound of a rhythmic breathing, but also much more, a sonorous noise. The mouth insists in this opening, lips parting, exuberantly displaying the mouth's tissues, fluids, tongue, and teeth. The face, otherwise a stable form, is now disturbed, contorted, formless. What initially appears like a momentary interruption of both soundscape and visual form continues, rhythmically, often convulsively, possibly *ad infinitum*.

At its most basic, laughter is this rhythmic opening of a mouth. Laughter sonorously opens the mouth, one in a series of orifices of the body and the paradigmatic opening of the face. Laughter is one of the extra-reasonable, animal-like activities of the mouth, alongside eating, breathing, spitting, or kissing. But the laughing mouth is also singular in that its mode of opening is unique. There is no incorporation of an object involved in laughter (as in eating), no expulsion (as in spitting or vomiting), nor a simple combination of the two (as in breathing). Likewise, there is no contact with an other, at least not immediately (as in kissing).

In laughter, the mouth opens, its "inside" touching the "outside," as if it wanted to speak or "communicate," and yet what is communicated is only the very opening of the mouth, its gaping. It is important to note that the word "mouth" refers to three locations of the human head: it is the opening itself, the orifice; the cavity behind this opening; and the outside of the orifice, the lips and surrounding cheeks. The mouth—inside, outside, and threshold— bears witness to the fact that the inside of the body is always also outside. Skin, the envelope wrapping the body and isolating it from its outside, is exposed as one of the body's fictions. Performing the structure of inside/ outside and in charge of both logos and animal functions, the open mouth is the site of an incommensurable "quasi-union."[24] It is not an accident that the mouth has been considered the organ most associated with passion, and thus with the quasi-union of body and soul.

Aristotle considered the diaphragm or midriff, which he thought responsible for the convulsions of laughter, to be the separating wall or fence between the animal parts of the body and the intellectual ones. As a convulsion of the diaphragm, laughter bursts on this fence between the lower and upper parts of the body, the nonplace where they intermix.[25] While Aristotle conveniently separated things at the level of the human trunk, he could not draw a dividing line *within* the mouth, which remains multifunctional and polyvocal, the mouth of sense and the mouth of the senses at the same time. The mouth is the threshold where the two dwell in common, often convulsively. There is something "mouth-like" about the subject formed by this "quasi-union."[26]

It is as if the opening of the mouth in laughter comes to remind us that the mouth has two Latin names: *os* and *bucca*. There is a mouth of orality and a mouth of buccality.[27] *Os/oris* is the ancestor of *oral* and *orality*. *Os* is the mouth, whether open or closed, connected to the voice and speaking. *Os* also means "face," "countenance," "expression," and "mask." The mouth it stands for is in fact often used as the metonymy of the face. As such, *os* is also "figure," figuring speech but also the other activities of the mouth on the model of speech. As for *bucca*, it is the more "primitive" mouth of breathing, sucking, eating. Always-already open, *bucca* is a rictus of the face. *Bucca* deforms the face. The first intuition is that laughter is buccal, not oral. But in fact things cannot be divided so neatly. The other mouthlike opening of the female body is *os* (one of the entries in the OED for *os* is "opening into the vagina"). This "thankless mouth" is "oral," even if it does not speak and is therefore necessarily ungrateful. And yet when we invoke what would seem to be an adjacent space, "the mouth of darkness," also a site of obscure, faceless activities, we invoke *bucca*. It is as if the mouth insists on remaining both *os* and *bucca*, a quasi-mixture of logos, verticality, and the light of the face, and animalism, cavity, and defaced darkness.

But does laughter come from the mouth? It is not at all clear. Jacques Derrida writes: "We must have a mouth for laughs and for laughing. Surely, we can laugh with our eyes [*on peut rire des yeux*], but it is difficult (even if not impossible) to imagine a human being laughing without something like an opening [*orifice*] other than the eyes. The opening in question may be presently visible and significant in the burst of laughter, or it may not; it is indispensable. For laughter as for so many other things, more than one opening is needed [*il faut plus d'un orifice*]."[28] As we will see, laughter is indeed produced through more than one opening of the body and addresses multiple senses of receiving bodies. Sight, hearing, smell are involved in laughter; and therefore eyes, ears, mouth, nose, to stay for now only with the face. Importantly for conversations on vision and modernity, the laughing eye becomes mouthlike, its eyelids lips touching each other, as in a kiss, rather than palisades closing to block intruders, to close shop, as it were.[29]

But laughter is not content to only touch the eye, even this mouthlike eye. Jean-Luc Nancy writes:

> Laughter bursts [*le rire éclate*] at the multiple limit of the senses and of language, uncertain of the sense to which it is offered—to the sight of color, to the touch of the mouth, to the hearing of the burst, and to the sense without meaning of its own voice [*au sens sans signification de sa propre voix*]. Laughter is the joy of the senses, and of sense, at their limit. In this joy, the senses touch each other and touch language, the tongue in the mouth [*Dans cette joie, les sens se touchent entre eux, et ils touchent au langage, à la langue dans la bouche*]. But this touch itself puts space between them [*Mais ce toucher lui-même les espace*]. They do not penetrate one another, there is no "art," still less a "total" art. But neither is there "laughter," as a sublime truth withdrawn from art itself. There are only bursts of laughter [*Il n'y a que des éclats de rire*].[30]

The limit of the senses, the laughing limit where the senses touch, for Nancy is also the limit of sense. After all, laughter is also a function of the voice, and thus necessarily in close proximity to language.

And yet the bodily origin of the laughing voice *qua* voice is itself enigmatic. The voice is acousmatic: it makes itself heard without its source being visible.[31] It looks as if the voice is coming out of the mouth, but in fact it is clear that we do not know where it comes from. In no other case is this clearer than when we laugh. Without an "origin," the laughing voice issues from a place in the body that goes deeper than the mouth. We speak of a "throaty laugh." We also speak of a "belly laugh." But although the throat may lend laughter some of its "grain," and the belly may be its resonance chamber, their status as the home of laughter remains elusive. At its most basic, laughter is breath, a sonorous column of air traveling through the body, without it being possible to assign a visual point of origin for its burst. Mladen Dolar suggests that every emission of the voice is a form of ventriloquism, a consequence of its acousmatic character.[32] This explains our reactions upon hearing a recording of our own laughter: our laughs can never be a match for who or what we think we are.

Where, then, does laughter come from? Nothing is less certain. The laughing voice remains rigorously acousmatic while participating in the disfiguring of the mouth.

It is important to emphasize, as Nancy does, that there is no "sublime truth" of laughter, withdrawn from "art." It is in fact only from within language, or rather at its limit, a limit exposed by the artifices of art, that we can hope to listen to echoes of laughter. As one such artifice, Khlebnikov's poem exploits the onomatopoeic dimension of the Russian word for laughter, challenging its reader to hear, in language, something that is no longer language. If Saussure argued that, unlike symbols, linguistic signs are arbitrary in the sense of being unmotivated, Khlebnikov's poem seems to be objecting vehemently. Saussure responded to such anticipated objections by arguing that, even if one acknowledges the symbolic origins of some "authentic onomatopoeia," once they enter language and in order for them to function as words, they lose their "suggestive sonority." On Khlebnikov's side, Derrida argued for the possibility of remotivation.[33] Remotivation works on words whose sound "strikes the ear" in certain ways and exploits an affective investment in this sound. The words thus reawakened end up contaminating their linguistic milieu, which becomes "relatively motivated" and inductive of further "onomatopoeia effects."[34] In Khlebnikov's poem, it is as if the very sound of laughter has seeped into the signifier, allowing us to laugh a little when we say the word "laughter." It is only through such art and its "artifices" that one can hope to touch on laughter.

THE LAST AVANT-GARDES As the names of Derrida and Nancy indicate, this book is also committed to the project of tracing an unconventional history of what we have come to call poststructuralism, and its relation to other twentieth-century intellectual and artistic movements. On the Anglo-American academic scene, we have identified this community of texts along structuralist/poststructuralist lines, but there are signs that we are learning to approach them somewhat differently. According to Badiou, what makes this generation of philosophers a generation is a fragile coherence around the insistence of a question, a set of common readings, a specific attitude to writing, and the exposure to the same political urgency.[35] Its actors also present us with a particular kind of intellectual community, which, perhaps appropriately, can be grasped as such only at the moment of its vanishing. What this book adds to this conversation is the suggestion that what brought this generation of very singular thinkers together is also the sharing of a friend in Bataille, and, through him, an exposure to a communal passion: laughter.

It was Walter Benjamin who, in an untimely fashion, can be said to have set the tone for what was to become a fascination with the promise of laughter. In 1934, Benjamin wrote "The Author as Producer," the essay that put forth his ideas about engaged art. The "engaged artist" he addresses here, whom Sartre would approach under the rubric of the "engaged intellectual," would become the "philosopher-writer-combatant" of the second half of the twentieth century.[36] In this context, Benjamin declares: "there is no better starting point for thought than laughter; speaking more generally, spasms of the diaphragm generally offer better chances for thought than spasms of the soul."[37] What the engaged artist is urged to do is return to art's "opportunity to expose the present."[38] Pointing to Bertolt Brecht's epic theater as exemplary, Benjamin argues that one does not do this by inducing feelings in the audience, including feelings of revolt. Rather, the goal is to "alienate the audience in a lasting manner, through thought, from the conditions in which it lives."[39] This leads Benjamin to the statement above: "Let me remark, by the way, that there is no better starting point for thought than laughter. . . . Epic theatre is lavish only in the occasions it offers for laughter."[40] The sentence comes as a digression ("by the way"), and yet what appears as a mere addition is also a concrete starting point. Art's goal is to alienate its audience from the conditions in which it lives; and it can do this by creating opportunities for thought-provoking spasms of the diaphragm, which promise to expose the laugher to the present. We have moved from "feelings" to "spasms." These spasms of laughter function not unlike Descartes's passion of wonder, to which Benjamin alludes when he describes the disclosure of the present as an "astonishment," Descartes's definition of excessive wonder.[41] Nothing more and nothing less is, then, at stake for Benjamin in laughter than the beginning of thought in something that seems to be of a completely different order—a spasm of the body.

The strongest formulation of the promise of laughter in the generation of writers and philosophers we call poststructuralist would come with Michel Foucault's opening paragraph to *The Order of Things*:

> This book first arose out of a passage in Borges, out of the laughter that shattered, as I read the passage, all the familiar landmarks of my thought [*le rire qui secoue à sa lecture toutes les familiarités de la pensée*]—our thought, the thought that bears the stamp of our age and our geography—breaking up [*ébranlant*] all the ordered surfaces and all the planes with which we are accustomed to tame the wild profusion of existing things, and continuing long afterwards to disturb and threaten with collapse [*faisant vaciller et inquiétant*] our age-old distinction between the Same and the Other.[42]

Laughter shatters and breaks and disturbs. It is not Foucault, you will have noticed in the French formulation, who laughs. The only thing that Foucault, his "I," can be said to be doing is read. Laughter laughs Foucault's thought, which, emphasis added, is *our* thought, the thought of a particular age and geography, of a particular "order of things." What this laughter brings, what it makes space for within our undifferentiated familiarity, is something Foucault condenses around the word "Other." Foucault describes the experience as unsettling: "This passage from Borges kept me laughing for a long time, though not without a certain uneasiness that I found hard to shake off."[43] Reading this passage, Michel de Certeau describes Foucault's uneasiness in terms of his being "overtaken by laughter, seized by an irony of things equivalent to an illumination."[44] The illuminative experience seems to reveal "the irony of things" within the "order of things." It is, as de Certeau puts it, a certain "experience of disappropriation" that laughter announces. Foucault is disappropriated; his thought is not his property. He is at the mercy of laughter, engulfed in laughter.

Firmly situated in the avant-garde of unintentionalism, Foucault found himself wondering: Where does *The Order of Things* come from? What are its conditions of possibility? What is its "situation"? More generally, in Benjamin's terms, what is the starting point of thought? In an attempt to answer these questions, Foucault recalled that at the beginning there was reading, and with reading came a burst of laughter. Peal after peal of laughter, accompanied by a hard-to-shake-off uneasiness. It all began with this burst of laughter. Not much of an answer, laughter-skeptics will say. What would it mean, Foucault's passage seems to insist, to take this answer, as we say, "seriously"? What would it mean to risk the proposal that the situation of new thought (and perhaps of the new more generally) is a burst of laughter?

On the terrain of the theoretical writing of the last decades of the twentieth century, the answer to this question has most often mobilized one or more in a series of conceptual figures: *kairos* (a modality of time), the middle voice (a matter of grammatical voice and a modality of action), *khōra* (a question of gender in relation to the two). They are neighboring concepts, some of their components overlapping over a zone (*zone de voisinage*) that resonates with laughter.[45]

When it comes to the time of laughter, Benjamin, like Khlebnikov, unambiguously imagines laughter, that spasm of the diaphragm, bursting into a radical present. Associated with other "passions of the present," especially joy and wonder, laughter is very much of the "now." It thus needs to be reconnected to that famous Greek word, *kairos* ("the right, opportune moment"). Having begun as a rhetorical term, *kairos* traveled into political philosophy, where it helps conceptualize the bursting of the present as "time for revolution."[46] *Kairos* implies that one talks or acts at the right, decisive, urgent moment, but not because one seizes the moment; rather, the moment seizes the subject. Time is ripe for things to happen. A caesura in chronological time, this is still a time within time, acquiring, however, a different quality. Time contracts. Time is "filled full" with "now," and it bursts. When it comes to laughter, in a certain sense one always laughs at the right time.[47] Most often, this "right time" is in fact acutely "inopportune" within the situation in which it bursts, and it is "opportune" only within the horizon it opens up itself.[48] What the burst of laughter bursts is time itself, producing a subject at the crossroads of freedom (laughter's "spontaneity") and necessity (its "overwhelming" quality). Laughter is a moment of affirmation, a *yes* to "now" as the time of a kairotic burst.

One is "swept" by laughter; "overwhelmed" by laughter; one is "cracking up" in laughter; one is "breaking up" in laughter; one "drowns" in laughter; one "faints" with laughter; one laughs until one "splits"; one "dies" laughing. Consider two of Milan Kundera's characters in *The Book of Laughter and Forgetting* attempting to enter a "battle" with laughter: "They were too weak. Laughter was stronger. Their bodies began quaking uncontrollably."[49] In part through its association with *kairos*, laughter risks triggering anxious thoughts of passivity. But if this is the case, Émile Benveniste reminds us that instead of an opposition between active and passive, Indo-European languages have historically known a triple distinction between active, middle, and passive. This distinction has subsequently developed into a symmetry, only initially not between active and passive, but between active and middle. Here is Benveniste: "passive is a modality of the middle. From which it proceeds and with which it keeps close ties even when it has reached the state of a distinct category."[50] Of interest here is the relation subject-action which the middle voice presupposes: "the middle indicates only a certain relationship of the action with the subject, or an 'interest' of the subject in the action."[51] The subject, in other words, is not the agent of an action exterior to it, but has an "interest" in the action. Through the action, the subject "achieves something which is being achieved in him—being born, lying [helpless or dead], imagining, growing, etc. The subject is somewhat 'inside' the process of which he is the agent."[52] To say that the subject has an "interest" in the action of the verb is to say that it "participates" in the action without predicating it. This is the relation between the subject of laughter and the action of laughing; like the subject of "dying" and "imagining" (with which it keeps its ties), the laugher is "interested" in laughter and "participates" in it.

What of the feminine overtones that come with the suspicion of passivity? The middle voice leads to an engagement with another important term for the thought of the generation we call poststructuralist: khōra ("place," "location," "region," "country"), around which questions of femininity are often posed. Coming from Plato's Timaeus, khōra is the prehistorical, asubjective, nontheological, nonplace needed to think the relation between the two categories of creation, the visible and the intelligible. Khōra needs to be there, to support their work, and yet it has no attribute that allows it to "be" itself. It is well known that Julia Kristeva connects chora (using the established spelling, by way of drawing attention to the long history of uses and abuses of the term in the philosophical tradition) to laughter, and the laughter of the mother specifically.

Drawing on Plato's metaphors of chora as mother or "imprint bearer," Kristeva proposes we revisit the term by reconsidering the relation between mother and infant child. In the first weeks of its life, the infant (ungendered animate "it") puts forth an invocation (in-vocāre), sending its very voice as a message of sorts. The mother receives the invocation; she acknowledges a call, which she does not perceive as a demand. The mother in fact becomes mother through this invocation; she fashions herself as mother on the voice she receives. Specifically, on Kristeva's account, what the mother receives is a laugh, voice as laughter and laughter as voice. This is not to say that the infant laughs. It is the dual "it" that the mother and child form at this stage that laughs.[53] This "it" is the space-time of a laughing voice. Regardless of how we settle the temporality of this scene, Kristeva's suggestion is that in this space-time the voice "scores a point: laughter."[54] "It" laughs.

Kristeva's argument is that we occasionally access chora synchronically— through laughter. Our bursts of laughter are a memorial to chora. The mother in us laughs again. If Derrida too, in spite of his desire to move beyond "all anthropomorphy,"[55] refers to the "gaping mouth of the quasi-banned discourse on khōra,"[56] Kristeva goes a step further, to hear the sound of laughter coming out of what Derrida calls the "cleavage" or "yawning gulf" of the choral "gaping mouth."[57] Derrida's question "Who are you, Khōra?" seems to point to a gaping mouth, laughing. This mouth does not need to be anthropomorphized, attached to a face or other facialized parts of the human body.

A mouth can be just a mouth, an opening for the insistence of laughter. "I've often seen a cat without a grin," thought Alice. "But a grin without a cat!" Kristeva nevertheless finds promise in the body *qua* body—nothing else, she knows from Mikhail Bakhtin, than a series of openings/gaping mouths, a place-making mechanism for laughter.[58]

It was Kristeva who, perhaps because of her work on *chora*, was most explicit about the centrality of laughter to the thought of her generation: "Every practice that produces something new (a new device) is a practice of laughter: it obeys laughter's logic and provides the subject with laughter's advantages. When practice is not laughter, there is nothing new, practice cannot be provoking: it is at best a repeated, empty act."[59] In the beginning there is laughter; it all begins with a burst of laughter. God must have laughed while creating the world—or, indeed, while "imagining" the very idea of a "world," a familiar image in many cosmologies.[60] Kristeva concluded: "Laughter is thus merely the *witness of a process* which remains the privileged experience of the 'artist': a sovereignty (of the subject and of meaning, but also of history) that is simultaneously assumed and undermined."[61] For the philosophical avant-gardes of the second half of the twentieth century, laughter was a means of thinking about temporality, action, and gender—in the same burst. Laughter's time is that of the force of *kairos*. The laugher is a passional "it," laughing in the middle voice. What laughter does is squeeze *chora* into a burst, a moment to be repeated in moments of imagination like the beginning of *The Order of Things*. The agency of the laugher is to be understood on the order of "participation": we participate in laughter. Glossing Bataille, the actors here insisted that this is no small thing: participation is also the order of our engagement in what we used to call "the revolution."

The voices of this generation were profoundly singular. They formed a community (in the precise sense Bataille gave to the term) that did not erase their singularity in the name of an identity but in fact accentuated and celebrated it. Their texts left behind traces of these singularities, but also a common passion for laughter, itself manifested in profoundly singular "bursts": Louis Althusser suggested that we should rethink the relation between Marxism and philosophy starting from Lenin's laughter.[62] Derrida wrote one of the foundational essays of deconstruction proposing a practice of reading that culminates in a burst of laughter.[63] Jean-François Lyotard's attempt to rethink our practices of reading and their libidinal investments passed through the necessity of the statement, "we laugh at critique."[64] Deleuze and Guattari struggled to hear Kafka's laughter, which they thought inextricable from the possibility of a form of politics inspired by Kafka.[65] Jean-Luc Nancy and Maurice Blanchot pushed Bataille's thoughts on a "community of laughers," a model for community *tout court*.[66] Nancy further explored the relation between the aesthetic program of modernity and laughter.[67] For his part, Jacques Lacan spoke of ri-en, hearing nothingness resonate with laughter.[68] Hélène Cixous entered a dialog with Bataille on the question of woman's laughter.[69] A community, then: singular bursts laughed together.

Laughter here is a necessary "beginning," the burst one describes retroactively in terms of "In the beginning there was laughter." A variant of Emma Goldman's famous dictum, "If I cannot dance I do not want to be part of your revolution," could read: "If I cannot laugh I do not want to be part of your revolution." This, because, once one spends enough time in laughter's archive, it becomes clear that the two go hand in hand. A "revolution" is nothing but a "beginning." What this constellation of texts helps us realize is that in the twentieth century, it was often through laughter that "revolution" was revolutionized.

WOMAN   An anecdote will help prepare the way for woman's entrance on this stage. It is the story of a miracle—the birth of Isaac in the Hebrew Bible. The story unfolds in two parts. In the first part, God announces that Abram and Sarai (soon to be renamed Abraham and Sarah) will have a child. Abram is over one hundred years old; Sarai is ninety. When Abram hears the promise, which has been repeated to him a few times but has so far remained without consequence, he "threw himself on his face and laughed" (Genesis 17:17).[70] Still somewhat skeptical, Abram prostrates himself before God; his laugh is a form of worship. Sarai's reaction is different. Overhearing a second announcement of the promised child, and acutely aware not only of her own body but also of Abram's, she "laughed to herself" (18:12). In his turn overhearing Sarai's inner laugh, God asks Abram: "Is anything too wondrous for the LORD?" (18:14) Confronted by what appears to be the accusation that she does not believe in God's wonder-making abilities, Sarai tries to withdraw her laugh: "Sarai lied, saying, 'I did not laugh,' for she was frightened. But He replied, 'You did laugh'" (18:15).

God, otherwise in a vengeful mood, does not punish Sarai for what appears to be her incredulous laugh. In due time, a child is born. God demands his name be Isaac (Hebrew *Yishaq*, "laugh"). Sarai concludes: "God has brought me laughter; everyone who hears of it will laugh with me" (21:6). In anticipation of Isaac's birth, as if by way of welcoming him, Abram and Sarai receive new names: Abraham and Sarah (17:5, 17:15). It is as if from now on Abraham and Sarah laugh a little when they say their own names. And since God's promise is that they will be the ancestors of a multitude of nations, who will bless them, these new nations will be blessing their new, laughter-inflected names. It is not immediately clear, then, if in the biblical account Sarah's laughter signals a lapse of faith, as God's words seem to suggest ("Is anything too wondrous for the Lord?"), or is in fact the ultimate proof of faith, as God's gift of Isaac and Isaac's name seem to suggest.

In the second part of the story, God demands the sacrifice of Isaac—of the promise of laughter, as it were. Sarah is not explicitly present here. Abraham needs to exclude her, perhaps because she is not trusted: not only to sacrifice her son, but also to sacrifice laughter. As for Abraham, he makes the leap of faith and is ready to offer Isaac in sacrifice, in fact offering a sacrifice not only of his son, but of his very moral existence in the name of a superior ethical order. This is all God needs and, at the very moment of sacrifice, he returns Isaac. God gives Isaac back—to Abraham, but perhaps even more so to Sarah and those she imagines laughing with her. Sarah, however, dies. Abraham's purchase of a burial site brings him his first piece of the land promised to him and his nation. Sarah's body is this land. Abraham remarries, unproblematically has six other children, and lives to be one hundred and seventy. Upon his death, he makes Isaac his sole heir and is buried with Sarah.

What Sarah's story reveals is another relation to faith and the possibility of miracle—another "Abraham."[71] Sarah has faith, and yet the miracle makes her laugh. God likes this mixture of faith and laughter, as if human faith needed a dose of laughter. It is, in fact, Sarah's laughing apparent skepticism that gives birth to Isaac. Sarah is ninety, but her mouth's opening in laughter is the sign of fertility out of which Isaac is born. Yes, you did laugh, God insists almost childishly. And you did well to laugh, he seems to imply. Sarah is willing to take her laugh back, to deny it. It is no easy thing, though. Once laughed, a laugh persists. God would not hear of it. Sarah's laughter reminds God that the miracle—that "wondrous" event—has to pass through her body ("Now Abraham and Sarah were old, advanced in years; Sarah had stopped having the periods of women. . . . Now that I am withered, am I to have enjoyment— with my husband so old?" [18:12]). It also has to pass through Abraham's body, old and recently circumcised. Laughter marks the acknowledgment that the miracle (in the broadest sense) is precisely the point where "the wondrous" meets the materiality of the body. It nonetheless announces a faith that translates into a somewhat skeptical/material openness to the possibility that, despite all odds, this is a felicitous, life-creating meeting point.

"Sarah" is the event here. Abraham already has a son, Ishmael, born of the handmaid, Hagar, and yet God insists that Sarah is the one to give birth to the promised child. She is to be the mother of nations. After a long life of infertility and waiting, "The LORD took note of Sarah" (21:1). Her reaction is a yes; not a "Here I am," but a laugh. This is the yes of the mother. Yes, I will have this child, I will be the mother of this wondrous child.

Sarah is otherwise a very quiet woman. She follows Abraham in his travels, quietly accepts playing the role of his "sister," and so on. Laughter is Sarah's "speech." It is only at this moment in her story that she speaks in her own name. What she says, however, is something only God understands, and even he needs some time to do so. For us mortals, the meaning of her laugh remains a secret. We hear only the sound of her voice, which is also the voice of the mother, laughing. Sarah welcomes the miracle with a laugh, she makes place for the wonder of Isaac through the fashioning of her mouth/body into an evental yes-laugh. Sarah is not, as it has been said, "incredulous."[72] She is hospitable to the miracle, welcoming it with a feminine touch of hospitality.[73]

If Sarah could be said to be a model on which to begin to think the structure of a specifically feminine evental decision, it will not come as a surprise to note that feminism has had its own tense relation to laughter. On the one hand, the figure of what has been called "the humorless feminist" is well established in any gallery of seriousness. In the tradition of caricatures depicting the suffragette as temperance fanatic and pleasure-spoiler, she is portrayed as extremely worried, angry, or bitter.[74] Laughter does not disturb the seriousness of her face. The most serious charge against her is not that she "does not have a sense of humor" or that "she does not get the joke," as the phrase "humorless feminist" would have it, but that she actually cannot laugh. Wrapped in her seriousness, she has forgotten how to laugh. In part due to her longstanding alliance with a Marxist tradition, whose great thinkers are not big laughers themselves, she has grown sour.[75] (What is there to laugh about in such bleak times, anyway?)

On the other hand, there are vocal "feminist laughers."[76] Rosi Braidotti, for example, imagines the very beginning of feminism as a laughing beginning, when "joy and laughter were profound political emotions and statements. Not much of this joyful beat survives in these days of postmodernist gloom, and yet we would do well to remember the subversive force of Dionysian laughter. I wish feminism would shed its saddening, dogmatic mode to rediscover the merrymaking of a movement that aims to change life."[77] It is an invitation many feminists accepted, not only in order to draw a dose of surplus pleasure from laughter, but also so that they can think about feminism's own conditions of possibility, the laughing *yes* involved in its "beginning."

READING/LISTENING   One hears all kinds of laughs: giggles and cackles, guffaws and chortles, sniggers and titters, burbles and chuckles. Writing "on" laughter has an important descriptive dimension. To read in laughter's archive is to decipher nuances. It is a voyage into the microscopic, into the difference of the bit of nuance. It is also an exercise in closeness, in intimacy. Close reading, or close listening, is intimate reading. An infinite spectrum of nuances— tones, timbres, accents, resonances—unfold in laughter. And yet we do not quite have a vocabulary to talk about laughter. Language has grown poorer and poorer, and insists on imposing the same word ("laughter") on laughs that— ontologically, aesthetically, ethically—often find themselves at opposite ends of the laughing spectrum. Description is an attempt to soften this injustice.

Traditionally thought of as largely ornamental or decorative, a question of excessive style, gratuitous pomp, and immodest erudition, description received an important blow from André Breton, who condemned its naïve claim to an unmediated relation to the real.[78] The necessarily useless "detail," description's harbinger, was likewise dismissed on account of its alleged claims to realist citationality. And yet there is a different story of description that can be told, one that insists on its materialism. Although description is never objective, a mimetic picture of objects in the world, it maintains a relation with a certain fantasy of the real. If it is to be thought of as a mirror, Michel Beaujour argues, this is the mirror of Narcissus, laying bare hidden details and showing things that stand not in front of our realist nose but precisely in our blind spot.[79] In other words, rather than citing the familiar, description defamiliarizes. When we describe an object in detail for enough time, we inevitably move away from realistic verisimilitude (does Werther describe Charlotte?) into the territory of dream and fantasy. Carrying erotic overtones, its pleasures having to do with lingering and detail, closeness, intimacy, and often perversity, description remains in close contact with the senses. When it comes to laughter, description relies mostly on the ear. The challenge here is to listen to laughter, its range of sounds, although description often also brings forth a synesthetic play of the senses, which makes it possible to talk about the color of laughter or its tastes.

Ultimately, description is one way of attending to Nancy's challenge: "We always *make* too much of laughter [*on en fait toujours trop sur le rire*], we overload it with meaning or nonsense, we take it to the point of tears or to the revelation of nothingness. . . . If possible, let's let it present—lose—itself [*laissons-la se presenter—se perdre*]."[80] Ideally, one would deictically point to laughter by way of description, in the same breath acknowledging and recounting the effects of its undeniable, if elusive, presence and its hermeneutic opaqueness.[81] Reading is caught between these two demands: to read, to listen to nuance and resonance, while allowing laughter to burst.

Attending to this double call, description often acquires aphoristic touches (Nietzsche and Bataille are exemplary here). One writes in bursts or fits. Aphorism moves toward laughter, without hoping to reach it, touch it, even less exhaust it. For its part, this book gathers under the subtitle, "Notes on a Passion." Notes follow a logic and a rigor of juxtaposition, a disjunctive arrangement that acknowledges, respects, and preserves the difference of the often divergent discourses and texts at play here.[82] The word "notes" also translates a teacher's writing habits. Drawing on its musical overtones, the teacher writes "notes," around which she and her students improvise.[83] Crucial in any note-writing exercise is the interval, the energetic white space between the islands of writing, where the interesting swimming happens.

The risk here, which one must take, is that we will have made too much of laughter. Description, of course, is never "mere description." Despite a long tradition that opposes it to narrative, description has its own narrative modalities. Think of the descriptive mode of the cinematic close-up. Although they function as lulls in the development of narrative, close-ups are stories within stories. They stop the main narrative clock of the film, but only so that more local but also more intense narratives can develop. Furthermore, description has its own argumentative modes. When Clifford Geertz proposes that ethnography is engaged in "thick description," he advocates both a narrative and an argumentative methodology. The ethnographer (a would-be literary critic) proposes an argument about the multilayered webs of meaning within which a phenomenon (a wink, for example) is produced, perceived, and interpreted. Often, these webs are not explicit, and can be strange and irregular, as well as indistinct, commingled or knotted into each another. Geertz imagines the work of the ethnographer as that of a rigorous, if always necessarily incomplete, description of a given network of signification.

For Geertz, human behavior is symbolic action—"most of the time; there *are* true twitches."[84] Laughter is such a twitch. There is, of course, an encyclopedia of rules for laughing. Conduct manuals are filled with them, although many remain implicit and do not take the form of written advice. There is also a range of keys in which laughing is interpreted (our "theories of laughter"). The ethnographer would read through and describe the layers of signification surrounding any given burst of laughter at both the production and receiving ends. But while Geertz believes the ethnographer can, at least provisionally, conclude that a given wink "says" something, laughter as such does not "say" anything, although it can illuminate the context in which it bursts. If the point of description is, in Geertz's terms, to "bring us into touch with the lives of strangers," the description of laughter does just that: it touches on the strangeness of laughter, and this strangeness brings us into the proximity of the stranger the laugher is.

ARCHIVE This book uncovers a limited and fragile archive of laughter. It invites us to spend time in this archive, in the hope that we might become somewhat intimate with laughter, dwell in its "field," and learn to follow some of its rhythms and listen to its shades of tone. Although it takes the "civilizing of laughter" as one of its premises, the book is primarily interested in twentieth-century laughers and friends of laughter. In that, it participates in the emerging, retrospective project that attempts to revisit the Western twentieth century and its political, scientific, philosophical, and aesthetic ventures. The question it asks is: How did the twentieth century laugh?

It is important to note at the outset that to talk about the laughing twentieth century is not to propose an alternative to the century of horrors, war, and genocide. In fact, in the twentieth century, laughter was often imagined as a way into horror. Let us remember that Khlebnikov's laughter found an echo in Marinetti's experiments with sound. Marinetti's "Bombardment" hears laughter amid the "orchestra of a great battle": "the orchestra pools muddying huffing goaded oxen wagons *pluff-plaff* horse action flic flac zing zing *shaaack* laughing whinnies the *tiiinkling jiiingling* tramping. . . ."[85] "Laugh like a bomb" is the phrase used in the vorticist "Manifesto," published in *Blast* and signed by, among others, Wyndham Lewis.[86] In a similar vein, T. S. Eliot's "Hysteria" locates the horror of war and the dizzying vortex of the present in the abyss associated with woman's laughing mouth: "As she laughed I was aware of becoming involved / in her laughter and being part of it, until her / teeth were only accidental stars with a talent / for squad-drill."[87] If laughter is a bit of the real, it is invoked in relation to joy, but also often to horror.

Each of the chapters that follow revolves around an anecdote. The assumption here is that the anecdote is the site where, for a brief moment, the fiction of biography meets the uncanny of lived experience.[88] The result is a form of theorizing that attempts to do justice to an event like a burst of laughter. Each of the anecdotes that serve as anchors for the chapters that follow is an enabling entry point into one twentieth-century project: modernism and its echoes in the African-American tradition (chapter 2), the philosophical avant-gardes (chapter 3), feminism (chapter 4), and cinema (chapter 5). Each chapter also revolves around one central figure through which each project is revisited (Ellison, Bataille, Cixous, Adorno). The result is not a comprehensive picture of these projects, but rather an episodic yet—I hope—illuminative perspective on each, starting from the laughs that burst at some of the most convoluted interstices of the century.

CHAPTER 1

THE CIVILIZING OF LAUGHTER

The concessions to *politeness* always contain *political* concessions.
Pierre Bourdieu

PROHIBITION A country road, a tree, two tramps by the side of the road—
Samuel Beckett's minimalist scene for *Waiting for Godot*:

> *Vladimir breaks into a hearty laugh* [bon rire] *which he immediately stifles* [réprime], *his
> hand pressed to his pubis, his face contorted.*
>
> Vladimir: One daren't even laugh any more [*On n'ose même plus rire*].
> Estragon: Dreadful privation.
> Vladimir: Merely smile [*sourire*]. (*He smiles suddenly from ear to ear, keeps smiling, ceases
> as suddenly.*)[1]

Vladimir breaks into a hearty laugh, but immediately cuts it short. While
laughing, he seems to remember something. Whatever it is that crosses his
mind, it amounts to a command to not laugh. Like a good child, Vladimir
stops. There is a brief time lag between the perceived command to stifle the
laugh and the achievement of a body and a face at rest, which for a while bear
traces of the laugh in the contortion of the face and the perceived imminence
of a piss.[2] "One daren't even laugh any more." Laughter is a provocation, a
matter of "Dare!": dare confront that invisible force giving orders. Vladimir
seems to think there has been a time, an indefinite past, when laughter was
allowed. But not any more. Not even laughter. This "dreadful privation" is
countered with the possibility of a smile. But to smile is unsatisfactory; to
smile is to "merely smile" (*sou-rire*). Vladimir is willing to try it. A good actor,
he puts on a smiling show, suddenly stretching his mouth from ear to ear,
freezing the pose for a short time, then stopping. "It's not the same thing,"
comes the conclusion of the experiment. Perhaps there is nothing "hearty" in

the smile, which remains an empty performance, a show. When the interdiction on laughter is countered with an invitation to smile, one still experiences a "dreadful privation." Later in the play, Vladimir laughs again:

> Laugh of Vladimir, stifled [il coupe court] as before, less the smile.
>
> Vladimir: You'd make me laugh if it wasn't prohibited [si cela m'était permis].[3]

The smile is not a lesser laugh, a matter of degree, but of a different register altogether. Vladimir tries it: it's not the same thing. Much has been written of Beckett's play and its "humor," yet little attention has been paid to this passage. Indeed, what are we to make of two tramps, characters in a self-described "tragicomedy," deploring a perceived interdiction on laughter? Who is whispering in Vladimir's ear? What is being whispered? By what authority? How did we get here?

CIVILITY   Only children laugh "heartily." The civilizing process has pruned laughter to a moderate size: we laugh moderate, civilized laughs. Openmouthed, loud, extravagant, passional laughter, what Norbert Elias calls "full throated, side-splitting laughter," is condemned by the Western polite world as indecorous, primitive, and vulgar. Only children, before they too are broken in, can allow laughter to run through their whole body. Elias's "Essay on Laughter" offers a new take on the civilizing process, one that assumes that "the civilizing of laughter" occupies a special place within it.[4] Laughter becomes the occasion to tackle, in Elias's words, "a limited and therefore more easily manageable key-problem for the opening of a wider problem-area which concerns man as a whole."[5]

We will sketch here the path on which "the civilizing of laughter" leads to what Vladimir suggests we could think of as a prohibition. For it is on this historical background that we need to place twentieth-century investments in laughter. Laughter intrigues twentieth-century writers and philosophers precisely because a lot of energy has historically gone into its management. It should be said at the outset that this is not a history; we will witness a constellation of moments forming an intricate and irregular mosaic, in which one can nonetheless trace the complex, convoluted, often contradictory, story of an interdiction on laughter.

If we are in search of beginnings, Erasmus of Rotterdam's 1530 De civilitate morum puerilium (On Good Manners for Boys) has acquired foundational status in the history of manners, which is crucial to an investigation of the civilizing of laughter.[6] For laughing is a question of manners, politeness, and good breeding. De civilitate was intended to be used as an educational tool; it was one of the main textbooks used in the teaching of Latin in the schoolrooms that emerged throughout Western Europe in the sixteenth century. The book witnesses and participates in the concomitant invention of the modern notion of the child and of the school. The child is that which lacks civility, and the school—providing an appropriate humanist education—is that which fills this lack. It is important to emphasize that the school in its originary moment teaches manners, something any modern educational system will do, whether manners are explicitly the main educational focus (as in "finishing schools") or are only implicitly taught and rewarded in institutional practice.[7] Instruction in manners is crucial to the everyday functioning of the school, and the school takes it upon itself to teach them through works like *De civilitate*. Thus regulations regarding appropriate behavior in the classroom are among the first to be addressed by early texts on manners, and laughter is one of the first things to be excluded from the educational setting.[8] It has remained taboo ever since. One of the most important things the school teaches children is how, when, where, and for how long to laugh.

Erasmus describes appropriate behavior in seven chapters: "On the body," "On dress," "On behavior in church," "On banquets," "On meeting people," "On play," and "On the bedroom." Under his first heading, "On the body," he gives very precise instructions as to the correct movement of the mouth. He advises that one's mouth should be neither "tight-set" nor "gaping open like an idiot's," but, rather, "formed with lips lightly touching one another."[9] One should therefore cover one's mouth when yawning and, more important, be wary of laughing:

> To laugh at every word or deed is the sign of a fool; to laugh at none the sign of a blockhead. It is quite wrong to laugh at improper words or actions. Loud laughter and the immoderate mirth that shakes the whole body and is for that reason called "discord" by the Greeks, are unbecoming to any age but much more so to youth. The neighing sound that some people make when they laugh is also unseemly. And the person who opens his mouth wide in a rictus, with wrinkled cheeks and exposed teeth, is also impolite. This is a canine habit and is called a sardonic smile. The face should express mirth in such a way that it neither distorts the appearance of the mouth nor evinces a dissolute mind. Only fools use expressions like: "I am dissolving with laughter," "I am bursting with laughter," "I am dying with laughter." If something so funny should occur that it produces uncontrolled laughter of this sort, the face should be covered with a napkin or the hand. To laugh when alone or for no obvious reason is put down to either stupidity or insanity.[10]

One should be—as in any other aspect of life—moderate with respect to laughter.[11] While there are acceptable forms of mirth, loud or immoderate laughs "that shake the whole body" should be avoided. If one has to laugh, one's mouth should not be gaping. It is the abyss of the open mouth, connected to laughter's animal sounds, as well as the animal-like exposure of teeth, that Erasmus advises against. Ideally, one would laugh a soundless laugh, with lips lightly touching one another. To laugh out loud is to expose a "dissolute mind," a mind in a state of disconnectedness, loose, lacking in consistence and firmness. A dissolute mind is a weak mind, verging on effeminacy. Folly is close by. The story of laughter is intertwined with that of folly and the feminine. To say that one is "dissolving," "bursting," or "dying" with laughter is to acknowledge an uneasy, anxiety-producing loss of control.

De civilitate presents its reader with an ideal, a mirror to look at and mold oneself accordingly in a lifelong, never-ending process. The other side of this mirror is offered through what Elias calls "Grobian reversal."[12] The figures of Grobianus and Grobiana—actively refusing civility and grossly indulging in its faux pas—work to produce a visceral appeal to a sense of shame. Grobianus and Grobiana are the imagined "before" of the civilizing process, a fictitious "state of nature," and its projected "outside." As such, they embody the very necessity of civility. For what one sees in the mirror will always also be a Grobiana, a reminder that one's work on the body is never quite finished. It will come as no surprise that, in a section of Grobianus and Grobiana titled "Of devouring, laughing, vomiting at the table, and other such like civilities to be observed," one is invited to laugh all the time, through all daily activities. Most importantly, one should laugh as one eats, in such a way as to spit the food back on the plate.[13] The place of laughter in this series of horrors, between "devouring" and "vomiting," is suggestive of its abject indecency. The reader is asked to witness the other side of the civilizing process, its reversal, and be ashamed. De civilitate and the Grobianus texts work in tandem toward the same goal: one side of the mirror presents an ideal; the other, its shameful underside. One urges restraint in laughter while the other works toward a growing sensitivity to embarrassment, shame, and abjection.

Humanist education goes hand in hand with Christian education, for which laughter is also an important concern. The Hebrew Bible offered the story of Sarah's laugh, which was understood in the Christian tradition as a sign of incredulity and ultimately a lack of faith. The Christian Bible was silent about Christ's laughter, a fact which led to a long theological debate about whether he actually laughed. One of the influential texts on this issue in the early modern period, Ludolf von Sachsen's Vita Christi, emphasized that since Christ's face is the image of dignity, majesty, and beauty, he simply could not have laughed.[14] The iconographic tradition depicts Christ as calm, peaceful, often smiling. But whether he laughed or not, Christ was laughed at, or, rather, "mocked," and the Christian tradition had to come to terms with the issue in light of the fact that laughter could potentially have Christ or God as its object. This was the pitiless, scoffing "laughter at the foot of the Cross."[15] In the horizon of Christian laughter, there would be the sentence "Woe to you who laugh now!" (Luke 6:25).

It should be clear, then, that Christian education could not leave the laughter of children to chance. Another warning served as a horizon: the forty-two children who "mocked" Elisha's baldness were cursed and consequently torn to pieces by two she-bears (2 Kings 2:23–25). Education, learning in Christian laughing matters, was needed in order to avoid such a predicament. Thus William Perkins, in *A Direction for the Government of the Tongue According to Gods Word*, allowed that, "As for laughter, it may be used: otherwise God would never have given that power and faculty unto man: but the use of it must be both moderate and seldome, as sorrow for our sinnes is to be plentiful and often."[16] Perkins reminds his readers that Christ wept three times but never laughed, and that raising laughter in church can only be the work of the devil. Calvin would make some amendments for laughter, but he too married the Christian and humanist traditions, insisting on sobriety. He approved of "laughter at the tears of our enemies, provided that it be not too lavish, but moderate and temperate and, for that reason, holy and approved by God."[17] There is a tension here between the acceptance of a very problematic Christian laughter "at the tears of our enemies" and the classic slogan of measure and gravity.

In Erasmus's view, unlike in that of many of his successors, only blockheads do not laugh at all. Modernity will know a few such blockheads, who will state plainly and clearly that laughter is to be avoided in all or most circumstances. As for Erasmus, he is also the author of *Moriae encomium* (Praise of Folly). Here he creates the fictitious voice of Folly, a woman and an advocate of laughter, who encomiates herself, her own folly.[18] The genre of the encomium—in this context praising something deemed unworthy of praise—works in ambivalent ways. Folly indeed sings her own praises and is quite convincing in her attack on the serious, polite, unlaughing world. But, like Grobianus, she also educates through aversion.[19] The reader of the encomium is called upon to make the necessary distinctions. Suture to Folly's laughter is not really an option; she is, after all, just a woman.

CACHINNATION The year is 1579. Having kept the manuscript in a drawer for twenty years, Laurent Joubert publishes his *Treatise on Laughter*. His goal: "leave nothing on the unusual topic unsounded."[20] The treatise is an early modern encyclopedia of laughing matters. Trained in the tradition of humanist medicine, Joubert begins by sketching a fictitious contest between the parts of the human body. Which one is most important? Which one can stand on its own? One obvious candidate lays its claims to the title: the hand. Joubert acknowledges its merits but soon dismisses it. After all, the brain commands and the hand obeys. The brain takes the lead in the competition but does not reign long. Another contestant appears and wins: the face. Only man has a face; animals do not. We carry it high, looking toward the sky, proud; the face is the signpost of our verticality. It is the site of social interaction—

the face-to-face—and therefore cannot be covered by either hair or clothes. It is the seat of beauty; art is content to represent the face as the mark of an individual. It is the mirror of the soul; passions are visible on the face; so is sickness. The kiss is of the face, and therefore love. The face is individual but the face of Marguerite de Navarre, to whom the *Treatise* is dedicated, is also, according to Joubert, the face of the French nation. Most of all, however, what makes the face stand out is its status as the throne of laughter, and Joubert agrees with the premise that laughter makes us human; laughter is the "effect of the most human passion there is."[21] As such, laughter will be paramount in the modern history of the face, which could be said to begin with Joubert's contest. The face and laughter come to define each other: man is the only animal with a face, which is why he laughs; and man is the only animal who laughs, which is in direct correlation with his face.

What is laughter? Joubert's catalog of definitions returns us to a materialism long forgotten today. Laughter is "a trembling and a noise"; "a sound producing movement"; "a movement which stretches the muscles of the face"; "the dilating of the parts of the mouth and of the face."[22] In laughter, "the chest shakes, the lungs produce an interrupted sound, the mouth opens, and the lips draw back."[23] To the question: What does laughter look like? Joubert gives a complex answer:

> Everybody sees clearly that in laughter the face is moving, the mouth widens, the eyes sparkle and tear, the cheeks redden, the breast heaves, the voice becomes interrupted; and when it goes on for a long time the veins in the throat become enlarged, the arms shake, and the legs dance about, the belly pulls in and feels considerable pain; we cough, perspire, piss, and besmirch ourselves by dint of laughing, and sometimes we even faint away because of it. This need not be proven.[24]

Laughter is a convulsion of the face. It involves a specific constellation of functions of the face: the mouth, the eyes, the cheeks, the voice. When laughter becomes a question not of a single burst but of a series of bursts ("when it goes on for a long time"), it also involves the rest of the body—arms, legs, belly, breast, veins in the throat. The body laughs. Extreme physiological changes might occur, for one can feel pain, cough, perspire, piss, besmirch oneself, faint. The body in laughter is a convulsive assemblage, whose parts shake and dance about, refusing to form a totality. The laughing face is itself bursting, its mouth suddenly stretched, its eyes sparkling, color splashing its cheeks with shades of red.

Joubert further complicates the scene of laughter:

> Some men, when they laugh, sound like geese hissing, others like grumbling goslings; some recall the sigh of woodland pigeons, or doves in their widow-

hood; others the hoot-owl; one an Indian rooster, another a peacock; others give out a peep-peep, like chicks; for others it is like horse neighing, or an ass heehawing, or a dog that yaps or is chocking, some people call to mind the sound of dry-axled carts, others, gravel in a pail, others yet a boiling pot of cabbage; and some have still another resonance, aside from the look on their face and the grimacing, so variedly diverse that nothing parallels it.[25]

Not only is laughter distorting the face into a grimace and shaking the body convulsively, but it also produces a certain, hard-to-define, sound. Joubert describes laughter's sound onomatopoeically; laughter sounds "like" geese hissing, horses neighing, the peep-peep of chicks, or the hee-hawing of asses. Even when laughter sounds like a pot of boiling cabbage or gravel in a pail, the description speaks to the ear of Joubert's reader; one is challenged to hear these sounds.

The choreography of the body in laughter is, however, only the outward manifestation of a passion. Which passion? The question seems simple, yet it has received a variety of answers, with a number of variables. For particular passions often blend into compounds, and a particular chemistry is needed to produce different compounds. Joubert offers a list: "The principal of these are joy, sorrow, hope, fear, love, hate, anger, pity, shame, impudence, zeal, and envy or malice. They are also called passions, troublings or perturbations of the soul in that they come from an appetite that does not proceed from reason."[26] Among the passions on Joubert's list, it is clear that laughter is a manifestation of joy. But things are not so simple. Like other early modern theorists of passions, Joubert adds that the joy associated with laughter is of a particular quality and is most often accompanied by other passions. For Joubert, laughter translates a combination of joy and sorrow. The particular constellation of movement and sound we call laughter, that trembling noise and muscular movement, transcribes the workings of a blend of joy and sorrow, expressing, in an Aristotelian vein, "a feeling over an ugly thing unworthy of pity."[27] Laughter marks the tension between the joy and the sorrow we feel when faced with this ambivalent situation.

Passions are located in the heart, which is why we say one laughs "heartily" (il rit de bon cœur), but in Joubert's account they are, or should be, governed by reason. That the human mind is to be conceived as a commonwealth and the commonwealth as a human mind, Joubert knows from Plato's Republic. The analogy is a commonplace of work on passions in the early modern period. Reason is to be sovereign in both; the prince is to be an embodiment of reason, ruling over the passions of the people. The reverse is also true: control over the passions yields political power.[28]

Joubert tells us there are two ways to govern: "one is as master, where one simply commands; the other is civil or political, where with authority one points out obligations. Reason governs the heart in the second way when with its advice it moves or calms the emotions, and if the heart resists the bit, reason has recourse to the first means, through which it can order the external members to do its bidding."[29] In other words, reason first tries to calm the passions, to show them in what direction they ought to move us. If the passions resist the authority of reason, the latter has recourse to another maneuver, directly commanding "the exterior," the body and the face, to not follow the movement of a given passion. Joubert trusts that things stop here and there is no need for what Erasmus identified as the last resort in government, censorship: cover the mouth with a napkin or the hand.

It seems, however, that sovereign reason is often at a loss when confronted with laughter:

> These are among the great marvels of laughter, how it escapes so quickly that it seems to come without our knowing it, almost sneaking out, and how sometimes, letting ourselves be overcome with laughter, we cannot stop or suppress it. For when we laugh until we split [*nous rions à tout rompre*], carried away by cachinnation [*amportés du Cachin*], it is not in our power to close our mouth or to have breath at our bidding, so that with the air lacking, sometimes one almost suffocates.[30]

Laughter seems to obey reason less than any other passion. A rebel, it sneaks in and overpowers reason. We cannot control our laughs, Joubert argues, much as we cannot control our bladder.[31] Laughter "bursts," "breaks," and "splits" us.

Not all laughs are the same, and not all pose the same threat to reason and its governance. What is needed is a typology of laughter, instrumental in the acquisition of the "*savoir-rire*."[32] There are two basic kinds of laughter. The first is modest; it is small, natural, and healthy. The second and problematic one is cachinnation (*le cachin*); it is bastard, illegitimate, and unhealthy. Cachinnation is an umbrella term for laughs that are "immodest, excessive, insolent, and too long."[33] The mouth, which shows a medium opening in modest laughter, is gaping indecently. While modest laughter is the laughter of the Aristotelian definition, cachinnation evades it. In this latter case, the same constellation of movement and sound occurring in modest laughter cannot be traced back to something ugly or inappropriate but unworthy of compassion. The laughter of tickling and infant laughter fall into this category. Something known as "dog laughter" (*le ris-chien*) belongs here too.

Cachinnation, Joubert argues, borders on madness. It can be caused by castration, poisonous bites, or epilepsy. A number of epithets come to define unhealthy, bastard laughter: sardonian, canine, Ajax, Catonian, Ionic, inept, tumultuous, asbestos. Modest, healthy laughter is in no need of epithets, it is simply called laughter. Language has slowly rid itself of most of these epithets, as we have slowly learned to laugh our small, modest laughs, which we, indeed, have come to call "laughter." The very word "cachinnation," widely used in the early modern period, slowly fades out of use.

Modest laughter is to be encouraged, because it acquires therapeutic qualities. A long tradition in the history of medicine pursues this idea.[34] Laughter is a remedy for a variety of health problems, heart disease in particular. In fact, to not laugh is worrisome for Joubert. And there are some people who do not laugh: "those who give themselves completely to study and contemplation, or to some great enterprise, are almost all *agelasts*, sad, rude, severe, and have knitted brows."[35] It is not difficult to discern the figure of the knit-browed philosopher here. At the other end of the spectrum, children and the young laugh more. So do women. While modest laughter has its clear advantages, cachinnation is dangerous. It renders effeminate. It makes fat. It causes fainting spells, coughing, and strangulation. One can even die laughing.

AN EXPLOSIVE CRY   Passions, Descartes would argue, are thoughts, but a special kind of thoughts: disturbed thoughts or, rather, thoughts that disturb the mind.[36] What makes passions distinct is their potential for putting the subject in a particularly confusing state: in the passional situation the subject is active and affected at the same time. Descartes makes the passions the site where the activity of reason is perverted by the perceived passivity of the body. Passions "happen" to a body which apparently deterministically "suffers" them, while reason struggles to contain a movement that contaminates it. According to Descartes's "rule of the inverse reaction," when the body acts the soul is passive, and the other way around. There is a back and forth, a reversal of transitive action, between the soul and the body. What is important, however, is that, more than anywhere else, the body and the soul touch and contaminate each other on the terrain of the passions. Cartesian "dualism" needs revisiting in light of the dialog between the *Meditations* and *The Passions of the Soul*, which makes it clear that the body and the soul "quasi-permix."[37]

For Descartes, passions are the necessary link between subject and action. They agitate us, orienting our associative processes and directing us to think what is useful for the self that the mind *and* the body form, their "quasi-union." They incite us and dispose us to will certain actions. Passions move us to action. However, different passions move us in different directions and, on Descartes's account, we need to train our will to focus the attention on what is essential. Like other early modern theorists of the passions, Descartes makes it his task to identify and define the passions, list and classify them, and meditate on what work needs to be done such that their dysfunctionality is kept to a minimum while allowing us to benefit from and cultivate some of them. How, then, can one create a self able to premeditate its reactions and make premeditation a matter not only of the future but of the very present?

The principle of habituation enters the stage. Through experience and with the help of the will, the soul creates premeditated habits, automatisms linking a movement to a thought such that the body reacts automatically when moved by certain passions.

There are six "primitive passions," Descartes tells us, in this order: Wonder, Love, Hatred, Desire, Joy and Sadness (a.69). They—and their combinations—all have their usefulness and they are all prone to "misuses or excesses" (a.211). Keeping oneself in what Descartes calls "a particular [state of] reflection and attention" (a.76) and with the help of the will, one can exploit the passions' usefulness while correcting possible "misuses and excesses." There is a need for what Descartes calls "a little skill [un peu d'industrie]" (a.50) with the use of which we can train and guide the passions. For example, Descartes elaborates, we laugh when we are tickled, but if we anticipate that this is about to happen, we can delay our response, and, in this temporal lull, distract ourselves, change the focus of our attention, and will ourselves to think something else. With a little bit of work, laughter can be avoided. The horizon here is "not to tend toward anything immoderately [de ne nous porter à rien avec excès]" (a.138).

There are exterior signs of the passions, and one can best read these signs when more passions are, as they usually are, commingled. Passions are visible on the face, the place where the workings of the soul are on display. The reading of "expression" becomes a most important everyday activity. It requires training and practice, especially since different passions produce almost identical expressions: "there are men who have almost the same look when they cry as others when they laugh" (a.113).

Descartes offers a definition of laughter en physicien:

Laughter consists in this: [1] blood coming from the right cavity of the heart through the arterial vein, suddenly and repeatedly swelling the lungs, compels the air they contain to come out forcefully [avec impétuosité] through the windpipe, where it forms an inarticulate and explosive cry [une voix inarticulée et éclatante]; and [2] the lungs as they swell and this air as it emerges each push against all the muscles of the diaphragm, chest, and throat, and thereby make the ones in the face that have some connection with them move. And what we call Laughter is only this action of the face, together with that inarticulate and explosive cry. [Et ce n'est que cette action du visage, avec cette voix inarticulée et éclatante, qu'on nomme le Ris.] (a.124)

Laughter is a motion, forceful, sudden and repetitive; and it is the sound of a bursting, inarticulate voice. Described en physicien, laughter is simply an action of the face. As for the passional chemistry needed to produce laughter: it always involves a dose of wonder, sometimes joy, sometimes hatred, sometimes both joy and hatred. In moderate doses, wonder is to be encouraged,

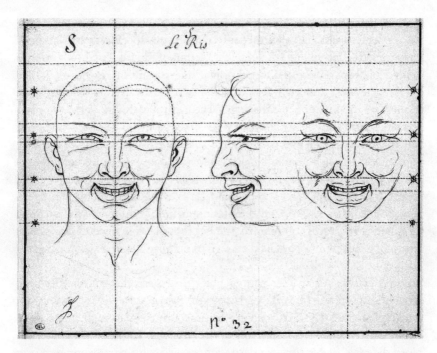

FIGURE 1.1
Charles Le Brun, *Laughter*. Musée du Louvre, Département des Arts Graphiques; Réunion des Musées Nationaux/Art Resource, New York.

for "it is useful in making us learn and retain in our memory things we have previously been ignorant of" (a.75). Wonder, the most interesting passion for Descartes, benefits science, revealing the horizon of what can be known. However, excessive wonder perverts the use of reason and should be avoided. Excessive wonder borders on astonishment, which "makes the entire body remain immobile like a statue" (a.73). Passivity lurks in the horizon of excessive wonder. Likewise, the immoderateness both of joy and of hatred is to be corrected.

Charles Le Brun, painter and Chancellor of the Paris Royal Academy, gave a lecture in 1668 on the expression of Cartesian passions.[38] In it, he described every nuance of a passion and, in order to illustrate his insights, drew a series of diagrams that accompany the lecture and, importantly, some future editions of *The Passions of the Soul*. Le Brun maps the passions, spatializes them, offering a geometry of the face. His diagrams sketch the face as a genderless bald head. Each head is divided into two symmetrical parts with the help of a vertical line, while eight horizontal lines make excess under the reign of the passions visible. An important diagram is "Tranquility," something of a degree zero of the face: calm, moderate, "normal."

Although Descartes allows that there are acceptable laughs as signs of useful moderate passions, Le Brun sees laughter, the specific constellation of changes in the face called laughter, that "action of the face," as itself immoderate. Noteworthy here is the horizontal line tracing the eyebrows, which become the most important feature of the face, their movement proportional to the level of "agitation" of the soul.[39] The eyebrows are the key to the reading of Le Brun's laughter diagram: "In laughter all the parts of the face go in one direction, for the eyebrows slope down towards the middle of the face, and cause the nose, the mouth, and the eyes to follow the movement."[40] This downward movement of the eyebrows, which the other features of the face follow, translates into a somewhat evil face. Eyes are fixed; the mouth opens in a spasm and seems suspended in its contraction. Thus drawn, the laughing face, not as an expression of a passion but in itself, is in need of correction. The soul is believed to be skilled enough to perform the necessary changes.

GLORY   Hobbes is stricter with laughter than Descartes, and he becomes stricter as he moves from the early work of *Human Nature* to the mature, systematic *Leviathan*.[41] For him, man is a natural creature of passion. The state of nature he imagines is a dominion of the passions, with one passion, vainglory, the most visible sign of a desire for power, acquiring preeminence over all others.[42] Violence is inevitable in this world as human beings struggle to impose their power on their neighbors. In order to avoid this predicament, which has death lurking on the horizon, man, also a natural being of reason, needs to find a solution to the problems posed by his own nature. Hobbes is not persuaded by the Cartesian "remedy" for the passions, especially Descartes's focus on the will, and he sets out to find another solution, this time on the terrain of political philosophy. The state is born; its material, brute "facts," are the passions.

After going through passions such as humility or courage, the Hobbes of *Human Nature* arrives at laughter: "There is a passion that hath no name, but the sign of it is that distortion of the countenance we call LAUGHTER, which is always joy."[43] It is important to emphasize that the passion that laughter marks through its immoderate distortion of the face—and the "sign" of which it is—has no name. For Hobbes, things that either have never happened and therefore cannot be remembered, or things that custom does not allow to be transformed into habit, do not have a name. Names are, as *Leviathan* puts it, "marks, or notes of remembrance."[44] Laughter is the sign of a passion that, for one reason or another, has never been "marked."

Hobbes goes on to offer a definition: "I may therefore conclude, that the passion of laughter is nothing else but a sudden glory arising from some sudden conception of some eminency in ourselves, by comparison with the infirmities of others, or with our own formerly."[45] Immoderateness is translated as arrogance, vainglory, an "eminency in ourselves." Hobbes would go through several formulations to the same effect before he reached his *Leviathan*, where a significant variation is at work. Here we have a system, and things that were not so clear to Hobbes in *Human Nature* now become clear. There are no more passions without a name: "*Sudden glory*, is the passion which maketh those *Grimaces* called LAUGHTER."[46]

"Sudden glory" is not just any passion. "Suddenness" is of interest if we remember that the first passion for Descartes, and an ingredient of laughter, is wonder—a newness or a freshness of perception, a "surprise of the soul." "Suddenness" is the one property of laughter to be agreed upon by theorists of laughter of all persuasions: if they cannot agree on anything else, they agree on laughter's "suddenness" or "spontaneity."[47] There are nuances of temporality among the passions. While they all occur "now," some of them do so with an eye either on the past (remorse or regret) or on the future (fear). Joy, sadness, and especially wonder are, however, simply of the "now."[48] This is why laughter, associated with joy, sadness, and wonder, bursts very much into a radical present.

Glory, the other ingredient of laughter as "sudden glory," interests us because it is, within Hobbes's system, the name of the paradigmatic threat to the well-being of the commonwealth. Given that, on this account, man is naturally given to comparison ("Joy consisteth in comparing himselfe with other men"),[49] Hobbes argues that joy, "arising from imagination of a mans own power and ability, is that exultation of the mind which is called GLORY-ING."[50] The source of our joy—leading to the grimace called laughter—is the operation of glorying. And glory is always the result of a comparison, when, perceiving a certain superiority over one's neighbor, the mind exults. It is on this argumentative path that *Human Nature* arrives at the Hobbesian theme of life as a race: "The comparison of the life of man to a race, though it holdeth not in every part, yet it holdeth so well for this our purpose that we may thereby both see and remember almost all the passions before mentioned. But this race we must suppose to have no other goal, no other garland, but being foremost."[51] The race helps us visualize the passions and, as always, the visual image helps us remember. The only *raison d'être* of the race is that, at the end of it, one finds glory. Laughter is an important part of this scene. Within the race, "To see another fall, is disposition to *laugh*. . . . And to forsake the course is to die."[52] Laughter furthers our sense of superiority in the race. In the fiction of the natural world Hobbes sketches, laughter marks the moment when one's fellow racer falls and the mind exults. It might be that Le Brun's diagram translates Hobbes's laughter more than Descartes's.[53] The 1734 English translation of Le Brun's *Conférence* reproduced a series of engravings made after copies of Le Brun's diagrams which, in a Hobbesian fashion, emphasized the cruelty of the laughing face.[54]

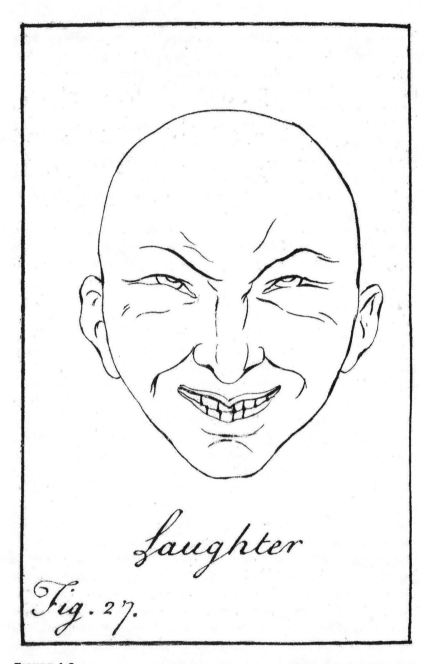

FIGURE 1.2

Charles Le Brun, "Laughter," from *A Method to Learn to Design the Passions, Proposed in a Conference on Their General and Particular Expression*, 1734. Huntington Library.

The very peace of the commonwealth, its first fundamental law and the horizon in which its members ought to live, is at stake in this laughter of the race. The passions, and glorying in particular, pose a threat not only to the governance of reason but to governance *tout court*. Anarchy, the Hobbesian absolute evil, lurks in the horizon of the passions.[55] All passions turn out to be variations on the same theme: vanity or pride or glory or *amour-propre*. Laughter, as "sudden glory," belongs to this series: "the apprehension of some deformed thing in another, by comparison whereof they suddenly applaud themselves."[56] Laughter is a form of self-applause. In relation to an other, it often borders on cruelty ("*Contempt*, or little sense of the calamity of others is that which men call CRUELTY").[57]

Civil society can be built only on nonglorious passions. Glory, and especially the vain glory laughter names, will need to be sifted into more social and more productive sentiments.[58] If one cannot love one's neighbor, one will need to cultivate benevolence and pity vis-à-vis his falling.[59] Glory will not disappear, but it will be translated into the more delicate "pride." As for the passion of laughter, it does not find its way into the socially acceptable and economically viable emotions and sentiments. It does not disappear either; it simply "falls into disrepute." Hobbes is one of the strongest voices in a choir that works toward laughter's falling into disrepute. But the choir is multivocal, complex, and often contradictory.[60]

GRIMACE/NOISE   The early modern discourse on manners is a form of practical philosophy, attending to the belief that the actions of the face can be changed if the soul wishes to conceal its passions. In a Cartesian fashion, the face is used to "dissimulate one's passions as well as to manifest them."[61] When Hobbes speaks of manners explicitly, he makes sure to warn: "By MANNERS, I mean not here, decency of behaviour; as how one should salute another, or how a man should wash his mouth, or pick his teeth before company, and other such points of the *small morals*; but those qualities of mankind, that concern their living together in peace, and unity."[62] Hobbes knows, however, that "the little things" and "the small morals," especially when they have to do with the management of mouths, are of concern for our life together, precisely on these two points: "peace" and "unity."

Two texts—and their dialog—are symptomatic when it comes to the place of laughter in the discourse on manners: the Marquis of Halifax's "The Lady's New Year's Gift; or, Advice to a Daughter" (1688) and Lord Chesterfield's *Letters to His Son* (1774). Halifax's "Advice" was addressed to his—at the time—twelve-year-old daughter, who would become Chesterfield's mother. Like Chesterfield's *Letters*, the "Advice" saw many editions over the following hundred years as it became England's main etiquette manual for women in the first half of the eighteenth century. Chesterfield's *Letters*, written between 1739 and 1765 and published in 1774, was reedited under the title *Principles of Politeness, and of Knowing the World*. The new edition consisted of selections from the letters, systematized under headings like "Modesty," "Elegance of Expression," "Cleanness," or "Laughter." In this form, the book was also published in Philadelphia in 1778, and, alongside a later edition suggestively titled *The American Chesterfield*, would become a reference point in the process of building the manners of the New World.[63]

Chesterfield wrote his *Letters* to his illegitimate son. Both the son's age and social status are to be considered in their reading, as Chesterfield's goal is to educate simultaneously the young and the deficient-by-birth toward acquiring a "decency" consonant with what he calls a "polite country."[64] In legal terms, Chesterfield's son is a *filius nullius* (nobody's son), and Chesterfield makes sure to repeatedly remind him of his position. He has no rights, and all he can inherit is a name and the privileges that can potentially come with it. The son thus needs to work hard; if he cannot be a nobleman, he will need to fashion himself into a gentleman. Manners become paramount; so does the control of laughter.

What Chesterfield believes is most needed in a young man's formation is "attention": "This steady and undissipated attention to one object, is a sure mark of a superior genius; as hurry, bustle, and agitation, are the never-failing symptoms of a weak and frivoulous mind";[65] "without attention nothing is to be done: want of attention, which is really want of thought, is either folly or madness."[66] Lack of attention is a form of folly, now closer to madness. The ever-present threat of effeminacy looms on the horizon. To lose control of one's attention is to be weak, frivolous, a woman. A certain kind of reading practice becomes the activity that most appropriately tests the limits of attention. But for Chesterfield, attention and its result, knowledge, are nothing if not conjoined with good breeding, with what he calls "the little things," which require a "second-rate attention."[67] He advises his son:

> A thousand little things, not separately to be defined, conspire to form these Graces, this *je ne sçais quoi*, that always pleases. A pretty person, genteel motions, a proper degree of dress, an harmonious voice, something open and cheerful in the countenance, but without laughing; a distinct and properly varied manner of speaking: all these things, and many others, are necessary ingredients in the composition of the pleasing *je ne sçais quoi*, which everybody feels, though nobody can describe.[68]

Among these "thousand little things" that he believes are a matter of "feeling," and thus cannot be either separated or described, Chesterfield goes on to isolate laughter:

Having mentioned laughing, I must particularly warn you against it: and I could heartily wish that you may often be seen to smile, but never heard to laugh while you live. Frequent and loud laughter is the characteristic of folly and ill manners: it is the manner in which the mob express their silly joy at silly things; and they call it being merry. In my mind, there is nothing so illiberal, and so ill-bred, as audible laughter. True wit, or sense, never yet made anybody laugh; they are above it: they please the mind, and give a cheerfulness to the countenance. . . . Not to mention the disagreeable noise that it makes, and the shocking distortion of the face that it occasions. Laughter is easily restrained by a little reflection. . . . I am sure that, since I have had the full use of my reason, nobody has ever heard me laugh.[69]

One's face should never give way to a laugh, but always maintain a controlled smile. Thinkers, "great minds," never laugh. This is a Hobbesian leitmotiv: "Great persons that have their mindes employed on great designes, have no leasure enough to laugh."[70] On Hobbes's account, as we have seen, only the weak laugh, those without genuine self-esteem, who use such gratuitous gestures to "recommend themselves to their owne favor."[71] If thought pleases, it produces a cheerful face. And cheerfulness is a form of controlled, polite, sober, smiling mirth, the sign of an interior "good nature."[72] As for laughter, it upsets aesthetic and moral requirements of control. It is a "shocking distortion of the face." The word "grimace," denoting a movement of the face affected by passion (any passion), will from now on be often associated with laughter. What "grimace" names is a geometrical breaking free from the outline of the calm, gentlemanly face.

An eloquent silence in Chesterfield's warning to his son covers over the fact that a "grimace" potentially opens the mouth. Teeth are not mentioned here, but Chesterfield implicitly draws his son's attention to the fact that a gentleman does not bare his teeth in laughter. At this time a gentleman's teeth would have most probably shown signs of decay, and many would have been missing. But while it would seem that toothlessness is an argument that can easily explain the "prohibition on laughter," in the early modern period the opposite argument also appears: by keeping the mouth closed, toothlessness discourages licentious acts, like "eating, laughing, and adultery."[73] In other words, not having teeth protects against the temptation of laughter.

Another important dimension in Chesterfield's warning is that laughter produces a certain sound, grouped together with other undesirable sounds under the umbrella of "noise."[74] Within a modern organization of sound, noise interrupts, interfering with rituals of communication and sociality. It carries resonances of discontentment and uproar. It is, in fact, laughter's affinities with noise that make it clear that the management of laughter is a question of class. Crowds and mobs make noise; gentlemen do not. If the body of a gentleman produces sound, this sound should fall under the two categories that fashion modern aurality: language and music. Bodily noises like coughing, burping, sneezing, and farting are *faux pas*. Even more so when produced with the same organs that produce language; only words come out of the mouth. Chesterfield's prohibition on laughter is a form of noise control.

The best argument Chesterfield can use in his persuasion exercise is, as always in instruction in manners, personal example. Within the parent-child cell, personal example (Have you ever heard *me* laugh?) works best. We do not know whether Chesterfield has ever laughed, but we—and the son-to-be-educated with us—are told the father himself has never been *heard* laughing.

PAINTING   Chesterfield is not preoccupied with women's instruction in manners. At the time he writes his *Letters*, Halifax, among others, had provided a code for women with regard to polite behavior. Halifax starts his lessons from a basic principle: "You must first lay it down for a foundation in general, that there is inequality in the sexes, and that for the better economy of the world the men, who were to be the lawgivers, had the larger share of reason bestowed upon them; by which means your sex is the better prepared for the compliance that is necessary for the better performance of those duties which seem to be most properly assigned to it."[75] Given this "foundation," the daughter must not attempt to change her lot. Her goal should simply be "compliance." In fact, at the end of the day, Halifax sees the daughter's situation as being in her favor, as she can learn to manipulate her husband to meet her needs. If Chesterfield gives his son advice on attention specifically in relation to his reading skills, Halifax warns his daughter against reading, as it might lead to "vain doubts." If the son should maintain his control by following the path of attention, a path to be best pursued through reading one thing at a time, for now the daughter should maintain hers by avoiding that path altogether. While the son is extolled to do everything he can to avoid falling into effeminacy, the daughter, already in its grip, is invited to comply. "No disquiet" is what a daughter should generally strive for: "Let your method be a steady course of good life, that may run like a smooth stream";[76] "in public be still and calm, neither indecently careless, nor affected in the other extreme."[77] But if laughter is to be avoided for the sake of attention, it is also to be avoided for the sake of the feminine ideal of statuesque stillness:

> It is not intended by you that you should forswear laughing; but remember that, fools being always painted in that posture, it might fright those who are wise from doing it too frequently, and going too near a copy which is so little inviting; and much more from doing it loud, which is an unnatural sound and looketh so much like another sex that few things are more offensive. That boisterous kind of jollity is as contrary to wit and good manners as it is to modesty and virtue. Besides, it is a coarse kind of quality, that throweth a

woman into a lower form, and degrades her from the rank of those who are more refined.[78]

It is from painting—and not from reading—that the daughter should take her models, because it is painting that at this time tries hard to illustrate the passions correctly, and does so with a nod to the day's rules of decorum. Modernity makes of the passions a matter of vision: since the passions arbitrarily paint themselves on a canvas-like face, the face needs to learn to compose itself, its muscles, into a work of art.

Le Brun drew two sets of drawings. First are his diagrams, meant to illustrate the text of his lectures on the expression of Cartesian passions. Second are his sketches, which acquire an important prescriptive dimension. "Laughter" is perhaps the most famous sketch. Although in his diagram the laughing face is immoderate and violent, and although most of his images depict vehement passions, when Le Brun sketches the laughing face (which appears to be a young woman's face, crowned with hair), she is still and calm, smiling timidly, inaudibly. Her head is slightly bent, as if in an exercise in flirtation. Her eyes modestly looking downward, she is appropriately embarrassed. It is as if she knows she is the bearer of a look, and is ashamed to be caught in the act. Color is not used, but she could be said to be blushing. There is no contortion of the face here, no grimace; laughter slightly dimples the cheeks. The eyebrows are moderately arched, remaining within the horizontal lines of the tranquil face. Laughter becomes one of the calm, soft, feminine passions—barely there.

Le Brun's *Conférence* went through three editions in the half-century following its presentation. The third edition, which appeared in 1727, skipped his theoretical gloss on Descartes and simply reproduced the sketches in magnified form. For it is visually that Le Brun's theory would work: like Descartes's *Passions*, his lecture would soon be forgotten, but the sketches he drew to illustrate the correct expression of the passions would reproduce themselves in the history of painting. Le Brun can be said to have established an aesthetic canon of facial movement which, in its turn, as Halifax's advice suggests, participated in an aestheticization of social life.[79] The aesthetic normality of the face would be class-determined. Passions like laughter signal the proximity of an anarchy-bound crowd, while the more refined, delicate emotions are the domain of a "feeling elite."[80]

EVELINA The domestic novel would take it upon itself to dramatize some of the principles put forth in explicitly prescriptive texts like Halifax's "Advice." One of the most popular (and symptomatic here) is Frances Burney's *Evelina, or The History of a Young Lady's Entrance into the World* (1778). The novel traces the vicissitudes of a laugh.

FIGURE 1.3

Charles Le Brun, *Laughter*. Musée du Louvre, Département des Arts Graphiques; Réunion des Musées Nationaux/Art Resource, New York.

The story is simple: Having been brought up by her adoptive father in the countryside, Evelina blunders upon her first encounter with the polite world. She laughs. Her burst is triggered by an overly polite gentleman, whose mechanical eccentricity translates into a "set smile on his face," an "invariable smile."[81] His problem is that he is polite out of politeness, which amounts to being impolite. As Chesterfield teaches, politeness is a matter of naturalness; to wear politeness excessively is a form of forbidden drag. The gentleman is addressing Evelina in an attempt to draw her attention to a *faux pas* of dancing rituals, when Evelina stops him: "I interrupted him—I blush for my folly— with laughter."[82] Shock on the faces of those witnessing the event: "when I looked around at Lord Orville, I saw such extreme surprise in his face,— the cause of which appeared so absurd, that I could not for my life preserve my gravity."[83] It is such a moment that Elias describes as marking the ever-receding "threshold of embarrassment."[84] Evelina sees herself reflected in the eyes of others, and the image that comes back to her is that of an abject Grobiana. "Refrain—Madam," eventually comes the response.[85]

The discourse on politeness stigmatizes laughter, and laughter stigmatizes Evelina. In Burney's novel, her burst makes her promiscuous in the eyes of the gentlemen witnessing the scene. The immoderateness of laughter translates into immodesty, which puts "delicacy" at risk. All orifices of a virtuous body need to be closed, wrapped tightly in an all-enveloping skin. To open one's mouth in laughter is to risk contamination. As if to follow up on this threat, throughout the novel Evelina is on the verge of becoming a "lost woman." Within the economy of the novel, it is with her burst of laughter that it all begins. Laughter is Evelina's stigma, a mark burned on her image, branding her irrevocably.

By the time she writes her letter to her adoptive father, Evelina has internalized the embarrassment of the moment. This embarrassment finds its expression on her face: "I blush for my folly." A reaction she herself finds absurd at the time of the event retroactively seems legitimate. Blushing, which Hobbes defined as "the apprehension of some thing dishonorable," translates this self-awareness.[86] Self-shaming has begun. Evelina apologizes for her burst, she distances herself from it, disavowing it. From now on, she will "take warning" whenever she feels a burst of laughter "coming."

Evelina is the tale of the struggle to stifle laughter lest the heroine be considered "a fool and half mad": "I could scarce forbear laughing"; "I really could not help laughing."[87] More and more, as the novel progresses, Evelina "improves," and she laughs or is on the verge of laughing less. Moreover, she becomes an arbiter in laughing matters as her letters pass judgment on those around her according to their laughs. Other characters in the novel laugh, and laughter marks them as outsiders to the polite world. Evelina's host, Captain Mirvan, is repeatedly described laughing immoderately. Evelina's lowly relatives, the Branghtons, laugh. Servants laugh. Drunkards laugh. Prostitutes laugh. They too attempt to hold laughter back; since they are "uneducated," however, their manners are closer to "savage manners." Laughter is one of the sites where it is clear that "savagery" has both colonial and class connotations. The "savages" are both out there, in faraway uncivilized lands, and within the territory of the "polite country."

Burney is aware of the prohibition on laughter *as* a prohibition. Her *Early Diary* tells the story of an imagined *Treatise upon Politeness*, which she would write in order to offer a comprehensive account of the "*newest fashioned* regulations."[88] The first injunction of the imagined treatise is not to cough: "'Not to *cough?*' exclaimed every one at once; 'but how are you to help it?' 'As to *that*,' answered I, 'I am not very clear about it myself, as I own I am guilty sometimes of doing it; but it is as much a mark of ill breeding, as it is to *laugh*; which is a thing that Lord Chesterfield has stigmatized.' . . . 'You may *smile* Sir,' answered I; 'but to *laugh* is quite abominable.'"[89] One of the virtues of the smile is that it is noiseless; the smile is an appropriate alternative to laughter, now a matter of the "abominable" (OED: "exciting disgust and hatred"). Burney's *Treatise upon Politeness* at the same time acknowledges and ridicules this norm, drawing attention to the existence of spaces where, despite the reign of polite behavior, one also found ways to laugh at the prohibition on laughter.

Burney is satirizing an injunction with which she is familiar, having perhaps heard it from Chesterfield, but also from a number of his followers. Preeminent among the latter is Anthony Ashley Cooper, Earl of Shaftesbury: "Consider the thing itself; at the bottom, what? Malevolence. Nothing else. Gall, venom. . . . See it in excess, see it when given way to and soundly followed. The characters it forms, the tempers, humours, morals of such as these."[90] Shaftesbury recommends reserve, frugality in laughter—if, indeed, such reserved laughter, he agrees, can still be called laughter: "How happy would it be to exchange this vulgar, sordid, profuse, horrid laughter for that more reserved, gentle kind, which hardly is to be called laughter, or which at least is of another species. How happy to exchange this mischievous, insulting, petulant species, for that benign, courteous and kind? this rustic, barbarous, immane, for that civil, polite, humane? the noisy, boisterous, turbulent, loud, for the still, peaceful, serene, mild?"[91] We are to imagine a laugh characterized by the following list of adjectives: reserved, gentle, benign, courteous, kind, civil, polite, humane, still, peaceful, serene, mild. Shaftesbury knows this could hardly be called laughter; this is something of a different register altogether—a "different species."

The words "emotion" and "sentiment" would come to be associated with the laugh Shaftesbury advocates. In fact, James Beattie speaks of "the risible emotion," which he couples with "sentimental laughter."[92] The latter is to be distinguished from malicious laughter, a mixture of hypocrisy and cruel joy, "one of the most hateful sights in nature."[93] Beattie agrees that sentimental laughter can in fact be no laughter at all, as the risible emotion can express itself in a grave, smiling face. What the ever more refined laughing face of a gentleman comes closer and closer to is a smile. Throughout this process, one in fact does not learn to laugh; one learns to smile. The "*savoir-rire*" is a "*savoir-sourire*."

Beattie sets the stakes high: "What improves individuals will in time improve nations."[94] The refinement of laughter becomes a sign of progress in the life of political institutions. "Good-breeding" is the rubric under which refinement is achieved:

> Laughter, which is either too profuse or too obstreperous, is an emotion of this kind. . . . [T]he restraints of good-breeding render society comfortable, and, by suppressing the outward energy of intemperate passions, tend not a little to suppress those passions themselves: while the unbridled liberty of savage life gives full play to every turbulent emotion, keeps the mind in continual uproar, and disqualifies it for those improvements and calm delights, that result from the exercise of the rational and moral faculties.[95]

Only the savage, those without good breeding, laugh passionately. Beattie proposes the possibility of a hierarchy of the politeness of countries, ranked according to "the very sound, duration, and frequency of their laughter."[96]

PRINCIPLES   Etiquette directives like the ones prescribed by Halifax and Chesterfield and dramatized in *Evelina* are never followed *ad literam*. After all, Chesterfield's son never became the orator his father's letters wanted him to be. He apparently was too shy and, ignoring his father's advice, secretly married an "inappropriate woman." Nor did Halifax's daughter become the model wife her father's advice wanted her to be. Her father-in-law, Lord Chesterfield, is said to have written on her copy of "Advice" the words "Labor in vain!" The epistolary messages can thus be said to have, at least in part   to use Chesterfield's word—"miscarried." As Burney's diary makes clear, despite the prohibition on laughter, people did laugh; that is, in certain ways, in certain spaces, at certain times, and at certain risks.[97] The very fact that such a range of normative texts on laughter exists is a sign not that there was no laughter but indeed that there was too much.

It is also clear that neither Chesterfield nor Halifax actually expected their offspring to follow their respective advice *ad literam*. It is on another level that advice works. Chesterfield writes about the role of his letters in his son's education: "I have laid the foundation of them [merit and manners], by the education which I have given you; but you must build the superstructure yourself."[98] The "principles of politeness" are to function as an invisible "foundation" in the son's formation. Chesterfield is a "founding father," and he knows that some of his prescriptions—the foundational ones—will stick to his son.

Halifax anticipates Chesterfield when he writes: "I am willing to begin with you before your mind is quite formed, that being the time in which it is most capable of receiving a colour that will last when it is mixed with. Few things are well learnt but by early precepts; those well infused make them natural, and we are never sure of retaining what is valuable till by a continued habit we have made it a piece of us."[99] The "principles of politeness" are to become "natural" and "a piece of us." It might be questionable whether Halifax can draw a picture for his daughter to look at—as in a mirror—and sculpt her body accordingly. But "continued habit," as well as repetition of rules regarding "the little things," infuse the body with cultural codes that become natural. They become our very "color," beyond the grasp of consciousness. Chesterfield writes to his son: "Your exercises in riding, fencing, and dancing, will civilize and fashion your body and your limbs, and give you, if you will but take it, *l'air d'un honnête homme*."[100] What gets "infused" and "civilized" and "fashioned" is the body. Through a very concrete form of "exercise," habits are drilled into a body and a face that come to appear "natural" and "a piece of us," giving us a certain "air," that *je ne sais quoi*.

Chesterfield's letters do nothing but repeat the same precepts of good breeding over and over again. This is the key mechanism of the civilizing process. Repetition is then followed by observation. Chesterfield draws his son's attention to the fact that he is being watched constantly from all directions: "I give you fair warning, that at Leipsig I shall have a hundred invisible spies upon you; and shall be exactly informed of everything that you do, and of almost everything that you say";[101] "for I have Arguses, with a hundred eyes each, who will watch you narrowly, and relate to me faithfully."[102] Hundreds of eyes, watching one's every move from all directions, translates into an autoscopic regime: whether watched or not, Chesterfield's son will be molding himself for an evaluative gaze. He will be composing himself, fashioning a body that interpellates its reader in a scopophilic mode: watch me and be pleased. On the horizon, there is the loss of paternal love in case of indiscipline: "be persuaded that I shall love you extremely, while you deserve it; but not one moment longer."[103] Eventually, there will come the time of examination: "I shall dissect and analyse you with a microscope, so that I shall discover the least speck or blemish. This is fair warning, therefore take your measures accordingly."[104] We have here what Michel Foucault describes as the three interrelated dimensions of a disciplining process: hierarchical observation, normalizing judgment, and examination.[105] Foucault's disciplinary techniques almost seem self-evident in the context of normative (explicitly didactic) codes for manners. They constitute that (not so) "hidden persuasion" which Pierre Bourdieu sees as "capable of instilling a whole cosmology, an ethic, a metaphysic, a political philosophy, through injunctions as insignificant as 'stand up straight' or 'don't hold your knife in your left hand.'"[106]

PHYSIOGNOMY/GELATOSCOPY   Physiognomic echoes resonate throughout the discourse on the passions and their expressions, and become paramount to a discussion of laughter in the nineteenth century, when physiognomy resurfaces with renewed persuasive force and acquires legitimacy in the reading of faces and bodies.[107]

Art history distinguishes between physiognomy (the study of facial features) and pathognomy (the study of expression). This is a temporal distinction: while expression is the episodic, fugitive trace of a passion or emotion on the face, physiognomy is the fixing of this expression, expression made face. Ultimately, however, physiognomy is a variation on the theme of expression. Johann Caspar Lavater, the "father of physiognomy," whose *Essays* were widely read in the nineteenth century, brought the two together in unambiguous terms: "The friend of truth considers these two sciences as inseparable. He studies them together."[108] And the fact remains that the distinction is often blurred in both artistic and interpretative practices. Many theorists of expression are also physiognomists. Conversely, physiognomists start from a theory of expression and build their notion of physiognomic perception and interpretation holding on to a notion of an educated beholder of pictorial representation who has learned to read the expressivity of faces.[109]

Physiognomy assumes that passions and emotions work on the face, and if one is repeated more than others it leaves a permanent "imprint" on the face, visible on "the animal at rest."[110] Repetition of the same state of mind, for which the soul has a "predisposition," thus "engraves" it on the face, forming a pleasing or not so pleasing "portraiture." Physiognomy assumes that the result of this repeated imprinting process is a somewhat fixed morphology of facial features. In other words, if one laughs often, laughter is gradually "imprinted" on the face. Since every time we laugh we agitate the same muscles, the face memorizes the laughing expression. In time, laughter writes itself on the face. An enlightened observer will be able to identify a "type" here: the laugher.

For Lavater, the face is a microcosm of the body and, like the body, it is divided into three parts: "The forehead, down to the eye-brows, the mirror of the intelligence: The nose and cheeks, the mirror of moral life: The mouth and chin, the mirror of animal life; while the eye would be the centre and summary of the whole."[111] Among the parts of the face, he singles out the mouth: "This part of the body is so sacred in my eyes, that I scarcely have the courage to attempt to treat it."[112] This, because the mouth is a complex physiognomic conundrum, a function of its multiple use value. At its most basic, the mouth both eats and speaks, and its two activities are in tension.

The mouth is also the most racialized feature of the face. The Italian physiognomist Paolo Mantegazza writes:

> Generally all the higher races have a moderately-sized mouth, with the lips rather thin and slightly curved. . . . [W]e agree in considering ugly a mouth which recalls our cousins, the anthropoid apes. A mouth is ugly if it is too large or too far from the nose, when the upper lip is a sort of long curtain. Unless we are sensual as some monkeys, we think a mouth with too fleshy lips very ugly, these nearly always going with a prominent snout, or, to speak scientifically, with a *prognathous face*. . . . [I]t is true that this type nearly always coincides with great sensuality.[113]

A protruding jaw, the signature feature of the prognathous face, equipped with thick lips and a big orifice, is considered the paradigmatic mark of animalism. The pleasures of lovemaking are thought to be visible on the mouth: "The yearnings of love and the passions of voluptuousness converge here as to their natural centre."[114] An open or half-open mouth is an invitation: "a half-closed mouth, always expectant of light kisses or savory morsels."[115] For the physiognomist, the upper lip, ideally neither too thin nor too fleshy, should dominate the lower lip, closing the mouth.[116] The problem of the prognathous face is that it most often reveals an open mouth. In Lavater's sketches of human profiles, racial others have open mouths; so do idiots and criminals. It often looks as if open mouths are open neither to eat nor to speak but, rather, by default—certain characters cannot keep their mouths closed.

For Lavater, the openness of the mouth translates degrees of morality: "And where could that vice express itself to more advantage than in the most moveable part of the face; in that which receives, more easily than others, the impress of our passions?"[117] And: "It is upon the lips,—or rather between the lips, that the depravity lurks."[118] On the horizon here is the idea that the mouth can acquire yet another use: the mouth can be a sexual organ. The thought has been lurking on the margins of "grimace" all along. Freud would come along to, in a signature gesture, put his finger on the issue, as well as express the anxiety still associated with it. Freud begins his speculations on the perversions starting from the deviation from the (normal) sexual aim associated with the mouth: "mutual approximation of the mucous membrane of the lips in the kiss has received a sexual value among the civilized nations, though the parts of the body do not belong to the sexual apparatus and merely form the entrance to the digestive tract."[119] Freud has in mind a mouth which acquires sexual resonances in relation to the kiss, but he knows that once the mouth is severed from its role in digestion (the entrance to the digestive tract) it can lay claim to being part of the sexual apparatus *tout court*. The mucous membrane enveloping the lips can then host a range of ever

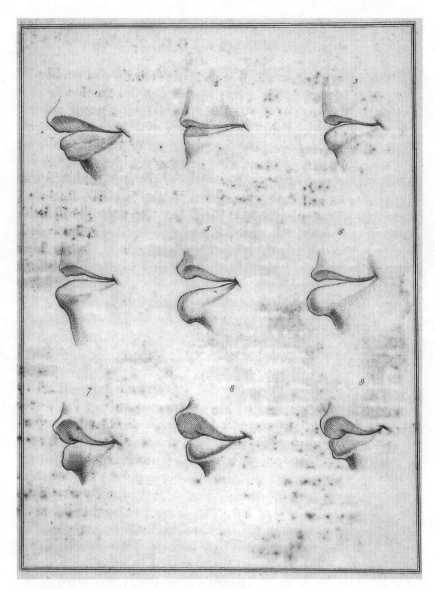

FIGURE 1.4
Johann Caspar Lavater, *Essays on Physiognomy*, 1810. Huntington Library.

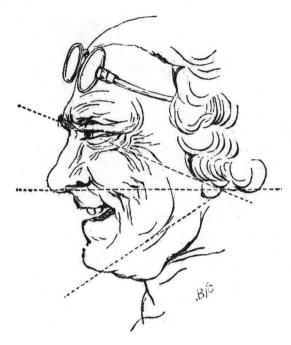

FIGURE 1.5
Charles Bell, *The Anatomy and Philosophy of Expression as Connected to the Fine Arts*, 1844.
Huntington Library.

more illicit activities. The problem artists, art theorists, and physiognomists face is how to visualize the scene of a mouth that can eat, speak, laugh, and have sex at the same time. A range of subterfuges will be found that will help domesticate the mouth's capacity to multitask such that the mouth will not speak when it eats or laughs, and it will not speak, eat, or laugh when it is part of the sexual apparatus.

Charles Bell's influential 1844 *The Anatomy and Philosophy of Expression as Connected to the Fine Arts* offered a diagram of a laughing profile and showed that, when the mouth opens in laughter, the lower part of the face encroaches on the higher, and this encroachment closes the eye. In other words, the problem with the face in laughter is that the excessive opening of the mouth almost closes the eye, the site of intellectual activity. The effect is that, in Bell's words, "the face loses all dignity and form."[120] This is why, according to Bell's earlier formulations of these ideas, only the "lowest class of Dutch painters, and the caricature draughtsman, have chiefly to do with broad laughter. It is too ludicrous and too violent a straining of the features for other compositions."[121] He concluded that the laughing face is a caricature—in itself.

When it comes to laughter, physiognomists learned from Giambattista Della Porta's 1586 *De humana physiognomonia*. An image of two men drinking and

FIGURE 1.6
Charles Bell, *Essays on the Anatomy of Expression in Painting*, 1806. Huntington Library.

FIGURE 1.7
Giambattista Della Porta, *De humana physiognomonia*, 1586. Huntington Library.

laughing recurred throughout the book, and their foreheads, mouths, eyes, and teeth were explained physiognomically. "There is nothing more stupid than an inept laugh," Della Porta declared.[122] He distinguished between different kinds of laughs, such as the coughing laugh or the high-voiced laugh, and generally advocated temperance, giving his approval only to the "little laugh." Della Porta's encyclopedic knowledge also led to a list of famous non-laughers or little laughers: Plato and Anaxagoras never laughed, while Horace and Crassus laughed very little.

For his part, Lavater saw in laughter an important key to the understanding of the moral truth of a face: "The laugh is the touchstone of the judgment, of the qualities of the heart, of the energy of the character: it expresses love or hatred, pride or humility, sincerity or falsehood. Why have I not Designers of sufficient ability, or sufficiently patient, to watch for, and to convey perfectly, the contours of the laugh? *A Physiognomy of Laughter* would be a most interesting elementary book for the knowledge of man."[123] The assumption here is that one should be able to distinguish and classify people according to their laughs. Gelatoscopy is the art of divination by laughter. Its premise: show me how you laugh, and I will tell you who you are.

Lavater revisited Le Brun's diagrams and unambiguously translated them into the language of physiognomy. Images 13, 14, 15, 16 on his plate with laughing faces depict idiots. Number 16, for example, is "naturally judicious, endowed with penetration, enterprising, and capable of perseverance. The traces of his imbecility are very slightly apparent only in the lips, and the

after CHODOWIECKI & LE BRUN.

FIGURE 1.8
Johann Caspar Lavater, *Essays on Physiognomy*, 1810. Huntington Library.

wrinkles of the cheek. . . ."[124] No face on the plate is to be admired, although a few are somewhat redeemed: 7 is "the profile of a good housewife," and 8 "an aged matron, active and experienced."[125]

As an exercise in gelatoscopy, Lavater performed a psysiognomic reading of Democritus' face. He argued that, despite the fact that tradition describes the laughing philosopher as a penetrating spirit and a creative genius, an attentive physiognomist can use his tact to reveal Democritus' real self by reading his laughter. Whatever Democritus' features might have been before he became the laughing philosopher, "The sarcastic grin, so different from the heavenly smile of pity, from the smile of tenderness granting indulgence or giving salutary counsel; so different, alas! from the smile of beneficent humanity, from the ingenuous smile of innocence and cordiality—that contemptuous grin converted into habit must inevitably disfigure the most beautiful, much more a singular face."[126] Laughter has left its permanent imprint on Democritus' mouth, disfiguring it. This mouth is now ugly even when it does not laugh. Nothing noble can be produced through a voice imagined to be housed in such a mouth.

According to Lavater, what is needed is work on laughter. In the nineteenth century, this work is undertaken from a range of perspectives, not all of physiognomic inflection. One fascinating account is the work of Pierre Gratiolet. For him, laughter is a "gesture of the voice" and is to be classified according to respiratory patterns.[127] But Lavater's call to design a physiognomy of laughter was to find its most attentive ear in George Vasey's *The Philosophy of Laughter and Smiling*. The essay is a culmination of a discourse that has no patience for laughter. Laughter is the source of all evils here, a hydra-headed monster. Vasey's argument: we laugh at a variety of undesirable things (crime, levity, frivolity); if only we did not laugh at them, they would slowly disappear. It is a utopia of a laughless world. The project of unlearning to laugh would be necessarily accompanied by that of learning to distinguish between different laughing faces and between laughing and smiling. An illustrated typology follows.

Vasey drew the profile of the habitual laugher relying on the following adjectives: ignorant, vulgar, uncultivated, silly, giddy, frivolous, superficial, shallow-brained, empty-headed.[128] What he called "inveterate laughers" are further described as coarse, brutal, and unfeeling.[129] Only the depraved, the dissipated, and the criminal are "addicted to laughter."[130] Those who become cultivated "seldom descend to laughter," and the wise, the prudent, and the thoughtful never laugh.[131] What they do is smile, and Vasey thought laughing and smiling could not diverge more: "The various species of laughter are all ridiculous, absurd, or impudent—vulgar or idiotic—presenting ugliness to the sight, and harsh and grating sounds to the ear. The various species of the genuine or amiable smile are all beautiful, whether of benevolence or kindness—sympathy or gratitude—admiration, veneration, or affection—they

DEMOCRITUS.

FIGURE 1.9
Johann Caspar Lavater, *Essays on Physiognomy*, 1810. Huntington Library.

are all sweetness and beauty. We suspect a laugh, we confide in a smile."[132] The problem with laughter is once again a function of its audibility, it being a "disagreeable noise . . . it invariably produces a silly, vulgar, unmeaning sound—whether it be a giggle or a grin—a compressed he! he!—an expanded ha! ha! or a downright broad horse laugh."[133] The smile, on the other hand, is "sweet and gentle silence."[134]

Vasey distinguished between four laughs:

1. The hearty laugh of the gentler sex
2. The stentorian laugh of the stronger sex
3. The superlative laugh, or, the highest degree of laughter
4. The giggling laugh, excited by boisterous fun and nonsense

None of these laughs is desirable. All laughers are dubious. The mouths opening to laugh them are often missing at least one tooth, a function of their aesthetic deficiency.

Not all nineteenth-century physiognomic voices were as vehement when it came to laughter.[135] Mantegazza's *Physiognomy and Expression* also dedicated a few pages to the issue, under the rubric "The Expression of Pleasure." He reviewed the physiognomic literature on laughter, going through typologies like Cornelio Ghirardelli's "*Laughing mouth and foul breath*," and their most frequent conclusion: "Those who laugh easily and in great bursts have large spleens, and are naturally foolish, vain, stupid, inconstant, and indiscreet. Those who laugh little and with moderation are prudent, astute, discreet, loyal, constant, and of brilliant intelligence."[136] After quoting such remarks abundantly, Mantegazza nonetheless claimed they were prescientific, and largely dismissed them. He eventually came to the conclusion that "Laughter, easy, copious, and frank, indicates a good soul devoid of vanity. This is one of the least misleading axioms of physiology. The hypocritical education of our age teaches us to restrain the expansion both of grief and of joy, and we grow unaccustomed to open-hearted laughter."[137] The problem, in other words, might be in the beholder, who simply has grown unaccustomed to laughter and now, like Vasey, sees evil everywhere and is not able to recognize a frank laugh. Mantegazza drew attention to the fact that many morally suspect types in fact do not laugh. Thus the haughty, the vain, the awkward laugh little so that they will not compromise their dignity; the envious, the wicked, the malevolent likewise rarely laugh. In other words, they too have acquired some amount of physiognomic savoir and now refrain from laughter lest they betray themselves. The art of dissimulation, which Lavater thought physiognomy could combat, had reached new levels of professionalism.

FACE-WORK The historical management of laughter is part of a face-producing mechanism, best described by Erving Goffman.[138] Goffman refers to the individual projection of a self as "face." He is quick to note that face is

1   2

3   4

FIGURE 1.10
George Vasey, *The Philosophy of Laughter and Smiling*, 1875. Harvard University Library.

not a biological entity; rather, it is diffused through social interactions (glances, gestures, statements, positionings). Such social rituals are nonetheless expressive orders and, as such, they remain dependent on the actual expressive work of faces. The smallest unit of social interaction is the fleeting facial move.

According to Goffman, daily social encounters consist of efforts to maintain face against possible threats to it, which can result in loss of face, embarrassment, and shame at the individual level and, in broader terms, social disequilibrium. The very possibility of these threats is a reminder that our face is "on loan" to us and we could lose it at any time. We thus do our best to not lose credit and maintain face. What Goffman calls "face-work" consists of operations whereby we maintain consistency with face and, in any given situation, devise a number of face-saving mechanisms. Tact, politeness, and poise are rubrics under which this is done.

What the story traced here shows is that certain kinds of laughs can lead to loss of face. Laughter is a threat to the expressive order of the smile, which has come to govern modern social interaction. In Goffman's terms, if the smile is a social ritual, the excessive laugh is its profanation. The body opens one of its most guarded orifices, and an explosive laughter "floods out." It is a social gaffe, and its effect is potential stigma.

Ritual orders are organized on accommodative principles and are inherently conservative. Goffman writes: "the person is willing to be subject to informal social control—if he is willing to find out from hints and glances and tactful cues what his place is and keep it. . . . He cooperates to save his face, finding that there is much to be gained from venturing nothing."[139] We thus "choose" to avoid certain laughs and to apologize for others. The "civilizing of laughter" does not lead to a prohibition on all laughter. But once one strips laughter of noise and grimace, what we are left with can hardly be called a laugh. The mouth begins to open, moves toward the possibility of a laugh, and then stops short of it. "You may smile," comes Burney's echo.

"It's not the same thing," retorts Vladimir in *Waiting for Godot*. In the twentieth century, a number of voices express their agreement.

CHAPTER 2

MODERNISM, OR AN EXTRAVAGANCE OF LAUGHTER

To comprehend the joke theoretically, therefore, is to address the problem of laughter. . . . Laughter imposes itself as the ineluctable problem.
Samuel Weber

LAUGHTER LOVERS   A people of laughers, Langston Hughes has called his people. His poem "Laughers," first published in Crisis in 1922 as "My People," goes through a series of roles associated with African-Americans (singers, storytellers, dancers, but also dishwashers, cooks, and waiters), to conclude that they are laughers: "Yes, laughers . . . laughers . . . laughers— / Loud-mouthed laughers in the hands / Of Fate."[1] "Yes, laughers . . . laughers . . . laughers" comes as a response to a doubtful question: "Laughers?" "Yes, laughers . . ." is the insistent answer, its insistence a function of the acknowledged irony of an African-American poet in 1922 describing his people as laughers.

"I love myself when I am laughing" is also Zora Neale Hurston's provocative statement, an attempt to claim membership with the same people of laughers. It is a response to Carl Van Vechten, who had taken a series of photographs of her laughing; but also to Hughes and his accusations that she had put on a "happy darkie" show and played the primitive. The sentence would be the site of Hurston's recuperation by 1970s feminism, becoming the title of her 1979 collection published by Feminist Press. It condenses an "attitude" that brought Hurston intellectual annihilation in the 1930s and posthumous fame. A list of adjectives describes the "attitude" within different contexts: quick-tempered, arrogant, rude, inconsiderate, unladylike; or, alternatively, enthusiastic, confident, unconventional, outspoken, free-minded. Photographs of Hurston laughing, marking this "attitude," have become her trademark. One sees them wherever Hurston's name appears. And then, "I love myself when I am laughing." What does Hurston see when her laughter returns to her in the form of a photograph?

What is clear is that both Hughes and Hurston are deeply invested in a wider struggle over African-American laughter. Hughes would write about Hurston: "To many of her white friends, no doubt, she was a perfect 'darkie,' in the nice meaning they give the term—that is a naïve, childlike, sweet, humorous, and highly colored Negro."[2] This description came in the wake of the fight between Hughes and Hurston over the authorship of their 1930 collaborative work, *Mule Bone: A Comedy of Negro Life*, which they imagined would be the first African-American comedy.[3] Their conflict is considered one of the most notorious "literary quarrels" in the history of African-American literature. "Playing the primitive" is in this context the insult one injured party throws at the other. But, in close proximity to the primitivist theme, the quarrel is also symptomatic of the desire to rescue African-American laughter from those to whom Hughes refers as Hurston's "white friends," known for their indulgence in fantasies of black laughter.

It would be Ralph Ellison who would take it upon himself to explicitly frame the struggle over African-American laughter, and to bridge the discussion between a wider modernism and the African-American tradition. In 1981 Ellison wrote a new introduction to the thirtieth-anniversary edition of *Invisible Man*—a twentieth-century novel if ever there was one. Four years later, in 1985, a key essay, "An Extravagance of Laughter," appeared in *Going to the Territory*, the only previously unpublished essay in the collection and the last text to be published by Ellison in book form during his lifetime. The essay told the amazing story of a 1936 burst of laughter. Ellison's views on laughter developed between these two texts, the new Introduction and "An Extravagance of Laughter." He would write: "It was a startling idea, yet the voice was so persuasive with echoes of blues-toned laughter that I found myself being nudged toward a frame of mind in which, suddenly, current events, memories and artifacts began combining to form a vague but intriguing new perspective."[4] A new, necessarily vague perspective over his own life but also over the century it spanned, put together through an eclectic editing of events, memories, and artifacts, became possible in the wake of this laugh.

It would be Ellison's attempt at a recuperative project, one that would struggle to hear a tone in a laughing voice. Ellison reminds us of the simple fact that laughter is a question of sound. But for him that means laughter is in fact a literary question. For Ellison believes that sound is not readily available in the immediacy of a range of sound practices, music in particular. His proposal is that we listen for echoes of laughter in a voice that speaks to us in the novel, his own novel, *Invisible Man*.

Ellison's story is crucial to the larger history of the laughing twentieth century. Let us recall that Badiou starts *The Century* on an intriguing note: "What is a century? I have in mind Jean Genet's preface to his play *The Blacks*. In it, he asks ironically: 'What is a black man?' Adding at once: 'And first of all, what color is he?' Likewise, I want to ask: A century, how many years is that?"[5] Badiou goes on to propose that "the century" is not a quantitative unit, a collection of an arbitrary number of years. Rather, the century coalesces around a series of thoughts the century thought, and the distinct manner in which its questions were asked. The relation between "What is a century?" and "What is a black man?" Badiou does not interrogate as such. And yet the twentieth century was also "the century of the color line," in W. E. B. Du Bois's famous formulation. There is an intimate relation between the two questions, one that goes beyond method and analogy. The twentieth century was profoundly implicated in the question "What is a black man?" because the figure of the black man has often been a foil for "the passion for the real." As we will see, this means that the century was also invested in the sound of his (and especially her) laughter.

PRIMITIVISM The "before" primitive people are thought to inhabit is a fantasy of unadulterated experience. It is well known that in early twentieth century a transgressive sexual impulse was attributed to the primitive. What is less known is that alongside the erotic fantasy (and in close proximity to it) one also found a fantasy of authentic, real, passional laughter. Bataille wrote in his *Story of the Eye*: "These orgasms were as different from normal climaxes as, say, the mirth of savage Africans from that of Occidentals. In fact, though the savages may sometimes laugh as moderately as whites, they also have long-lasting jags, with all parts of the body in violent release, and they go whirling willy-nilly, flailing their arms about wildly, shaking their bellies, necks, and chests, and chortling and gulping horribly."[6] Having passed through Chesterfield's school, Westerners have tamed both their erotic impulses and their laughter. The imagined return to one is also a return to the other. Bataille is drawing on a long tradition of philosophical anthropology, but also on early-twentieth-century avant-garde movements, precursors of modernism. And modernism is a site where laughing primitivism found a welcoming cradle.

On the American literary scene, Gertrude Stein's "Melanctha" could be said to have set the tone in this direction, at the same time as it announced the complexity and profoundly ambivalent dimension of modernist primitivism.[7] In "Melanctha," Stein's exploration into "real, strong, hot love" stands in need of passionate characters, "the kind of people who have emotions that come to them as sharp as a sensation."[8] What seem to be African-American characters (who are obviously *not* African-American) make the incursion into "excitement," "wondering," and "animalism" possible. All these terms are laughter-inflected.

Melanctha is a wonderer, a southern female *flâneur*, "keen in her sense for real experience."[9] Melanctha walks and wonders and learns. At the level of form, in search of this "real experience," indistinguishable from a sexual impulse, Stein's story fashions itself on an overly fictitious dialect, which draws attention to the figure of the African-American primitive while nonetheless exploring the formal effects of the use of dialect. Alongside its idiom, Stein's story is in need of an atmosphere, something we used to call "local color," here a function of a synesthetic amalgam of perception. In this context, the primitive's laughter is simply "in the air": "[they] glistened in their black heat, and they flung themselves free in their wide abandonment of shouting laughter."[10]

In "Melanctha," it is one's most important characteristic to be able to laugh "the wide, abandoned laughter that makes the warm glow of negro sunshine."[11] The phrase is repeated enough times to announce a cliché, perhaps a physiognomic type (the "black laugher"), an echo of the reader's own attachment to both physiognomy and primitivism. Nonetheless, all the characters in Stein's story are measured against it. Rose Johnson is a "real black, tall, well built, sullen, stupid, childlike, good looking negress . . . laughed when she was happy but she had not the wide, abandoned laughter that makes the warm broad glow of negro sunshine. Rose was never joyous with the earthborn, boundless joy of the negroes. Hers was just ordinary, any sort of woman laughter."[12] Rose stands no chance in the search for "real, strong, hot love," as she remains sullen in her desire to "do the right thing." In contradistinction, Melanctha, a "graceful, pale yellow, intelligent, attractive negress," is "impulsive and unbounded."[13] She nonetheless laughs a "hard forced laughter."[14] Melanctha has what it takes, but she tries too hard and the result is a harsh laughter: "you got a laugh then so hard, it just rattles."[15] Only Melanctha's lover, Jeff Campbell, initially unimpassioned, looking for a regular, respectable, secure life for himself and his people, "laughed, and his was the free abandoned laughter that gives the warm broad glow to negro sunshine."[16] The lesson he eventually learns is to stop thinking, abandon himself to passion, and feel "deep, hard and right."

One of the most controversial figures of American modernism, Carl Van Vechten, admired and promoted Stein's story, and was inspired by it. His novel Nigger Heaven is after a "vital instinct" the "civilized races [are] struggling to get back to."[17] In the economy of the novel, to watch people in Harlem dance is to watch "people who live."[18] The answer to the modernist question, "Does life live?" is, "It does in Nigger Heaven." That to-be-recuperated vital instinct is place-determined. It is to be found in "Harlem," which turns out to be a mix of music, dance, and laughter. In Nigger Heaven, laughter accompanies music, sometimes it covers over it, sometimes it explodes when music stops. It is a rhythm, which is also the rhythm of dance. Like "hot love," laughter is at the same time alluring and horrifying. A space where sexuality follows "the beat of the African rhythm," Harlem resonates with an "uncanny horrible laughter."[19] Coming from an invisible depth "the civilized races" have forgotten, this laughter is perceived as the sign of life itself.

The impulse to search for what is imagined as a lost vital instinct is revealed in *Nigger Heaven* as untapped material for literature, the it modernist writers should pursue. In a central scene in the novel, an aspiring African-American writer is advised to write about it and only about it. If he and others like him will not, white writers will. And so they did. It is the impetus for *Nigger Heaven* itself, and for what was to become an important thread in American literary modernism. This scene in *Nigger Heaven* can serve as a framing device for modernism's attentiveness to "the passion for the real": "The whole place [Harlem], contrary to the general impression, is overrun with fresh, unused material. . . . God, boy, let your characters live and breathe! Give 'em air. Let 'em react to life and act naturally. . . . [Harlem] has more aspects than a diamond has facets."[20] The network of intertextuality around the scene includes African-American writers like Nella Larsen, who expressed her admiration for *Nigger Heaven* and ambivalently explored some of the same themes in *Quicksand*. But it was Sherwood Anderson's bestseller, *Dark Laughter*, that drew out the modernist stakes in the laughter of the primitive.

The main character in *Dark Laughter* is after something he cannot quite describe. He leaves his wife and his repetitive newspaper job in Chicago in search of it. He associates this elusive something with life on the Mississippi and memories of his mother: "Song, laughter, profanity, the smell of goods, dancing niggers—life everywhere."[21] Were Mark Twain to write about life on the Mississippi in his time, however, he would have to write of "song killed, of laughter killed, of men herded into a new age of speed, of factories, of swift, fast-running trains."[22] How can one go back? How can one position oneself such that one can exclaim: "Dance life! Awake and Dance!"[23] Premodern, preindustrial, anachronistic yet vital "dancing niggers" and their laughter on the river offer a glimpse of one possible solution: "Standing laughing— coming by the back door—with shuffling feet, a laugh—a dance in the body."[24] More than the characters of *Nigger Heaven*, whose life in New York has alienated them from that "vital instinct," they seem to know about "life," which necessarily resonates in the "slow lazy laughter of niggers."[25]

The last scene of *Dark Laughter* draws the necessary conclusions. The second male character in the novel, a small-town industrialist attempting to live "the Ford way of life," has reached a dead end:

> Fred wanted to laugh. He tried but couldn't. . . . What one does is to smile. . . . Why couldn't Fred laugh? He kept trying but failed. In the road before the house one of the negro women now laughed. There was a shuffling sound. The older negro woman tried to quiet the younger, blacker woman, but she kept laughing the shrill laughter of the negress. "I knowed it, I knowed it, all the time I knowed it," she cried, and the high shrill laughter ran through the garden and into the room where Fred sat upright and rigid in bed.[26]

Fred (rigid, sterile, and unlaughing) has just been abandoned by his wife, Aline, who leaves him for "the other man," on account of her own search for that elusive something. Aline's aspiration goes in the direction of "something primitive like a nigger woman in an African dance."[27]

The African dance is a loaded trope in relation to the figure of the primitive, bringing images of Josephine Baker to mind. Indeed, if the impetus behind Dark Laughter is to say "Dance life! Awake and Dance!" the desired life is imagined dancing the syntax of Josephine Baker's rhythmic combinations. Nigger Heaven has a lot to say about what it imagines as "this African beat. . . . This love of drums, of exciting rhythms, this naïve delight in glowing color."[28] It is something that gets associated with an imagined jungle and its sounds: "The band snored and snorted and whistled and laughed like a hyena."[29] Baker improvised on the fantasy, capitalizing on it.[30] That this is a fantasy of "Africa" is perhaps best illustrated by Edmond Gréville's 1935 film Princess Tam Tam, which has Baker play a Tunisian girl, going to Paris and pretending to be an Indian princess, the viewer being all the while aware of Baker's iconic status in Paris, as well as her background as an African-American woman from St. Louis. Paul Colin's well-known prints, like other visual images of Baker, often depict her in an open-mouthed laugh. That the paradigmatic figure of the modernist dancer is also laughing should not come as a surprise. Since Nietzsche, dancing and laughing have held hands as thresholds toward an "elsewhere."[31] In this context, laughter is a primitive dance of the body. Rigid, smiling Fred, unresponsive to the rhythms of the imagined African dance and irritated by laughter, insisting on keeping up the pretense, does not match the fantasy, and is left behind.

"Dark laughter" is a version of the Freudian "dark continent," a matter of space, color, feminine sexuality, and both fascination and horror. The phrase appears twice in Anderson's novel, once to describe the laughter of the two African-American servants ("The air on the hilltop was filled with laughter—dark laughter").[32] The second time "dark laughter" is invoked is in a Parisian scene. During a small gathering in Paris after the war, a female journalist tells the story of an orgy. The end of the war, itself the epitome of a mechanized, assembly-line modernity, seems to announce the end of pretense, perhaps the very end of "civilization." The thought of one's being alive, of still being alive, calls forth a "hunger for the limit," which the orgy pushes to its own limit.[33] This Parisian scene, the mediator between "Africa" and "America," is a space of "dark laughter": "Rose Frank laughed, a queer high nervous laugh—dark laughter that."[34]

Anderson's novel suggests that "dark laughter" is an elusive thing, which it associates with what it perceives to be the secret of the primitive: "Word-lovers, sound-lovers—the blacks seemed to hold a tone in some warm place, under their red tongues perhaps. Their thick lips were walls under which the tone hid. . . . Afterwards when he thought of that moment Bruce always remembered the singing voices of the negro deck-hands as colors. Streaming reds, browns, golden yellows coming out of black throats."[35] This secret, hidden in the primitive's body, in her mouth, is translated as tone. This is a matter of both color and sound: sounds are pouring out of sound-loving mouths like colors. Not any colors, but a mixture of reds, browns, and golden yellows.[36] From the perspective of this nexus of texts, it is as if modernism takes on the project of attempting to catch up with the "hunger for the limit" as intuitively felt in this tone. The task of the modernist writer is to push his perceptive apparatus to eavesdrop on a tonal secret. *Dark Laughter* reminds us how Gauguin tried just that in his paintings, experiments in the red, browns, and especially golden yellows he found in Tahiti.[37]

If, *pace* Badiou, the passion for the real cannot be divorced from the century's project of creating a "new man," in its turn the latter cannot be conceived apart from a search for new social spaces.[38] The laughing primitive is a function of an attempt to produce space differently, the foil for which are fictional spatial constructs like "Africa," "the Mississippi," or "Harlem." Arguably, *Dark Laughter* is already aware of this. If it is not, it took Ernest Hemingway's *Torrents of Spring* (suggestively subtitled *A Romantic Novel in Honor of the Passing of a Great Race*) to frame laughing primitivism as a modernist fantasy of space. The 1926 novel is a parody of *Dark Laughter* and the modernist constellation around it. One finds in Hemingway's novel the assembly line, the war, the Parisian orgy, impotence and the search for "life," the walking and the wondering, the vital instinct—and laughter. Hemingway's "notes to the reader," with their invocation of figures like Stein, Anderson, and Dos Passos, offer a minimalist, caricatured sketch of the modernist literary game. Primitive laughter is revealed to be a function of this game.

Pushing the primitivist theme, Hemingway uses Native American characters: "Here among the simple aborigines, the only real Americans, he had found that true communion."[39] Modernist anthropology is part of this scene: "It is true that before starting this story we spent twelve years studying the various Indian dialects of the North."[40] So is woman: "Would it help him to want a woman?"[41] In the wake of the Parisian experience of sexual disillusionment, it indeed helps if one is faced with the "fact" of a naked Indian woman: "something stirred inside him, some vague primordial feeling."[42] But on the "background" of the literary game is, as in Anderson's novel, the sound produced by two laughing African-American characters. One is a black cook: "From out of the kitchen, through the wicket in the hall, came a high-pitched, haunting laugh. Scripps listened. Could that be the laughter of the Negro?"[43] The other is a black bartender in an Indian bar: "Sharply, without explanation, he broke into high-pitched uncontrolled laughter. The dark laughter of the Negro."[44] In Hemingway's parody it is "the haunting sound of a Negro laughing" that haunts modernism.[45] How "black" or "dark" is this laughter? The first time the black cook is mentioned, the novel makes sure to suggest, as if in passing, that "perhaps the chap was only sooty from the stove."[46]

The question of what anthropology has to say about laughter imposes itself here. Let us recall that, as part of his research for *Expression*, Darwin, an amateur anthropologist, sent a questionnaire to a number of functionaries of the British Empire to inquire about the laughter of "different races of men."[47] Two questions were asked about laughter: "When in good spirits do the eyes sparkle, with the skin a little wrinkled round and under them, and with the mouth a little drawn back at the corners?"; "Is laughter ever carried to such an extreme as to bring tears into the eyes?"[48] Darwin received a number of reports: "Sir Andrew Smith has seen the painted face of a Hottentot woman all furrowed with tears after a fit of laughter"; "the Chinese when suffering from deep grief, burst out into hysterical fits of laughter"; "the aborigines of Australia express their emotions freely, and they are described by my correspondents as jumping about and clapping their hands for joy, and as often roaring with laughter."[49] But Darwin also acknowledged in a note that he knew of the Weddas of Ceylon, who never laugh.[50] Darwin's "evidence" is slim, but his ambivalence when it comes to laughter finds resonances in anthropological writing. Mary Douglas writes: "We know that some tribes are said to be dour and unlaughing. Others laugh easily. Pygmies lie on the ground and kick their legs in the air, panting and shaking in paroxysms of laughter."[51] This, however, is a misleading path; the question is not an empirical one. The primitive is invoked in literary modernism, as often in anthropological writing, not as evidence but as fantasy. This is a fantasy of difference—the difference of authentic, uncivilized laughter, which seems to need a screen for its projection. The primitive is this screen. It will come as no surprise that a whole orchestra of laughs responds to the violence of this screen in the African-American tradition. Enter Ellison.

INVISIBLE LAUGHTER   Readers of *Invisible Man* often forget that it is laughter that takes us to the invisible man theme: "Then I was amused: Something in this man's thick head had sprung out and beaten him within an inch of his life. I began to laugh at this crazy discovery. Would he have awakened at the point of death? Would Death himself have freed him for wakeful living? But I didn't linger. I ran away into the dark, laughing so hard I feared I might rupture myself."[52] The Invisible Man is not "real," he is a product of a blond man's imagination, and yet he comes close to ending the blond man's life. "Would he have awakened at the point of death?"—the Invisible Man asks. But the point is not whether the blond man would have awakened; rather, the Invisible Man awakens himself at the point of the blond man's death. He awakens to his own "situation," through a laugh so strong that it might "rupture" him.

In an essay titled "Manners," which Ellison undoubtedly read, Ralph Waldo Emerson helped to set the standards for American manners. Some of his formulations are critical to an understanding of this episode in *Invisible Man*.[53] Emerson lays down the following tenets: "The gentleman is a man of truth, lord of his own actions, and expressing that lordship in his behavior; not in any manner dependent and servile, either on persons, or opinions, or possessions."[54] A gentleman worthy of the name is not defined in positive terms. Emerson tells us only what the gentleman is not—he is not "servile"; he is not an "underling." Relevant here is Emerson's description of a self-reliant gentleman's face: "A gentleman never dodges; his eyes look straight forward, and he assures the other party, first of all, that he has been met."[55] An American Underground Man, the Invisible Man discovers his invisibility in not being assured by the blond man he bumps into that he has been "met" in an Emersonian way.[56] Realizing that he is invisible to the blond man, the Invisible Man bursts out laughing. The more extravagant laughter is, the more it affronts gentlemanly ideals, which require measure and deliberation. "A gentleman makes no noise," Emerson wrote.[57] Through his laughter, the Invisible Man claims the right to make noise.

But, as we have seen, if laughter is about sound, it is also about a particular choreography of the mouth, related in a perverse way to Chesterfield's commandment "thou shall always smile." The smile has complex and ambivalent nuances in African-American semiotics, and requires a careful reading. Let us remember that the Invisible Man, upon leaving college, plans a series of encounters with important white New Yorkers. How to present oneself before a "superior" is one of the leitmotivs of the discourse on manners, and of what Ellison calls "race manners."[58] The Invisible Man elaborates:

> When I met the big men to whom my letters were addressed I would put on my best manner. I would speak softly, in my most polished tones, smile agreeably and be most polite; and I would remember that if he ("he" meant any of the important gentlemen) should begin a topic of conversation (I would never begin a subject of my own) which I found unfamiliar, I would smile and agree. My shoes would be polished, my suit pressed, my hair dressed (not too much grease) and parted on the right side; my nails would be clean and my armpits well deodorized—you had to watch the last item. You couldn't allow them to think *all* of us smelled bad.[59]

He adds:

> I would hardly speak above a whisper and I would always be—yes, there was no other word, I would be *charming*.[60]

It is not hard to recognize Booker T. Washington at work here. In his attempt to bring his students' bodies into the arena of citizenship, he set out to polish them. Paying attention to one's nails, teeth, armpits, shoes, and buttons is one of the most important things students learned at the Tuskegee Institute. Speaking softly and following the other person's lead as to topics of conversation is one of the most basic rules of good manners, and it becomes one of "race manners." So it is that Tuskegee worked on the body and appropriate speech acts, from "the rising bell" to "the retiring bell," through a marching routine under the heading "keep them busy."[61] All, Washington believed, with the goal of "ingrafting them [the students] into American citizenship."[62] In the tradition of Chesterfield's *Letters*, sifted through the work of American founding fathers, Tuskegee was to become a "finishing school," teaching manners to a series of deficient sons on their way to becoming proper citizens.[63] "Smile agreeably and be most polite" or simply "smile and agree" is what "race manners" recommend as the African-American way of being "charming."[64] This is also the mechanism that, through repetition, transforms the bodies of Tuskegee students into what in *Invisible Man* is called an "automaton"—a smiling invisible puppet. The Invisible Man's laughter in the Prologue noisily bursts through this smile.

But let us also remember that W. E. B. Du Bois's *Souls of Black Folk* famously opens with the question: "What does it mean to be a problem?"; and the reply: "At these I smile, or am interested, or reduce the boiling to a simmer, as the occasion may require. To the real question, How does it feel to be a problem? I answer seldom a word."[65] The response to the problematic question is a certain smile. The smile of double consciousness is a polite smile, but also much more. There is a tension between what the face reveals (a smile) and an emotional world "beneath the surface." Hurston elaborates: "And the Negro, in spite of his open-faced laughter, his seeming acquiescence, is particularly evasive. You see we are a polite people and we do not say to our questioner, 'Get out of here.' We smile and tell him or her something that satisfies the white person because, knowing so little about us, he doesn't know what he is missing."[66]

Louis Armstrong's smile, perhaps the most famous African-American smile, plays with this ambiguity, at times uncovering, seemingly in acquiescence, a not-so-polite, open-faced laughter. Armstrong, we need to remember, acquired a series of nicknames—Dippermouth, Gatemouth, Satchelmouth (Satchmo). Through a metonymic displacement, he is but a Mouth. That Armstrong's mouth has been said to be "grinning" should not come as a surprise. If, in the Aristotelian tradition, laughter is that which differentiates us from animals, when inappropriate or in excess, it also brings us dangerously close to animals, such that many kinds of laughter are described with reference to animal sounds (horse laugh, dog laugh, etc.). The racial dynamics of the nineteenth- and twentieth-century United States led to an understanding of humanity alongside a particular choreography of the smiling/laughing mouth. In the wake of a strong physiognomic tradition, which often presented itself as a gelatoscopy, African-Americans neither smile nor laugh: they "grin." American culture's designation of the African-American smile as grinning needs to be understood on the continuum between the smile of "smile and agree" and that of double consciousness. Crocodiles and hyenas grin: while apparently smiling in acquiescence, the mouth perceived to be grinning is also thought to be showing its teeth. The Invisible Man's laughter bursts at the heart of this complex network of intertextuality.

BLUES-TONED Ellison's *hommage* to Armstrong comes in the form of the statement: "My strength comes from Louis Armstrong."[67] This strength is in a complex relationship to what Ellison calls "blues-toned laughter." Armstrong's "What Did I Do to Be So Black and Blue?" is the background to *Invisible Man's* Prologue, lending it its organizing affective quality. But what does not often enter the discussion of Ellison's relationship to Armstrong is the latter's "Laughin' Louie." Recorded by Armstrong and his orchestra in 1933, "Laughin' Louie" combines Armstrong's trumpet numbers with his laughter, and lyrics written by Clarence Gaskill. Given the reading of Armstrong's mouth as "grinning," his "Laughin' Louie" had an ambivalent reception, critics being confused as to his laughter's relation to his "grin" and the "happy darkie" show Armstrong is also accused of having performed.

In the song, Armstrong introduces himself as "Laughin' Louie" and his orchestra confirms his self-baptism with a prolonged "Yes." "Laughin' Louie, I'm Laughin' Louie / Yeah man, I'm Laughin' Louie, yes sir, / Ain't no phooey, Laughin' Louie." A story follows: "I wake up every morning and I have to laugh / Cause I look on the wall and see my photograph!" Armstrong laughs. "They call me Laughin' Louie." It seems that Armstrong arrives at his laughing name when confronted with his own photograph. What photograph does Armstrong see or, rather, what photograph does Gaskill imagine Armstrong seeing? Most photographs of Armstrong are portraits, showing Armstrong's face smiling or laughing. The song can be said to be a variation on "I love myself when I am laughing." In fact, I love myself so much when I am laughing that I will call myself Laughin' Louie. Armstrong goes on to perform a number on his trumpet. He stops every now and then to laugh. The members of his band join in. It is a laughing jam session.

Armstrong's precedent in mixing music and laughter is George W. Johnson's "The Laughing Song."[68] Thought to be one of the first black recording artists, Johnson recorded his song many times between 1890 and 1900. Strongly within the minstrel tradition, the song sold thousands of copies. It is the first time that the "talking machine" laughed. The song's lyrics recall an interpellation as "darkey" ("As I was coming 'round the corner, I heard some people say / Here comes the dandy darkey, here he comes this way . . . / His heel is like a snow plow, his mouth is like a trap, / And when he opens it gently you will see a fearful gap . . .") to which Johnson responds with laughter ("And then I laughed . . . [laughter] I couldn't stop from laughing . . . [laughter]"). The lyrics go on to warn the audience that, in case the song does not please, all one can do is laugh ("And then I laughed . . . [laughter]"). Johnston, in other words, laughs when interpellated as "darkey" and confronted with the image returned to him, especially that of an excessive mouth—a "fearful gap" and a "trap."

Johnson is laughing upon being hailed into the ideologeme of race ("Hey, darkey!").[69] Laughter is a response to hailing, raising crucial questions about the very notion of response. For what is a response? What does it mean to respond, and especially to respond properly? Usually thought of as a matter of commensurability and propriety, a response (re-spondere: to promise in return) is a matter of reciprocity. A response is a response to something, whether a speech act or an action, which it struggles to commensurate. A response is by its very nature a "good response." In the world of emotion, anger is such a "good response," carrying overtones of a demand for redress. To laugh is to refuse to respond in the terms of the interpellation. One is being hailed (hailing is always a felicitous speech act), but the laughing yes that returns pushes the play of affirmation and negativity to new levels of ambiguity. It is no surprise that the subject produced or confirmed in the acoustic mirror of this hailing will laugh again.

In Invisible Man laughter thus bursts in moments of crisis, when, as in the scene in the Prologue, it threatens to "rupture" its character. The Invisible Man encounters his first major crisis following the discovery of what his former teacher's letter contains. Back in his room after reading the letter, the Invisible Man laughs: "I sat on the bed and laughed. They'd sent me to the rookery, all right. I laughed and felt numb and weak, knowing that soon the pain would come and that no matter what happened to me I'd never be the same. I felt numb and I was laughing."[70] Laughter marks such moments after which "I'd never be the same." The eating and enjoying of a yam in the streets of New York punctuates another development in the life of the Invisible Man: "I let out a laugh, almost choking over the yam as the scene spun before me."[71] At the thought that, ironically, his "brothers" want him to become a new Booker T. Washington: "Suddenly I felt laughter bubbling inside me."[72] After the Rinehart episode: "I fell into a fit of laughing."[73] After the Sybill incident and preparing for the riot: "I ran blindly, boiling with outrage and despair and harsh laughter."[74]

In an attempt to intervene in the conversation on minstrelsy, Ellison would insist that black laughter has no place in the white world—within the minstrel show or outside it. It irritates white sensibilities to the point of being more or less explicitly prohibited: "despite the fact that the whites had done everything they could think of to control the blackness of Negro laughter, the Negroes continued to laugh."[75] Ellison will emphasize this repeatedly in order to rescue Armstrong from his critics. Not only is Armstrong not an Uncle Tom, he is in fact offering us something very powerful, if one has a keen enough ear to hear. Ellison's "strength" comes from a very specific sound he hears in Armstrong's laughter. In Armstrong's wake, Ellison's genius is to have proposed that if the Invisible Man is not seen, he is heard. We hear what we cannot see; we hear the laugh of the invisible man.[76]

THE LAUGHING BARREL   Coming, like most of his essay writing, as a post-script to *Invisible Man*, Ellison's 1985 "An Extravagance of Laughter" is an apology. Or at least this is its frame. In 1985, Ellison explains, an apology is long overdue to Erskine Caldwell, and the occasion of Caldwell's eightieth birth-day serves as the impetus for its delivery. Ellison plays with the two senses of the word *apology* as, on the one hand, acknowledgment of offense given, and, on the other, in the tradition of Plato's famous rendering of Socrates' *Apology*, justification, without any admission of blame, of one's opinions or conduct. Ellison apologizes for something, an attack of laughter, while in the process delivering his *Apology*. This is the last text Ellison published in book form during his lifetime. "An Extravagance of Laughter" is his final "defense," his "response." This response comes in the form of laughter, and is an argument about tone.

What Ellison needs to apologize for is a burst of laughter he failed to control while joining Hughes, "an old hero and new-found friend," in the audience of Jack Kirkland's 1936 staging of *Tobacco Road*, Caldwell's famous novel. Fifty years later, across the century, an apology is in order because this was not any kind of laughter, but laughter "of a particular quality" and, more importantly, an "*extravagance* of laughter."[77] In inappropriate quality and quantity, Ellison tells us, laughter can be very offensive, even in the theater. Extravagant laughter announces a certain "attitude" and a "rudeness crisis." Ellison knows that his laughter in the theater is the laughter of "a young man who was so gross as to demonstrate his social unacceptability by violating a whole *encyclopedia* of codes that regulated proper conduct no less in the theater than in society at large."[78] Extravagant laughter is a Grobian offense against "proper conduct," in the theater and outside it.

There is something Ellison sees on the stage of Caldwell's *Tobacco Road*, although his laughter is only tangentially related to the story unfolding on the stage. He is witnessing the "horsing" scene, in which a whole sexual chore-ography is performed using clichés of African-Americans not being able to restrain their passions, specifically their sexual appetite.[79] It is at this moment in the play that Ellison starts laughing: "he [Caldwell] placed the yokelike anti-Negro stereotypes upon the necks of whites, and his audience reacted with a shock of recognition."[80] Somehow the Lesters in the play have become "black." Within Caldwell's novel, we need to remember, a group of African-American passersby gather outside the Lesters' yard and watch the spectacle of the horsing scene: "The negroes were laughing so hard they could not stand up straight. They were not laughing at Lov, it was the actions of the Lesters that appeared so funny to them."[81] In the theater, Ellison joins in. In both instances, one sees the scene on stage, from a minimal distance, and one laughs.

This is how, laughing and seeing Hughes's disapproving face, Ellison remembers the laughing barrel joke, a joke African-Americans tell to describe the prohibition on their laughter. The joke is a folkloristic explanation of why "race manners" do not tolerate certain kinds of African-American laughter. The laughing barrel joke goes like this: There is a small Southern town in which Negro freedom is so restricted that Negroes are not allowed to laugh in public. Because, however, they do not seem to be able to control themselves like rational beings, the town provides them with huge whitewashed barrels labeled FOR COLORED into which any Negro who feels like laughing should place his head. This arrangement has important secondary effects, because most often the Negro's initial laughter is doubled by a second laughter triggered by the image of himself laughing upside down in the barrel. Further and more disastrous complications follow. The laughter coming out of the barrel becomes so contagious that whites passing by find themselves compelled to join in. When this includes figures like the mayor, the lawyer, the cotton broker, the Baptist minister, and the whiskey brewer, things become serious. Because now the whites cracking up assume that the Negro involved is not only laughing at himself laughing, but is also laughing at them laughing. Who is laughing at whom? Indeed, "the most vicious of vicious circles," inescapable because this laughter has no easily discernable motivation or target.[82] The joke tells about white anxiety and irascibility in the face of black laughter, which is to be muffled by the laughing barrel. The barrel is designed to mute certain kinds of sounds, yet it is not quite successful. Laughter still comes through the barrel; its noise still interferes with the life of the city. There is no punch line to this joke; the joke resides in its own circularity. It is the vicious circle that makes the story a joke. And laughter explodes all the more the moment one acknowledges the vicious circle. Laughter, as it were, is a response to the story of laughter.

Within the framework of Ellison's laughter in the theater, triggered in part by the scene on stage and fueled by the memory of the laughing barrel joke and Hughes's unlaughing face, stories about his early days in New York are told.[83] They too work to prolong Ellison's laugh. One such story acquires particular relevance: One day Ellison meets a City College student in a bookstore.

They exchange ideas about literature—to be exact, about T. S. Eliot. Ellison knows *The Waste Land* well, its footnotes having served as one of his inventories in the process of fashioning himself into a "Renaissance Man."[84] At first, Ellison sees in this encounter evidence of a racially emancipated New York; he can have a one-on-one conversation with a white student! But when Ellison uses what he thinks is a clumsy formulation, the white student immediately corrects him, showing him his place. Then the white student starts to laugh. Ellison bursts too. Two students, one white, one black, laughing in a bookstore.

The two laughs sound different, they are of different qualities: "But while he laughed in bright major chords I responded darkly in minor-sevenths and flatted-fifths, and I doubted that he was attuned to the deeper source of our inharmonic harmony."[85] Ellison, with his dreams of becoming a musician, is familiar with sound: he can discern nuances in laughter. Laughing in the theater, Ellison recalls the white student laughing in major chords and his own laughter unfolding in minor sevenths and flatted fifths. One laughs in triumph; the other "darkly" laughs his "blues-toned laughter." One laughs scornfully; the other laughs his laughter at wounds. One laughs a laughter that "corrects"; the other laughs at himself and the "joke" of "the inharmonic harmony" the situation performs.

Laughing as he remembers the bookstore incident, Ellison translates his laughter in the theater into a musical idiom too: "a cacophony of minor thirds and flatted-fifths voiced fortissimo by braying gut-bucket brasses."[86] Laughter is a discordant sound, what musicologists call a cacophony, a harsh, unpleasant combination of sounds. It is voiced fortissimo, a matter both of loudness and of exaggerated emotion (under "fortissimo," the OED speaks of a "high pitch of excitement"). And yet to call laughter a cacophony is to underscore, albeit negatively, its musical potential. To Ellison's ear, his laughter sounds as if it was produced by brass instruments. Ellison's laughter is an unrestrained burst, a loud and harsh cry. Armstrong has his own "Gut Bucket Blues."

It is as if through laughter Ellison goes back to his first love, music. As if one can describe the sound of laughter only glossing a vocabulary used to describe another familiar nonverbal discourse. This is what Douglas Kahn calls "the musicalization of sound," the means by which sound, any sound, is translated into music. It is worth pausing to ask what it would mean to try to listen to the sound of laughter without recourse to music, without its musicalization. This, however, is not Ellison's project. Ellison is interested in cross-fertilizing two practices he finds most promising in the African-American tradition: music and laughter. In this, he is closer to what Jacques Attali describes as the project of reorganizing the political economy of sound by channeling noise into music. Ellison's laughter hinges on this project, even as it draws on a different lineage.[87] Ellison's story: He wants to become a composer but changes careers to turn to writing and, on the new aesthetic terrain, struggles to recapture a barely perceptible sound, a vibration that goes by the name of "blues-toned laughter."

THE AMERICAN JOKE "Why does one laugh at a negro?" Bergson asks; and volunteers an answer: "I rather fancy the correct answer was suggested to me one day in the street by an ordinary cabby, who applied the expression 'unwashed' to the negro fare he was driving. Unwashed! Does not this mean that a black face, in our imagination, is one daubed over with ink or soot? . . . 'A negro is a white man in disguise.'"[88] Suggesting that such connections follow the logic of "dreams dreamt of the whole of society," Bergson tells us that a "negro" is an eccentric white man in a particular form of disguise: he has painted his face.[89] Theories of the comic confirm that we tend to laugh at disguises (the Aristotelian mask); and so we laugh at the "negro" whom we perceive to be in disguise. One could think of minstrelsy as the literalization of Bergson's theory: since we laugh at disguises, we laugh at the black man whom we perceive to be in disguise, and, in order to draw a surplus of pleasure out of this discovery, we devise a game in which a white man paints his face and walks around pretending he has forgotten his disguise. We laugh during the minstrel show and we laugh after the minstrel show when some black faces remain "unwashed." Black men are white performers who have forgotten their face paints are on, and are walking around and driving in cabs absentmindedly.

But the safe game is not that safe, Ellison seems to reply: "When the white man steps behind the mask of the trickster his freedom is circumscribed by the fear that he is not simply miming a personification of his disorder and chaos but that he will become in fact that which he intends only to symbolize; that he will be trapped somewhere in the mysteries of hell."[90] The mask is tricky; one might put it on and not be able to take it off anymore. The white entertainer puts on the mask and then is afraid of being trapped in it. This is how Ellison can argue that the African-American becomes the model for "the American." In his self-fashioning, the American needs to put on a mask, and that mask is always in a sense the blackface. If, as Ellison sees it, the American is in the business of projecting a second self and dealing with the second selves of others, he can always become someone else, but this someone else will always in some ways be "black." Indeed, in Alan Crosland's *The Jazz Singer* (1927), a Jew puts on the blackface in order to perform his modernity and Americanness.[91] He becomes American, but, like the Lesters, in the process he has also become "black."

Ellison, laughing in the theater while getting a glimpse of the "American joke" on stage, is lost to laughter. We must repeat that his laughter is inappropriate *even* in the theater. There are rules as to when one laughs and how one laughs in the theater, which has its own acoustic regimentation, delineating language, music, and noise. All theaters have their laughing barrels. It is important, however, that laughter should irrupt in the theater because, Ellison writes, "When American life is most American it is apt to be most theatrical."[92] American life being theatrical, dramatizing its Americanness, it is in the theater that this Americanness becomes most visible. The "gift of laughter" indeed has something to do with the theater. But this does not necessarily mean that the project here, as Jessie Faucet (but also Hughes and Hurston of *Mule Bone*) believed, is to bring African-American laughter on stage.[93] A gift is for giving: the gift of "the gift of laughter" is to make the theatricality of American life visible as theatrical, and it is in the theater that this is most likely to happen. Laughter interrupts and subtly displaces our enchantment with a naturalized, Gatsby-inspired notion of Americanness.

DOUBLE CONSCIOUSNESS   Ellison's "An Extravagance of Laughter" is a rewriting of Baudelaire's well-known essay "On the Essence of Laughter." There is something in the fact that the Sage (the sage *par excellence* being Christ) withdraws from laughter. Baudelaire elaborates: "The Sage trembles at the thought of having laughed; the Sage fears laughter, just as he fears the lustful shows of this world. He stops short on the brink of laughter, as on the brink of temptation."[94] What is the temptation of laughter? It is not clear; but what is clear is that both Baudelaire and Ellison are tempted. For laughter, Baudelaire goes on, "is intimately linked with the accident of an ancient Fall."[95] Laughter has to do with the ancient Fall; only the fallen laugh. There is no laughter in paradise, just as there are no passions and just as there is no interruption, no noise. Likewise, there is no laughter in the golden age to come at the end of time, with redemption. Absolute knowledge does not know laughter. Laughter comes with the fall, and is the very mark of fallenness. (In fact, could it be that it was a burst of laughter that caused the expulsion from paradise?)

The fall has two interrelated dimensions: a little, literal fall (the familiar example in theories of the comic: we laugh at the person falling in front of us on the sidewalk, slipping on a banana peel); and the big Fall, the Fall from paradise, the failure to amount to the requirements of the grand design. But any fall is also a fortunate fall, a fall into something. Ellison would say that he laughed and he trembled and therefore gained "a certain wisdom."[96]

To laugh at the person falling in front of us is to forget our own fallenness. It is to pretend we are laughing at the other's fall; we would never have fallen. But in fact we are always-already fallen: we always laugh at ourselves in laughter. Baudelaire suggests that it takes a philosopher to acknowledge the ontological status of the laughing subject: "The man who trips would be the last to laugh at his own fall, unless he happened to be a philosopher, one who has acquired by habit a power of rapid self-division and thus of assisting as a disinterested spectator at the phenomena of his own ego."[97] Baudelaire credits the philosopher with the knowledge of the subject's fallenness into alterity. When the philosopher laughs, which is not often, he knows he is laughing at the other that he himself is. It is not that Ellison would like to identify with the philosopher, but Baudelaire's negative statement resonates with his own explorations into "the essence of laughter." One has acquired "by habit" the power of rapid "self-division" necessary to laugh at oneself. That power is called double consciousness. One indeed laughs until one "splits." Baudelaire himself refers to a doubleness necessary to laughter; laughter has to do with a "contradictory double nature."[98] This is Ellison's addendum to Baudelaire: philosophers or not, we always laugh at ourselves in laughter; laughter is a "blues-toned laughter at wounds."

Throughout the theater episode Ellison experiences himself through a "self-division" as he is able to watch himself laugh through the eyes of a "lucid self." Ellison's rewriting of Baudelaire:

> So, laughing hysterically, I felt like the fat man whom I'd seen slip and fall on the icy sidewalk and who lay there laughing while a passerby looked on in bewilderment, until he got to his feet still laughing and punched the one man who had joined in his laughter square in the mouth. In my case, however, there was no one to punch, because I embodied both fat man and the passerby who was so rash as to ignore Baudelaire's warning. Therefore I laughed and I trembled, and gained thereby a certain wisdom.[99]

Laughing in the theater, Ellison is both the man who falls and the man who watches. The fallen man starts laughing—at his own fall. The man watching, the passerby that the lucid self is, joins in. And the man who falls would like to punch the lucid one. Only there is no one to punch—the tension is within one's own consciousness.

The situation in the theater: Ellison falls. Ellison watches. Ellison laughs. Ellison laughs. Ellison is ready to punch Ellison. Ellison laughs all the more. The drama of laughter is played out by many Ellisons, a small crowd of laughers. Laughing, Ellison offers his take on Du Bois's double consciousness. In the context of the American joke redeployed in Baudelairean terms, there is no immediate distinction between "an American" and "a Negro," as in Du Bois's famous formulation "an American, a Negro; two souls, two thoughts, two unreconciled strivings; two warring ideals in one dark body. . . ."[100] In the moment of laughter described by Ellison, one is being "torn asunder," there are two selves, but all one can say about them is that they are laughing at each other across the "American joke," the vicious circle of laughter momentarily blurring the distinction between "an American" and "a Negro."

TONE The Prologue to *Invisible Man* has its protagonist listen to Louis Armstrong's "What Did I Do to Be So Black and Blue?" The Invisible Man's ear slowly learns to discern "a voice of trombone timbre" in the song.[101] It is the voice of an old woman mourning the death of her master: "'I dearly loved my master, son,' she said. 'You should have hated him,' I said. 'He gave me several sons,' she said, 'and because I loved my sons I learned to love their father though I hated him too.'"[102] When the Invisible Man asks her who can be heard laughing upstairs, the old woman tells him that her sons are laughing. She adds: "'I laughs too, but I moans too. He promised to set us free but he never could bring hisself to do it. Still I loved him. . . .'"[103] In the blues, specifically in the trombone timbre in which the voice of the old woman comes through (the trombone being the instrument that can best imitate laughter), one can hear the laughter and the moaning of the old woman who has come to love and hate her master at the same time. Although the laugh and the moan that make the old woman's blues and that Ellison "quotes" in the Prologue can be heard only through a double mediation (in the depth of Louis Armstrong's song within Ellison's text), when Ellison describes his novel as "one long, loud rant, howl and laugh," he positions it in a direct relationship to this woman and her trombone timbre blues and laughter. The episode functions as a warning that there are those subaltern voices that can also be heard in the text of *Invisible Man*—if one has, like its eponymous character, a keen enough ear to hear.[104] What the Invisible Man is straining to hear is an undulation of sound, a differential vibration. To put this in somewhat different terms, the problem is not so much whether the subaltern can speak but whether a certain tone in the subaltern's laughter can be heard.[105]

The history of African-American sound is marked by an insistence on tone. As Barry Shank argues: "The tonal difference, particularly the difference in overtones or harmonics, is an audible trace of the earliest white investigations into a specific black difference in African-American musical practice."[106] It is via this tone—the perceived quantum of African-American difference—that laughter becomes intimate with the blues and "the lower frequencies."[107] Laughter acquires a blues tonality and it might be said, by contagion, that the blues acquire a laughter tonality, partaking of that "throaty sound" coming out of the laughing barrel. A number of blues and jazz musicians play with laughter-toned sounds.[108]

If *Dark Laughter* is after a tone in laughter, which it imagines as the secret of the primitive, Ellison is struggling to recuperate the same tone from the primitivist tradition and its avatars and, through an encounter with the African-American blues, rewrite it as blues-toned laughter. The modernist assumption here is that tone fastens to laughter, giving it an amplitude, without acquiring an expressive function.[109] It is a resonance that finds its echo in a careful listener, who nonetheless will also to a certain extent miss it. Tone names a quality of sound: there, insisting and persisting in time, rendering time itself sonorous, but always also elusive. Close-listening is the stretching of an ear perceptive of tone, an affective opening to tone. What tone does is attune us to sound, here to certain frequencies in the underground laughter that resonates in the voice of an invisible man.

CHAPTER 3

THE PHILOSOPHICAL AVANT-GARDES, OR THE COMMUNITY OF LAUGHERS

I solicit everything negative that a laughing man can experience.

Georges Bataille

LAUGHING WITH HEGEL   Bataille's laughing specter haunts the twentieth century. Spanning its early decades and their surrealist experimentations, the collective trials of the 1930s, the war and the emergence of what was to become postwar French philosophy, "Bataille" is a productive entry point into a discussion of what philosophy and literature were in the twentieth century. A number of faithful readers—Maurice Blanchot, Jacques Derrida, Jean-Luc Nancy—form a community around Bataille, whose main concern is the very future of the thought of community.[1] Importantly, as articulated in this context, the thought of community is alert to the possibility of a relation between laughers.

Like many philosophers of the twentieth century, Bataille is reacting to Hegel. Derrida understands Bataille well when he says that he has taken Hegel's self-evidence as a "heavy burden," the only way to take Hegel "seriously," which is also the only way one can hope to laugh at Hegel.[2] According to Hegel, what makes man is his negativity, whereby he separates himself from and opposes nature. Man can become conscious of his negativity, the very principle of action, that which allows the human animal to act *as* man, only through an encounter with death. In order to overcome servitude, essentially the servitude of nature and of the animal, human freedom must raise itself to the "height of death," go through its trial, and dwell in the anguish that surrounds it.[3]

Bataille endorses Hegel, to the point of repetition, up to what he identifies as Hegel's blind spot: the moment where the life exposed to the risk of death is in the end held back and reinvested. Rather than having a genuine tête-à-tête with death, Hegel is in fact delaying the encounter, therefore limiting its stakes. Within the economy of freedom thus sketched, death becomes productive. Man makes himself a "work." Freedom remains servile. What Bataille calls for, by way of repeating what he thinks is most challenging in Hegel, is an absolute expenditure, the gift of death. Only death as gift, the joyful abandonment in the face of death, precisely what Hegel feared would be an "absolute dismemberment" (*Zerrissenheit / déchirement*),[4] can bring forth an "existence without delay."[5] Through the shredding or tearing of the self, death can become one's "honest measure."[6]

In his revision of Hegel, Bataille calls for what Derrida has called "a Hegelianism without reserve," which is also "a Hegelianism struck by laughter." This is synonymous with a "negativity without reserve," which, however, precisely through its excess, exceeds negativity. In Derrida's words, this means "to exhibit within the negative, in an instant, that which can no longer be called negative. And can no longer be called negative precisely because it has no reversed underside, because it can no longer permit itself to be converted into positivity."[7] This is ultimately an affirmative moment (nonpositively affirmative, Michel Foucault calls it),[8] a yes-saying or rather yes-laughing negativity. It is this affirmation, imagined by Bataille as a moment of joy and laughter in the face of death, that distinguishes his account of the encounter with death from what Simon Critchley calls tragic theories of finitude.[9]

If Bataille repeats Hegel, up to a certain point Derrida repeats Bataille. Derrida too is complicitous with Bataille without reserve, having followed him in an important lesson in reading: a form of discipline whereby one takes a text very seriously, is very close to it, knows it rigorously, in its totality as well as in its "details," and, from within, in a perverse intimacy, submits it (here complicity gives way to betrayal) to a barely perceptible trembling that has the potential to spread and lead to a point where laughter bursts and the text dislocates itself. At the point of laughter, trembling acquires an affirmative dimension as one creatively "steals" some of the text's concepts and reinscribes them into a new configuration. This, in Derrida's reading, is how Bataille reads Hegel, submitting Hegelian lordship to a trembling that almost imperceptibly transforms it into its nondialectic opposite: what Bataille wants to retain under the name "sovereignty."[10]

In order to speak about the possibility of an unworkable or inoperative encounter with death, an encounter that would not reabsorb and sublate death into the self-sufficiency of a subject, Bataille introduces the phrase "inner experience." Acutely aware of the inadequacy of this register of language, he suggests that the encounter with death remains of the order of what the word "experience," despite a range of infelicitous connotations, still touches. Experience is of the order of the everyday, lived and felt, although on the margins of the possible and the livable. Inner experience is close to a mystic experience, albeit in a perverted relation to "God," here the name of "an obscure apprehension of the *unknown*" (5).[11] As we will see, Bataille insists that laughter offers a way into inner experience.

It is impossible to tell what happens at the moment when "inner experience" befalls us, but it is clear that this moment is not in any way reassuring: "I abandon all hope for a logical harmony and dedicate myself to *improbability*" (70). Or: "I wanted experience to lead where it would, not to lead it to some end point given in advance. And I say at once that it leads to no harbor (but to a place of bewilderment, of nonsense). I wanted non-knowledge [*non-savoir*] to be its principle" (3; OC, 5: 15). Inner experience will solve nothing, it is not a weapon or a tool; one cannot invest in it, put it to work. The sovereignty one reaches at its summit does not want to persist, even less to govern or instruct. It is essentially nonconservative (not interested in conservation). Derrida calls it "ungrateful"; one will not be able to amortize one's investments in it; there will be no reimbursement, retribution, salary, or thanks.[12]

Inner experience is, most of all, not an investment in a subject's resurrection in the midst of a death-induced anguish. Happiness and security are out of the question; risk and torment are welcomed: "I call experience a voyage to the end of the possible of man" (7). Death becomes a seductive opener of unknown paths: "Like a marvelous madwoman [*une insensée merveilleuse*], death [*la mort*] unceasingly opened or closed the gates of the possible" (xxxiii; OC, 5: 11). As an encounter with death, inner experience is neither "inner," since "dying" does not happen to a self, let alone an "inner self"; nor "experience," a word that carries resonances of its post-factum utility.

Bataille desires death; he is "dying to die" (120). His singularity among a range of philosophical figures of the twentieth century who meditate on human finitude manifests itself in an important variation on the Freudian death drive: despite the anguish and in part because of it, Bataille longs for death; not the state of being dead, the ultimate rest, but the very moment of death. Blanchot puts it well, in a sentence in *L'Amitié* Bataille quotes: "such a flash [*éclat*] was more desirable than erotic pleasure. I don't see anything: *that* is neither visible nor tangible in any imaginable way; not intelligible. *That* renders painful and heavy the idea of not dying" (122; OC, 5: 142). The idea of not dying, of living without death, is insupportable, much more than the idea of a life without erotism. In fact, death and erotism become indistinguishable here as the horizon of desire; as Jean Baudrillard puts it, "they exchange their energies and excite each other."[13]

Inner experience is profoundly paradoxical, marking the impossibility of a juncture between life and death, a juncture at which "The door must remain open and shut at the same time" (92). There is desire to die and there is desire to live to see oneself die, to be witness to death. In order to talk about this impossible situation, Bataille introduces the theme of dramatization. He invokes the Irish and Welsh tradition of the wake. If, "in order for man to reveal himself ultimately to himself [*se révèle à lui-même*], he would have to die, but he would have to do it while living [*en vivant*]—watching himself ceasing to be [*en se regardant cesser d'être*]," the wake gives him the means to envision such a situation.[14] The only way for us to "experience death" is by means of a subterfuge. The generic name for such a subterfuge is "sacrifice": "In the sacrifice, the sacrificer identifies himself with the animal that he struck dead [*l'animal frappé de mort*]. And so he dies seeing himself die [*meurt-il en se voyant mourir*], and even, in a certain way, by his own will, one in spirit with the sacrificial weapon [*de cœur avec l'arme du sacrifice*]."[15] The wake is a variant of sacrifice: "It is the death of an *other* [*la mort d'un autre*], but in such instances, the death of the other is always the image of one's own death [*l'image de sa propre mort*]."[16]

The experience of death is detoured through the death of the other. One goes to a wake (think *Finnegans Wake*), where one eats and drinks with the dead lying in the open coffin. One keeps vigil over and takes care of death, which, properly speaking, is neither the dead man's nor "mine." The scene dramatizes inner experience: "Thus, at all costs, man must live at the moment that he really dies [*où il meurt vraiment*], or he must live with the impression of really dying [*l'impression de mourir vraiment*]."[17] Inner experience cannot do without this kind of subterfuge, without dramatization, without sacrifice.[18]

Bataille has no illusion that sacrifice exceeds its status as subterfuge, and yet he argues for the "authenticity" of the experience. This authenticity is a function of the fact that, ultimately, "It is not necessarily a question of dying but rather of being transported 'to the level of death.'"[19] One needs to live with death, dwell in it, love it—if possible, *be death*.[20] One needs to imbue one's actions and one's words with "the feeling of dying [*le sentiment de la mort*]."[21]

Bataille "dies laughing," because laughter has the intensity of and is imbued with "the feeling of dying." He punctuates the "experience" of death with a burst of laughter, a form of a "joy in the face of death": "gaiety, connected with the work of death [*liée à l'œuvre de la mort*], causes me anguish [*l'angoisse*], is accentuated by my anguish, and in return exacerbates [*exaspère*] that anguish: ultimately, gay anguish, anguished gaiety causes me, in a feverish chill, 'absolute dismemberment,' where it is my joy that finally tears me apart [*l''absolu déchirement' où c'est ma joie qui achève de me déchirer*]."[22] What tears apart is a nocturnal joy experienced as a burst of laughter.

Not only does Bataille propose laughter as the model for inner experience, but he methodologically imagines laughter as the interruption of Hegelian logic. Bataille reaches a point in his reading of Hegel where the exclamation "But it's a comedy!" imposes itself.[23] He laughs, not in response to this comedy (within its horizon), but *at* it, at its being a comedy. And he laughs all the more knowing that sacrifice is a comedy, too. Bataille laughs at Hegel and, in the same burst, laughs at himself. If there is something here that exceeds the comedy, it is laughter. For there is laughter and laughter. And if an initial burst is transitive, a laughing *at*, having "comedy" as its object, subsequent bursts become intransitive, dispense with the object, simply laughing. Laughter is necessary to this scene because Bataille wants to hold on to "experience." This word would disappear from the vocabulary of most of Bataille's readers, with important consequences for the understanding of the role of laughter here. Derrida writes:

> Laughter alone exceeds dialectics and the dialectician: it bursts out only on the basis of an absolute renunciation of meaning [*il n'éclate que depuis le renoncement absolu au sens*], an absolute risking of death, what Hegel calls abstract negativity. A negativity that never takes place, that never *presents* itself, because in doing so it would start to work again. A laughter that literally never *appears*, because it exceeds phenomenality in general, the absolute possibility of meaning. And the word "laughter" itself must be read in a burst, as its nucleus of meaning bursts [*dois se lire dans l'éclat, dans l'éclatement aussi de son noyau de sens*] in the direction of the *system* of the sovereign operation. . . . The burst of laughter makes the difference between lordship and sovereignty shine, without *showing* it however, and, above all, without saying it.[24]

Unlike Barthes, who finds in Bataille "an unexpected materialism" of laughter,[25] Derrida makes laughter a textual affair ("the drama is first of all textual").[26]

And yet if inner experience is subterfuge, simulation, a project, the laughter that irrupts at its summit is passional, and thus remains an experience. Laughter touches on the very principle of inner experience: "to emerge through project from the realm of project" (46). Laughter emerges in the midst of "project," but, in the repetition of its bursts, it escapes its realm, attaining its own sovereignty. One, of course, betrays the experience, transforming it once again into project, the moment one "says it," the moment one starts writing. Hence Bataille's ambivalence about literature, itself a project that will struggle to emerge from the realm of project and push language, the very instrument of betrayal, to a limit where laughter can once again be heard.

RESPONSIBILITY   Bataille can be said to be the only one to have taken Nietzsche seriously, when in *Beyond Good and Evil* the latter declared: "I would go so far as to venture an order of rank among philosophers according to the rank of their laughter."[27] In such a ranking of philosophers, Bataille would be foremost, having, in his own words, "delivered [him]self into a kind of dive, which tended to be vertiginous, into the possibility of laughter."[28] Bataille goes as far as to say that his philosophy, if it can still be called that, not only finds its impetus in the experience of laughter but does nothing but think about laughter. His assumption is that if philosophy is to say anything about laughter, it needs to *start* from the experience of laughter.[29]

Bataille's description of an ecstatic burst in *Inner Experience* explains a lot of what is at stake here. It is worth an extended quote:

> Fifteen years ago (perhaps a bit more), I returned from I don't know where, late in the night. The rue de Rennes was deserted. Coming from Saint Germain, I crossed the rue du Four (the post office side). I held in my hand an open umbrella and I believe it wasn't raining. (But I hadn't drunk: I tell you, I'm sure of it.) I had this umbrella open without needing to (if not for what I speak of later). I was extremely young then, chaotic and full of empty intoxications: a round of unseemly, vertiginous ideas, but ideas already full of anxieties, rigorous and crucifying, ran through my mind. In this shipwreck of reason, anguish, the solitary fall [*déchéance*] from grace, cowardice, bad faith profited: the festivity started up again a little further on. What is certain is that this freedom [*aisance*], at the same time as the "impossible" which I had run up against, burst [*éclatèrent*] in my head. A space constelled with laughter [*un espace constellé de rires*] opened its dark abyss before me. At the crossing of the rue du Four, I became in this "Nothingness" [*néant*] unknown—suddenly . . . I negated these gray walls which enclosed me, I rushed into a sort of rapture [*ravissement*]. I laughed divinely: the umbrella, having descended upon my head, covered me (I expressly covered myself with this black shroud). I laughed as perhaps one had never laughed; the extreme depth of each thing opened itself up—laid bare, as if I were dead. [*Je riais comme jamais peut-être on n'avait ri, la fin de chaque chose s'ouvrait, mis à nu, comme si j'étais mort.*]
>
> I don't know if I stopped, in the middle of the street—concealing my transport [*délire*] under an umbrella. Perhaps I jumped (no doubt that's just an illusion): I was illuminated convulsively; I laughed, I imagine, while running. (34; OC, 5: 46–47)

It is a singular experience, triggering the thought that perhaps no one has ever laughed before. One laughs as if for the first time—and as if for the last time. A moment of intense clarity, laughter lays things bare: "as if I were dead." At the summit of the experience, "I" falls into a "space constelled with laughter" (how not to think here of *chora*, that "riant spaciousness"?).[30] Laughter is an experience of space—the outside of the "I" experienced as the inside of "my" laughter. This space is an "abyss" in that it swallows the subject, which joyfully abandons itself, its subjectivity, to it. In being an experience of space, this is also, as we will see, an experience of community, the spacing of this laughing singular self in relation to other singularities.

The event is something that can be recounted only in the past tense. It all happened fifteen years before the moment of writing—perhaps earlier, the date is not important. The "I" that tells the story was not quite there when his laughter burst (Bataille later refers to this "I" in the third person: "the man with the umbrella" [36]). In the same way one cannot say "I am dead" in the present tense, one cannot say "I laugh" in the present tense. Laughter can only be predicated as "I laughed." But did "I"? Can one tell the story of a fifteen-year-old laugh? Some details are vivid—names of streets, the post office. They are not, however, "impressions" or "reminiscences," as Bataille imagines Proust would describe them.[31] Bataille makes it clear that the experience never becomes the object of memory, because in that it would be linked to an author, it would become an event in a biography, and thus lose its connection to the unknown: "What is hidden in laughter must remain so" (155). Is it possible it was all an illusion? Bataille asks, and has to acknowledge that this too is a possibility. And yet it is the intensity of the experience that, beyond any memory, does not allow it to drift into the realm of fantasy. Words borrowed from mysticism—"transport," "rapture," "ecstasy"—translate the "I"'s incorporation into the event. Jumping and running, on the other hand, are modalities of the body having been rendered light by the experience. Lightness marks it as an erotic experience—laughter and "I" touch each other in ecstatic, pleasure-giving ways.

This, Bataille insists passionately, exposing himself to equally passionate misunderstanding, is not only the model of our encounter with thought (the thought of non-knowledge or "God") but also the model on which one enters historical events. One's participation in historical events is a function of passion. There is something "strange" about our decisions to be part of certain events, a strangeness we encounter in "the strangeness of a laugh."[32] There can be no freedom without what Bataille calls "freedom of temperament" (23). One joins with history, its kairotic "now," in the same way (and at the same time) as one joins a burst of laughter.

The experience of laughter teaches Bataille an important lesson: sovereign is he who knows when to lose his head. At stake is Bataille's take on *kairos* and the possibility of an evental instant. Derrida would put it in explicit terms: "Bataille has a thinking of the instant, what he calls sovereignty. It has to do with the instant of the erotic experience of the sacred, laughter, bursts of laughter; that's the instant."[33] What Bataille's sovereign laughter brings forth is a joyful, erotic, passionate relation to the unknown of thought and history, which we perceive as the impossible.

One indeed loses one's head in this experience. But one also, Bataille insists, recuperates the passion of revolutionary spirit, which is itself *acéphale*. As Denis Hollier puts it, Bataille is best understood in terms of his "impatience to make oneself be carried away by the desired storms, and be reaped by tempests sown by the winter wind."[34] It is important to emphasize, however, that passion, particularly the passionate joining with history, does not foreclose responsibility. In dialog with Bataille, Derrida speaks of an "aporia of responsibility," distinguishing between two forms.[35] One is a general responsibility, a Kantian sense of duty within the horizon of a *de facto* knowledge and community. Importantly, *pace* Kant, this responsibility requires a violent sacrifice of the passions. The other form of responsibility is an absolute responsibility, a transgression of duty as a response to a secret call of the other ("God"). This second form of responsibility could easily be called irresponsibility in that it remains and insists on being passional, an affective opening to the undecidable dimension of history: "Continuity horrifies me. I persevere in disorder, loyal to the passions of which I really know nothing, which upset me in every sense" (117). Derrida describes an "ethics of irresponsibilization," whereby one acknowledges the aporia at the heart of responsibility and takes it on as a challenge. Bataille is irresponsible in this sense, which is also the only ethical imperative he knows, and the only way he can think the structure of evental decision.[36] Absolute responsibility is a responsibility to the silent, secretive, and passional gods within us. Remaining open to their call is the only guarantee that our revolutions do not always amount to a change of costume.

PHILOSOPHER! It is through laughter that Bataille explains the beginning of his project. He does so by way of an anecdote: In 1920, he met Bergson in London.[37] He was twenty-three, had recently been going through a series of mystic and religious experiences, and was completely unknown. Bergson was fifty-nine, held the chair of philosophy at the Collège de France, was a member of the Académie Française, and had published extensively. Bataille describes the encounter:

> I take myself back twenty years in time: at first I had laughed, upon emerging from a long Christian piety, my life having dissolved, with a spring-like bad faith, in laughter. Of this laughter, I have already described the point of ecstasy but, from the first day onward, I no longer had any doubt: laughter was revelation, opened up the depth of things. I will reveal the revelation out of which this laughter arose: I was in London (in 1920) and I was to have dinner with Bergson; I had at that time read nothing by him (nor moreover had I read much by other philosophers); I had this curiosity—while at the British Museum I asked for Laughter (the shortest of his books); reading it irritated me—the theory seemed to me to fall short (for this reason, the public figure disappointed me: this careful little man, philosopher! [*le personnage me déçut: ce petit homme prudent, philosophe!*]). But the question—the meaning of laughter which remained hidden—was from then on in my eyes the key question (linked to happy, infinite laughter, by which I saw right away that I was possessed), was the puzzle [*l'énigme*] which at all costs I will solve (which solved, would of itself solve everything). (66; OC, 5: 80)

Bergson had offered a variation on the Aristotelian definition of the laughter of comedy: we laugh at the person falling in front of us so we correct a certain automatism or mechanical inelasticity, a clumsiness or rigidity. For him, laughter has a crucial social function, that of correcting dangerous eccentricities. These can be bodily, mental, or character deficiencies, which, from the sociological standpoint Bergson wants to inhabit in *Laughter*, are nothing less than sources of misery and potential causes of crime. Bergson's sociology is mixed with a dose of moralism; in correcting our "manners," laughter "makes us endeavor to appear what we ought to be, what some day we shall perhaps end in being."[38] A certain kind of arrogance is at stake: "In laughter we always find an unavowed intention to humiliate, and consequently to correct our neighbor."[39] Laughter is a useful social gesture, to be used in the formation and reproduction of a group.

Reading Bergson's "little book" in London, Bataille is "impassioned."[40] Not only had Bergson instrumentalized laughter, making it work in the service of calculable results, but he managed the task of making laughter conservative, in the service of the same.[41] "This careful little man, philosopher!" Bataille's encounter with Bergson—and the laughter that punctuates the occasion—help him to understand the stakes in laughter. They have little to do with ridicule, correction, and humiliation, although laughter will be a testing ground for the possibility of community. Moreover, laughter will have nothing to do with comedy (comedy is of interest, perhaps, only when it comes to the Bataille-Bergson encounter in London). Bataille also understands that if philosophy (or sociology) cannot do justice to laughter, this is because the experience of laughter demands new modes of writing, a new "literature." In the writing Bataille can be said to inaugurate, philosophy and literature will become indistinguishable in light of this demand.[42]

COMMUNICATION "No doubt Bataille has gone farthest into the crucial experience of the modern destiny of community," writes Nancy.[43] Bataille's laughter is paradoxical, being at the same time a solitary and communal experience: "No doubt, it suffices that a single individual reach the extreme limit: for all that, between him and the others—who avoid him—he keeps a link. Without that he would only be an oddity [*étrangeté*], not the extreme limit of the 'possible'" (38–39; OC, 5: 51).

Bataille wrote about community passionately, throughout his life. But between 1937 and 1939 the exigency of community imposed itself with renewed urgency within the communal experiment that was the College of Sociology, attended by Roger Caillois, Michel Leiris, Alexandre Kojève, Pierre Klossowski, Jean Paulhan, and, briefly, Walter Benjamin. It is important to note that in this context, Bataille and the other members of the College were in the business of studying two communal formations. One is "society as we know it," also referred to as the *de facto* community. Bataille (in 1938, with an eye to neighboring Germany) described this community on the model of the army: "at this very instant, in the face of our impotent remonstrations, the military spirit *alone* dictates the fate of hypnotized masses, some overwrought, others appalled [*les une surexcitées et les autres atterrées*]."[44] These masses are hypnotized by the myths the community recites to itself by way of revisiting its foundation or origin. Its members commune through the recitation of myth, becoming one as community. This "one" can easily be put to work in the community's name, hence "the militaristic spirit."

But the College was mainly invested in exploring what Bataille calls (again, inadequately) "elective" and "existential" communities. Without substance or cause, such communities gather at the very level of existence: "the essential objective of their gathering together is existence [*des hommes prétendent s'y réunir en posant l'existence comme un objet essentiel de leur réunion*]."[45] This, because, "there exists at the basis of human life a principle of insufficiency" (81). This principle is unsurpassable. We do not complete ourselves through community, as if filling a lack. There is nothing tragic about insufficiency, thus there is no need for a project of becoming sufficient. We have nonetheless created mechanisms that give us the illusion that we are separated, isolated, self-sufficient individuals. Bataille insists that we need to be reminded of our insufficiency. Some states (laughter) expose us to it, and thus expose the very "essence" of community as an ontology of insufficiency.

In his reading of Bataille, Nancy emphasizes the "existential" dimension of community; existence is existence in-common, as being-self and being-with are co-originary; there is an "originary and ontological sociality," what Nancy calls compearence (*comparution*, "showing up together").[46] For his part, Blanchot emphasizes the "elective" dimension of community; while being-with is ontological, community nonetheless presupposes an "encounter." Friendship and love become exemplary of elective communal relation. We are not friends and lovers with just anyone; we "elect" our friends and lovers, even if not actively. They are singular and irreplaceable. This "election" remains a function of an encounter or event, which is possibly distant and nonsynchronic.[47] If Nancy qualifies community as "inoperative" (*désœuvrée*), accenting its unworkability in relation to death and myth, Blanchot qualifies it as "unavowable" (*inavouable*), intensifying the "secret" that binds its members.

Blanchot and Nancy agree that community is of necessity beyond what is common (identity) and beyond the commonwealth (the contract). It is the community of those who, not sharing an identity, share its lack. This lack of identity is what makes community. To use a word dear to Bataille, this is a formless (*informe*) community that redefines the word community as such beyond recognition. It is a community *without a form*—whether an essence, a leader, a myth, or an art.[48] Communal forms continue to exist, but community is an operation of subtraction from these forms. A series of twentieth-century meditations on community starts here.[49] Often called the "negative community," this community is founded (without acquiring a "foundation") on the retreat or subtraction of its work.

Community is thus not a number of individuals plus contract, as political philosophy would have it; community is co-originary with the very being of those who "communicate" within it. "Communicate" will indeed be the predicate of "community," beyond any technocratic "theories of communication," and in fact beyond the hope of a transfer of messages ("I have little chance of making myself understood" (117), writes Bataille.) Our very existence communicates with other existences, and it is an existence only insofar as it communicates: "communication is a phenomenon which is in no way added to Dasein, but constitutes it" (24).

COMMUNIFYING LAUGHTER   In the course of the development of his thoughts on community, Bataille turns to laughter—the "operation of laughter." He fears that the argument about community unpacked so far is too abstract. What he is describing is lived experience, "acutely felt," which is in need of another mode of argumentation.[50]

Bataille thinks about laughter in order to come to understand the workings of community, and he thinks about community in order to try to understand laughter. It is in the context of his work in "sacred sociology" at the College that Bataille decides that "the analysis I am about to undertake will offer what I believe is a correct answer to the problem of laughter," which is "one of psychology's most complex and maddening [*désespérants*] problems."[51] It is what we would call "the example" that Bataille wants his listeners at the College and his subsequent readers to retain: "There are two existing forms of perceptible human interattraction [*d'interattraction humaine sensible*], first sexual interaction—which cannot be considered social in the precise sense of the term—then laughter, which, I will now demonstrate, constitutes the specific form of human interattraction."[52] Two examples of laughs follow: "A child, who is a few weeks old, responding to an adult's laughter, represents unambiguously the classic example of immediate laughter [*rire immédiat*]. On the other hand, a young girl full of charm and full of humanity who cannot help laughing [*ne peut pas s'empêcher de rire*] each time she is told about the death of someone she knows, as I see it, laughs a *mediated* laughter [*un rire* médiatisé]."[53] The point is to say that laughter, our laughter, oscillates between these two laughs, both communal, albeit in different ways. It retains something of the apparent immediacy of the infant laugh, as well as the joy this laugh "communicates," and at the same time it is mediated by the "news" of death.[54]

The operation of laughter is a "roundabout way" whereby individuals laugh together, in a sense always at death and with death but, in that, communal laughter becomes objectless. While sexual arousal, Bataille's other example of communifying movement, has an object, "laughter hid [*dérobait*] the object from attention and bound the process into an intense and exuberant human communication of joy."[55] In contrast to what has become his "reputation" in the wake of his work on erotism and Foucault's translation of his notion of transgression, Bataille prefers a laughing orgy to a sexual orgy as a model for communication.

Bataille describes the emerging "community of laughers" on the model of contagion:

> Each isolated existence emerges from itself by means of the image betraying the error of immutable isolation. It emerges from itself in a sort of easy flash [éclat]; it opens itself at the same time to the contagion of a wave which rebounds [un flot qui se répercute], for those who laugh [les rieurs], together become like the waves of the sea—there no longer exists between them any partition as long as the laughter lasts; they are no more separate than are two waves, but their unity is as undefined, as precarious as that of the agitation of the waters. (96; OC, 5: 113)

To laugh is to enter the space of the sea and a fragile "compound being" (être composé), formed by isolated singularities that remain singular and yet, in laughter, become permeable to a common movement and communicate. "Be that ocean," Nietzsche's slogan, finds its echo in Bataille's wavelike community. Laughter produces a fragile, formless unity; there is no partition between laughers as long as the laughter lasts. Laughter is a communal experience of space, space as sea, reminding of "the brilliant immensity of space" (77). Bataille hears the sea itself laughing, laughing its absence of limits and the joyful coexistence of singular waves exposed to the touch of other waves. It is important to emphasize "as long as the laughter lasts [tant que dure le rire]" because unity here is a moment, a "point." The unity of waves can easily decompose. It is, however, an "infinite moment" in that, in its being a sonorous event, it has the potential of reverberating infinitely.

Bataille comes to describe a contagious contagion (la contagion [la compénétration intime de deux êtres] est contagieuse) whereby the form of intimate communication involved in the laughter of two people (two friends, two lovers) becomes itself contagious and "susceptible to indefinite reverberation [susceptible d'une répercussion indéfinie]."[56] Contagion is contagious, and thus we move from the two to the multiple. In this sense, the laughter two individuals share is already "the same as the shared laughter of a roomful of people [le même que le rire commun de toute une salle]."[57] If we are not quite there in our laughs, our headlessness is a function of their communal dimension: "the intensity in this case is one that is devoid of personal significance. To a certain extent, in principle, laughter between two people supposes a state that is open to all comers [le rire entre deux êtres suppose un état ouvert à tout venant]."[58] Rather than being the closed "freemasonry" Bergson imagined, the community of laughers is infinitely open. It is a confirmation that Bataille's laughter cannot be (or remain) a reactive laugh, the laughing at that excludes, closing the gates of community. In fact, as a state of communication, laughter displaces the very problematic of inclusion/exclusion on which the thought of community has been articulated.[59]

It will be asked: Why laughter? Most readings of Bataille, as well as engagements with second-order commentaries, do not quite know what to make of laughter in this context. Laughter is thought to be one of Bataille's idiosyncrasies, an oddity that can be safely put aside. In response, Bataille would underscore at least five things:

1 *Laughter is insufficiency.*   Bataille rereads the well-known scenario of the man slipping on the banana peel in terms of insufficiency: "Laughter arises from differences in level, from depressions suddenly produced. If I pull the rug out from under . . . the sufficiency of a solemn figure is followed suddenly by the revelation of an ultimate insufficiency (one pulls the rug out from under pretentious beings). I am made happy, no matter what, by failure experienced. And I lose my seriousness by laughing. As if it were a relief to escape the concern for my sufficiency . . ." (89). When someone falls in front of us, what is revealed is not a mechanical inelasticity in need of correction (Bergson's response) but an ontological insufficiency. We laugh at ourselves when we laugh at the falling man; laughter is a common experience of "failure."[60] It is this failure, exposing us to our common insufficiency, that founds community.[61]

2 *Laughter is passion.*   Bataille emphasizes the excessive nature of passion, which destabilizes our self-sufficiency. Passion is by definition excessive. Passion is also by definition *this* passion, even if different passions touch on each other and contaminate each other. For Bataille, the passion par excellence is laughter. He is responding to Aristotle in emphasizing the excessiveness of passional laughter. Having made man a laughing animal, Aristotle asked for moderation in laughing matters.[62] For Bataille, laughter is not worthy of the name unless it is excessive. The phrase "to die laughing" also names the necessarily hyperbolic dimension of laughter.

3 *Laughter is communication.*   Laughter is what Bataille calls "a state of communication" (112). We do not cease to communicate, and yet there are certain states when communication is experienced *as* communication. Laughter is such a state. Pulling the rug from under the subject and the object, laughter exposes their communication: "And above all *no more object* . . . there is no longer subject-object, but a 'yawning gap' between the one and the other and, in the gap, the subject, the object are dissolved; there is passage, communication, but not from one to the other: *the one* and *the other* have lost their separate existence" (59). Bataille would ultimately argue that writing offers a model of communication that comes closest to this subject/object relation.

4 *Laughter is acéphale.*   In one of his descriptions of ecstasy in *Inner Experience*, having recounted his transformation into a tree, Bataille tells about how he became a flame:

The upper part of my body—above the solar plexus—had disappeared, or at least no longer gave rise to sensations which could be isolated. Only my legs—which kept me standing upright, connected what I had become to the floor—kept a link to what I had been: the rest was an inflamed gushing forth, *overpowering*, even free of its own convulsion [*jaillissement enflammé, excédant, libre même de sa propre convulsion*]. A character of dance and of decomposing agility (as if made of the thousand idle futilities and of life's thousands moments of uncontrollable laughter [*des mille fous rires de la vie*]) situated this flame "outside of me." And as everything mingles in a dance, so there was nothing which didn't go there to be consumed. (127; OC, 5: 148)

There is somebody or something in this experience—a burning passion. A flame is an "it" with neither head nor tail. It is a rhythmic convulsion. Bataille is aware of affinities the Greek word *gelos* shares with heat, fire, and flames; the laughter of the gods is, after all, "inextinguishable." As for the Latin *rideo*, it plays with resonances of "dancing."[63] Laughter is an experience of such a dance, an "inflamed gushing forth," in which the subject is consumed, joyfully. The now-proverbial and much-abused "death of the subject" is understood by Bataille as a death by laughter.

5 Finally, and perhaps most challengingly, Bataille discovers that at the summit of the experience one finds a laughing woman.

GOD Bataille uses the word "virile" to describe community, and his arguments draw on all-male models like the army and the church. Hollier writes: "Virile unity is not the uniting of man and woman. It is man's unity confronted with woman."[64] Woman is the principle of dispersion and thus, as Freud made clear, she has no place in virile communities. This community is a brotherhood, founded on the exclusion of woman. Confronted with what he perceived to be the "impotence" of Western democracies in the face of Nazism, Bataille imagined decision as "virile" (if not necessarily unproblematically active).

And yet woman is all too present in Bataille's elective and existential communities. Having proposed that Bataille's lovers remain subject and object, where man is subject and woman is object, Nancy would allow that, "on another register and in another reading of Bataille's text, it is not certain that love and *jouissance* do not pertain essentially to the woman—and to the woman in man."[65] A few years later, and in an explicit meditation on laughter, Nancy gives Bataille yet another reading, and offers the statement: "*Perhaps it is always a woman's laugh ...*".[66] Bataille's well-known, provocative statements about his distrust of "poetic femininity" notwithstanding, is it possible that at the summit of inner experience, the self-that-dies laughs a woman's laugh? To die laughing, indeed.

Bataille comes closest to this suggestion in "Madame Edwarda," the story he wrote in 1941, at the same time as "The Torment," the fragments that make up the second part of *Inner Experience*. Bataille conceived of "Madame Edwarda" as the necessary companion to *Inner Experience*. An exercise in erotic literature in the tradition of Sade, the story recounts an adventure its narrator has with the title character, a Parisian prostitute. The climax comes at its close, which has Madame Edwarda open her legs.[67] The sight is one of horror and joy:

> She was seated, she held one leg stuck up in the air [*une jambe écartée*], to open her crack [*la fente*] yet wider she used fingers to draw the folds of skin apart. And so Madame Edwarda's "old rag and ruin" loured at me [*les "guenilles" d'Edwarda me regardaient*], hairy and pink, just as full of life as some repulsive octopus [*une pieuvre répugnante*]. . . . "Do you mean," I protested, "here in front of all these people?" . . . I sank down on my knees and feverishly pressed my lips to that running, teeming wound [*la plaie vive*] . . . Her bare thigh caressingly nudged my ear, I thought I heard a sound of roaring seasurge [*un bruit de houle*], it is the same sound you hear when you put your ear to a large conch shell . . . Edwarda and I were losing ourselves in a wind-freighted night, on the edge of the ocean [*une nuit de vent devant la mer*].[68]

Philosophy has not had a lot to say about kissing, Derrida would remind us[69]—up to this point, that is, when philosophy, if this still is philosophy, concentrates the operation of ecstasy in a kiss, opening into community. Edwarda urges the narrator to look ("You want to see my rags? she said. . . . But no, you have to look: look!").[70] Instead of a look, he offers a particular kind of touch.

"I am God," Madame Edwarda declares, pushing blasphemy to unprecedented heights.[71] Initially astonished, the narrator comes to understand that she is right. Edwarda is "entirely black, simply there, as distressing as an emptiness, a hole."[72] God is this "simply there," a hole, an abyss. Bataille's passion for Edwarda is his "passion for the real": the impossible presence of an absent God. Bataille's sympathies remain with her. Hollier notwithstanding, the "community of lovers" is the community of two the narrator in this scene forms with Edwarda. Love imposes itself here on two accounts: "we cannot conceive of ultimate collapse in a way other than in love" (120); and, "love has the rigor of death."[73] Let us not forget that the scene of this kiss is a public scene, open to a contagion that reverberates and communifies. The community of lovers is at the same time a community of two and of a multitude.[74]

If Madame Edwarda's "rags" (*guenilles*) are at the heart of this communifying movement, this is because "I lusted after her secret and did not for one instant doubt that it was death's kingdom [*la mort régnât en elle*]."[75] Madame Edwarda's "wound" is, however, also life's kingdom. This too is a mouth, a set of lips framing the opening into the void. We have reached a point where Bataille suggests that woman's "crack" is yet another opening for laughter. The "repulsive octopus" laughs—an inhuman/divine laugh. What Madame Edwarda does in spreading her legs is "expose" herself. The gesture partakes of "the operation of laughter," the spacing of the inside and outside of the mouth. Woman is exemplary here because she is thought to be this exposure; she is "mouth-like." Nancy touches on this in *The Inoperative Community*, acknowledging the family connection between woman's "breach" and the open mouth: "The open mouth [*la bouche, quand elle s'ouvre*] is not a laceration [*déchirure*] either. It exposes to the 'outside' an 'inside' that, without this exposition, would not exist . . . [the mouth] is—perhaps, though taken at its limit, as with the kiss—the beating [*le battement*] of a singular site against other singular sites."[76] Bataille is tempted to think of the kiss—the kiss at the end of "Madame Edwarda"?—as a laugh. He is tempted to ask whether one could kiss and laugh at the same time. For that, however, one needs new words, new figures, a new literature.

LITERATURE   Blanchot revisited "Madame Edwarda" alongside Marguerite Duras's short *récit*, *The Malady of Death*. The *récit* tells the story (that in fact never becomes a story) of two solitary existences, for a short while lived in common. This is what Duras's *récit* names "love." Blanchot's reading of Duras suggests that what makes this "couple" a community is the impossibility of becoming one. The two lovers remain singular, solitary, their "union" partaking of the structure of what Bataille calls the "community of those without community."

Blanchot's reading of Bataille with Duras is a reaction to Nancy's *The Inoperative Community*. Nancy's meditation on community, Blanchot fears, has not accounted for sexual difference, or not sufficiently. We do not have many facts in Duras's story, Blanchot seems to say, but one thing is sure: there is a man and there is a woman. This is the only truth: there are men and there are women. What kind of relation is at stake in the two of sexual difference? What community do a man and a woman form, before any story? While the first part of *The Unavowable Community* is a reading of Bataille, the second part is an attempt to think community on the model of sexual difference.[77]

In his reading of Duras, Blanchot reaches a point where "Madame Edwarda" imposes itself as an intertext. Speaking about "the complicity of the word death," Blanchot comments on "the abyss, the black night discovered by the vertiginous emptiness 'of the spread legs' (how not to think here of 'Madame Edwarda'?)"[78] How not to? "Madame Edwarda" imposed itself on the thought of community that was *Inner Experience* and now imposes itself on *The Unavowable Community*. With and against Nancy (and with a certain Bataille), Blanchot concludes his thoughts on Edwarda: "that exhibition conceals her [*la dérobe*] by handing her over to an ungraspable singularity (one can literally no longer grasp her) and thus, with the complicity of the man who loves her momentarily with an infinite passion, she *abandons herself*—it is in this that she symbolizes sacrifice—to the first comer (the chauffeur) who does not know, who will never know that he is in touch with what is most divine or with the absolute that rejects any assimilation."[79] If community cannot be thought apart from an engagement with the figure of the other, the one whom *de facto* communities necessarily exclude, the community thought by Bataille/Blanchot is a "community of others." There is indeed an other in community; but this is all there is; there is no "same." Blanchot's reading of Bataille slowly becomes a parallel engagement with Emmanuel Levinas. This, on two counts: if for Levinas woman is an exemplary other as the bearer of the feminine principle, Blanchot grants Edwarda her radical singularity *within* the feminine. Secondly and most importantly, Blanchot reminds Levinas that if Edwarda is the other, it is hard to speak of relation on the model of respect. Edwarda is not respectable. She is not a decent, respectable neighbor. She is "God," but she is also base. Let us not forget, moreover, that Edwarda is not a face. One cannot, with Levinas, facialize the relation to the other into a face-to-face. She is a set of holes, mostly a mouth. Bataille suggests a double effacement: the subject is disfigured as face, but so is the other. Relation loses the visibility of the face-to-face; what is left are mouths—multiple, nonsymmetric, abyssal.

Nancy, too, returned to Edwarda. He did so through a poem in prose by Baudelaire, "Desire to Paint," in an oblique dialog with both Blanchot and Duras. It could be said that Nancy becomes receptive to Derrida's repeated warnings about the traps of a thought of community articulated as a fraternity: "the word [fraternity] privileges some 'virility.' Even if he is an orphan, a brother is a son and therefore a man. In order to include the sister or woman or daughter, one has to change words—generously—and then change the word 'generosity' while one is at it."[80] Nancy's response, a reworking of an essay initially titled "Laughter in the Throat of Death" into "Laughter Presence," is his own take on "the community of lovers" coupled with the thought of "to die laughing." Importantly, it is a very different exercise than *The Inoperative Community*, an engagement with art and literature, Nancy's own acknowledgment of the limits of philosophy.[81]

Baudelaire's "Desire to Paint" presents us with a painter burning with the desire to paint a young woman, a "beautiful regretted thing."[82] She is gone, has disappeared, and the painter struggles to catch her in his painting. If only he could, he would have caught beauty itself. But what the poem metonymically describes is the bursting of a face. The desire to paint is the desire to paint the "inexpressible loveliness" of the lower part of a face, its burst into a wide, grand mouth. Nothing less, the poem suggests, than the desire to paint a miracle. The miracle of laughter is here that of a red-on-white explosion, a volcanic eruption on the terrain of painting/art.

The woman of the poem is beautiful, nocturnal, mysterious, and surprising. She is the bearer of a certain grace, which is at the same time the vulgar grace of a *fille*. (How not to think here of Madame Edwarda?) She is a prostitute and in that, for Baudelaire too, God-like. Her job is to spark desire, which is the desire to die, modified here as the desire to die painting the opening of a mouth in laughter, an important variation on "the malady of death" for the world of aesthetics. The woman is not a body; she is not even a face, only a fragment of a face, its lower part. Most of all, she is the opening of a mouth, red and white. The woman is also a set of eyes, sparkling in the dark. A lamp of sorts, her eyes illuminate the scene of painting. The painter needs this lighting. He needs it to see himself slowly dying. The impossible painting, the painting no painter can paint, would be a self-portrait: the painter would paint his own death under a laughing woman's gaze.

Nancy reads and rereads Baudelaire's poem, his own reading a series of bursts. In one of them, he emphasizes that "laughter has never really found its place, in the erotico-aesthetic dialectic of philosophy. I mean laughter 'itself,' and not the comic, humor, or irony."[83] For, indeed, we have learned to deal with humor, the comic, irony—and the ridiculous, jokes, the grotesque, etc. Laughter passes through them without yielding to them. Laughter is a burst, it can only be a burst, an index of a certain presence. Nancy is tempted to say that this is not the presence of something, but presence itself. Laughter, Nancy suggests, seems to take us from art's flirtation with beauty to its desire for the sublime: "laughter reveals itself—it does nothing but reveal itself—as the sublime flower of the impossible and the painting of the unrepresentable. Laughter as pure presentation: it is an extremity that art has rarely reached [*touché*]. . . . The laughter of sublime beauty is pure presentation."[84]

And yet there is no art of pure presentation. Baudelaire's poem cannot represent laughter; all it can give us is a vision of a never-to-be-painted painting of a mouth opening before a dying painter. For, indeed, the mouth opening in laughter is painted—red. Lipstick, the poem can respond. But no, the "inexpressible loveliness" of red on white can only be that of a canvas. There is no sitter on this scene, the woman is always-already gone, disappeared. When the poem begins, she is already a trace. The redness of her mouth, which seems to present us with woman at her most "real," is painted. What the poem does is speak about the consumption of painting, torn (*déchiré*) by the desire to commensurate the sublime unrepresentability of a woman's laughter.

"To die laughing" marks the juncture of life and death, when, for an instant or a burst, laughter opens the gates of death at the very heart of life. If only the painter, who is witnessing the scene through the mediation of woman, that nocturnal being, could seize the moment and paint. If "to die laughing" marks the crossroads where laughter and death burst at the same time, we are now at a point where we see that we are talking about *woman*'s laughter and the *painter*'s death occurring at the same time. He laughs her laughter and dies—laughing. At the moment of death, he enters her laughter.[85]

If the scene of painting is an asymptotic curve of desire, perhaps the desire to paint is always the desire to paint that which desire cannot catch up with: a woman-laugh. This woman is both a muse, a mediator of art and death, *and* a knowing, witchy old hag, an avatar of the "Thessalian Witches" Baudelaire's poem invokes. She is—and this might have been Zeuxis's death[86]—both a Venus and an old crone, their coexistence a function of a certain nightwood under a sinister, intoxicating dancing moon. The woman in Baudelaire's poem, that "beautiful regretted thing," is, after all, always-already gone, having perhaps unnoticeably become an invisible old hag. But if she is gone, disappeared, the trace she leaves behind is the haunting, reverberating echo of a laugh.

Painting can only be late for the encounter with the laughing woman. It struggles to be on time, but it necessarily fails. The mouth will have burst, the painter will have died laughing, but the painting will have been only a desire. What is unknown in laughter remains unknown. Unlike what Bataille saw in Proust, literature's arresting of and capitalizing on the unknown, Nancy sees Baudelaire's painter abandoning himself to the grace of an open mouth, at the risk of death. This is a literature that abandons faces and figures for the abyss of the deadly beautiful unknown of the mouth and of a voice that resonates in it, a voice that, the actors here would insist, does not say anything yet is far from being silent.

LITERARY COMMUNISM   We need art and we need literature to touch on this.[87] Bataille warned that "literature" is a most inadequate word: "What I see: poetic facility, diffuse style, verbal project, ostentation and the fall into the worst: commonness, literature" (49). To write in the wake of an experience like a burst of laughter is to "falsify the accounts" (66). Moreover, because of its own mythical dimension, literature has the power to seduce, to masquerade as nonproject. Bataille repeatedly emphasizes that at the moment of inner experience there is no language. The exigency of inner experience would seem to be silence. In order to communicate, one would need to be silent. Yet Bataille is writing. He cannot not write. This, among other things, because Bataille knows silence is already a "literary attitude" (68). So he writes, trying to smuggle literature from the literary. "Communication" becomes an ever more ambiguous word, now standing both for an ontological condition and for a literature, no longer an operative myth, that carries the promise of "touching upon the 'extreme limit'" (149).

In the last reckoning, it is writing and literature that offer Bataille a glimpse into a community founded on a new relation: "the gesture of writing, which alone permits one to envisage slightly less conventional human relations, a little less crafty than those of so-called intimate friendships . . .".[88] In order to be able to speak about a literature hospitable to this notion of communication, one has to leave the author behind: "*the putting to death of the author by his work*" (151). Now that Barthes's and Foucault's almost mythical "beheading" of the author has become an institutionalized cliché, this might seem easy. Bataille, however, knew that the beheaded body has its ways of searching for a head. He located this search in the "unbearable vanity" (81) of the author (himself).[89] No matter how passionately he struggled, the author seemed to return: "the impossible spider, not yet crushed, that I am, so poorly dissimulated in its networks of webs" (128). The vanity of the author asks for recognition; literature returns to project, yielding returns for the ego of the author, who circulates it as his property, on the appropriate paths.

If literature is to be communication, there can be no linguistic model of sender-message-receiver (author-work-reader). Ideally, one would say: "Thus I speak—everything in me gives itself to others . . ." (130). What Bataille calls literature is an anonymous, communifying writing. Bataille returns in this context to an imagery of the sea: "The self in no way matters. For a reader, I am any individual: name, identity, the historical don't change anything. He (the reader) is any one and I (the author) am also any one. He and I, having emerged without name from . . . without name, are for this . . . without name, just as two grains of sand are for the desert, or rather two waves losing themselves in two adjacent waves are for the sea" (50). Literature is a sea in which author and reader communicate. Author and reader touch each other, on the model of two waves, themselves lost in other waves, barely distinguishable in the larger sea.

This literature, Bataille knows, draws on the tradition of erotic literature. In being an exposure, it responds, as Blanchot puts it, to the exigency of "saying everything" (*tout-dire*).[90] Literature concentrates the operation of exposure, without rest. Bataille, like Sade, thus wrote passionately, even as he despised the idea that he might become a writer or create a work. What Blanchot calls "the main impropriety," the true scandal, is to write and to write ceaselessly. The true revolutionary is never at rest and never gives literature a rest. It is a state both Sade and Bataille thought incompatible with bourgeois morality (inherently conservative, a resting); not for the morally outrageous "content" of their literature, nor for a certain style or genre, but for the scandal of their passion for writing, the putting in motion of literature.

Literature is indistinguishable here from a certain practice of reading and listening. We need new ears to listen to the communal voice of the sea. Blanchot would call this voice the neutral, and Beckett would become exemplary of a writing that claims its main task is to listen: "Well, waiting, we chat. Yes, listening to the voice."[91] What one hears in the folds of this writing is a certain murmuring or rumbling. Baudelaire's "Desire to Paint" presents itself as sound, a rhythm of *désire, déchire, mourir, jouir, rire*. It would be convenient, falling back on the old literature, to call this sound rhyme. But the voice is not musical, even if poetry and painting would be happy to defer to a third sister art. What literature makes audible is the nonmusicalized sound of a voice. If one reads / listens carefully, one slowly begins to hear its distant laughter.[92] What Blanchot calls "literary communism" is our exposure to this laugh.

To reread Bataille today is to get a glimpse of a reverberating moment in the twentieth century when the lack of essence of our being-in-common was imagined as a literary experience, a function of a tripartite constellation of, in Nancy's words, "a certain death, an inconceivable star, and the grace of a tart shaking with laughter [*une mort certaine, un astre inconcevable . . . et la grâce d'une fille secouée de rire*]."[93]

CHAPTER 4

FEMINISM, OR "SHE'S BEAUTIFUL AND SHE'S LAUGHING"

Old women, unmanned, free
Of children, embarrassment, desire to please,
Hooting grossly, without explanation.

U. A. Fanthorpe

LAUGHING HEADS The anecdote Hélène Cixous tells at the beginning of her 1976 essay "Castration or Decapitation?" ("Le Sexe ou la tête")[1] has a Chinese background, but, given its origin in Sun-tzu's *The Art of War*, it has acquired mythical dimensions in the Western world too.[2] It is the story of a Chinese king who wants to test the feasibility of a military strategy by having his one hundred and eighty wives (three hundred in some versions) trained in the art of war. He gives the task to Sun-tzu, an expert in military science. Sun-tzu starts by arranging the women in two rows, each headed by one of the king's two favorite wives. He wants to begin by teaching them the rhythm of the drumbeat. Right turn! The women burst out laughing. Left turn! More fits of laughter. Sun-tzu personally takes up the sticks to beat the drums, and repeats the drill several times. No change: the more he tries, the more the women fall about laughing. Sun-tzu understands that they will not stop. He is left with no choice, he needs to take drastic measures. The king is not so sure anymore—they are his wives, his own pleasure is at stake. Sun-tzu reminds him that he has been put in charge. An order is an order. When an order is clear and the troops do not perform, it is the fault of the officers. Sun-tzu beheads the two women commanders. They are replaced and the exercise starts again. Now the women turn right and left, they march forward and backward. All in silence and with never a single mistake. Ask them to do anything, Sun-tzu tells the king, and they will not disobey. Sun-tzu is made general, and goes on to win many wars.

The story is of interest because it emphasizes that women respond with laughter to the attempt to bring them onto the terrain of military science. Laughter is what they do together. It defines them as a group, a community that makes Sun-tzu lose control. In her version of the story, Cixous does not give us all the details of Sun-tzu's state when faced with the women's laughter: "Sun-tzu was enraged, his eyes suddenly opened wide, his sound was like a terrifying tiger, his hair stood on end under his cap, and his neck broke the tassels at the side."[3] Sun-tzu needs to prove the viability of his strategy, and his reaction to the women's laughter—that which threatens his system with failure—is of hyperbolic dimensions. Otherwise famous for his wisdom, Sun-tzu is at a loss. His carefully thought-out theory of the art of war is in danger of being discredited. Violence, spectacular violence, is at this time the only solution to the problem posed by the laughing women. Their two commanders are beheaded. Silence sets in. It is the sign that now the women are ready. They will do what is being asked of them, and they will do it con- scientiously. They will march as if they have never done anything except prac- tice the art of war. They become mute, malleable bodies. They too have in fact been decapitated, they too have lost their laughing heads—to silence.

Every detail of this story counts, Cixous emphasizes. The "detail" of interest here is laughter, the "little thing" laughter is. The question is not why the king's wives laugh or what they are laughing about. Rather, the question worth asking is, Why is laughter the name of that which disturbs Sun-tzu, the master? And, later, why does laughter return as the name of that through which Cixous conveys her vision of change? In other words, what happens here by way of laughter?

The silence that covers the women in the Sun-tzu story has its acoustic dimensions, one can hear its taunting sound. The bodies that silently follow orders, turn left and right without mistake, are eloquent.[4] "The Laugh of the Medusa," the essay with which Cixous's name is still first and foremost asso- ciated, and which is credited with having brought laughter to the main stage of feminist theory, is an exercise in hearing.[5] Cixous struggles to hear echoes of laughter within the many folds of silence at the end of the Sun-tzu story. In this sense, the 1976 "Castration or Decapitation?" comes before the 1975 "Laugh of the Medusa." The Sun-tzu story offers a "representative anec- dote" within which "The Laugh of the Medusa" can be read. In her suspi- cion of any kind of origin-finding project, Cixous writes "the beginning" as a postscript.

"The Laugh of the Medusa" is a call, something like a manifesto.[6] Impera- tive sentences like "Let's get out of here!" or "Write!" call the reader to join the "I" writing in the "we" to come. Are you coming? The first act of read- ing we are asked to perform in encountering the essay is an initial *yes*. This *yes* places the reader in the "now" of Cixous's writing. Only once such a reading premise is established is the content of the call apparent. And what the essay calls its reader to do is hear laughter. Retrospectively, more than thirty years after its publication, this call appears as an opportunity to revisit the feminist twentieth century—at the point of its laughter.

HYSTERICAL WITCHES   The beheaded laughing heads in the Sun-tzu story somehow return. Not in a direct way, as if one could unproblematically go back to a time before women were trained in the art of war, a time before women started marching. But indirectly, by way of a long detour that goes through a series of other laughing figures. For there are some women known for their laughter.

In *The Newly Born Woman*, Cixous and Catherine Clément struggle to hear the laughter of the witch. The witch, Clément tells us, is cursed, for she too has once laughed at a master: "We learn that she has been damned ever since, in a mythical time, she laughed at Christ's passage—accursed laughter that she will carry within her until the end of time."[7] The witch is eccentric, a woman outside of the family structure, sexually ambiguous. She is also a foreigner, present briefly at the Sabbath and then gone, flying. But she is laughing—a loud, open-mouthed, insistent laughter that persists in the ears of those present once the Sabbath is over. When the witch takes off, Clément tells us, we are left with the haunting image of her flight and the echo of her laughter.

In modern times, the witch's laughter slowly becomes associated with the figure of the hysteric. Clément writes: "When she [the witch] is caught, when the scene of inquisition is formed around her, in the same way the medical scene later forms around the hysteric, she withdraws into herself, she cries, she has numb spots, she vomits. She has become hysterical."[8] With the hysteric, we move into modernity, to another form of discipline, no longer spectacular, or rather, spectacular in different ways. The discipline the hysteric is subjected to is subtler and more efficient. A whole arsenal of knowledges and institutions is deployed to methodically administer her disorder.

The hysteric is silent, she is mute (Cixous: "Silence: silence is the mark of hysteria").[9] Linguistic usage has coined the phrase "hysteric laughter" when in fact laughter is rarely among the hysteric's symptoms.[10] The hysteric has fits and spasms, she is convulsed: symptoms/stigmata that connect her to the medieval witch and the possessed. But if the hysteric is silent, she is so in that she does not speak (nor does she have an "expression"), which does not mean that she is completely silent. Augustine, Charcot's star hysteric at the Salpêtrière, lets out a series of piercing cries. Dora coughs. What both Augustine and Dora have is an attitude that translates into a certain tone of voice in which the sounds they make come out. This elusive attitude nonetheless functions as a show stopper: the hysterical theater finds itself at an impasse.

Dora only laughs at Freud, at his attempts to find a cure and to "bring her to reason": "She [Dora] had developed into a mature young woman of very independent judgment who had grown accustomed to laugh at the efforts of doctors, and in the end to renounce their efforts entirely."[11] This is how Freud retroactively imagines and sketches Dora: laughing at his efforts and eventually leaving him before his work is done. Dora does not use the poses that made Augustine famous, her *attitudes passionnelles*, which often gaped her mouth into a mute laugh.[12] Suspicious of Charcot's use of photography (psychoanalysis is, after all, the art of listening to the voice), Freud still paints a portrait of Dora. He has her sit for him, and he exercises his excellent talents as a portraitist of the literary variety. It is his contribution to the *tableau* hysteria is.

Cixous will want to retell Dora's story, remixing that which Freud has put in order, that which he had "brought to reason."[13] Her 1976 play *Portrait of Dora* comes in the wake of "The Laugh of the Medusa," the same year as "Castration or Decapitation?"[14] It is a "portrait" too, but one that does not quite belong to the tradition of portraiture. Cixous makes a point of insisting that she puts Dora on stage, for the theater is "the land of others," a space where "their words make themselves heard, and their silences, their cries, their song, each according to his/her own world and in his/her foreign tongue."[15] Dora speaks on stage, which, Cixous believes, is the closest one can be to speaking as an other. Most importantly, *Portrait of Dora* gives the silent, muted Dora a voice; not one through which "to tell her story," but one which is itself an intervention, before it begins to speak. The stage directions describing Dora's voice when she first enters the stage read: "in a tone of voice that shatters the silence abruptly, somewhere between a threat and a demand."[16]

Echoes of the hysteric and the witch's laughter find resonances in yet another figure that needs to be added to the gallery of women laughers—the old hag. A witch figure herself, she too is outside the marriage market and free of its constraints. Women's texts return to her again and again. One amazing text in this category, published in 1974, is Leonora Carrington's novel *The Hearing Trumpet* (*Le cornet acoustique*). Its main character is ninety-two years old and is abandoned by her family to the whims of an organization called the Well of Light Brotherhood:

Then a terrible thing happened to me. I started to laugh and could not stop. Tears poured down my face and I covered my mouth with my hand, hoping they would think I had a secret sorrow and was weeping and not laughing.

Mrs. Gambitt stopped her exercise on the harmonium. "Mrs. Leatherby, if you are unable to control your emotions, kindly leave the room."

I left and sat down on the nearest bench where I laughed and laughed and laughed. Of course this was irreverent behaviour but there was nothing I could do about it. Even when I was still a young woman I was occasionally overtaken by spasms of uncontrollable laughter, always in public. . . . Marlborough seemed to always be present when I was overtaken by my spasms, which he was pleased to call Marian's maniac laughter. He always enjoyed seeing me making an exhibition of myself.[17]

A docile body, silently following the absurd game of the institution she finds herself in (a "brotherhood"), the old hag is nonetheless free. She has nothing to lose. She uses the prosthetic trumpet of the title selectively, to hear what she wants to hear and to play deaf when there is no point in straining to hear. The moment of laughter's irruption is occasioned by the unquestioned daily routine of the institution. It is "irreverent behavior," for routine is a most serious thing. Marian knows that laughing and crying verge on indistinctness when accompanied by tears, so she tries to camouflage her laughing as crying.[18] The attempt fails and Marian is punished. While the laughter of the young woman in the theater needs to be contained lest she should "make an exhibition of herself," the gross hooting of the old hag is in no need of containment—she can laugh, that is, within the already contained walls of the senior home.[19]

MEDUSA Having alluded to the three main figures in the gallery of laughing women—the witch, the hysteric, the old hag—Cixous goes on to suggest that we need to listen to echoes of these laughs in a rather unpredictable place: Medusa's story. "The Laugh of the Medusa" becomes an exquisite exercise in reading. For ever more finely tuned reading ears are needed to hear Medusa's laughter.[20]

Medusa is one of the three mythical Gorgon sisters, daughters of the sea gods. She is raped in Athena's temple, and the goddess punishes her for violating her space by transforming her into a snake-haired monster: anyone who looks at her is turned to stone. Medusa is the only mortal Gorgon and Perseus, with the use of a mirror that reflects her image while shielding him from her gaze, is able to kill her by cutting off her head. At the moment of decapitation, Medusa becomes mother: Pegasus and Chrysaor spring out of her blood through her neck. But Medusa's story does not end here—that is, with her death. The story of her head continues. It becomes Perseus's trophy and his most lethal weapon. From now on, Perseus identifies himself as "I, Perseus, son of Jove and Danaë, / Conqueror of the snaky-headed Gorgon."[21] The head becomes instrumental in that, having fought the monster that threatens Andromeda, his bride-to-be, Perseus uses it to confront her former suitor, Phineus. The head is eventually given to Athena, who puts it on her shield and uses it to ward off danger, of any kind.

Freud adds an important fold to the myth of Medusa. He argues that to decapitate is to castrate: Medusa's decapitated head triggers the fear of castration. Structurally, then, Medusa's head is in the place of the paradigmatic castrating object: the penisless female genitals. To look at Medusa's head is to see the female genitals in all their lacking threat. "We read in Rabelais of how the Devil took to flight when the woman showed him her vulva," Freud writes.[22] He argues, however, that the other element in Medusa's mythological makeup, her hair of phallic serpents, works in the opposite direction, assuaging the horrified viewer. Medusa's power to petrify (what the French call *méduser*) turns out to be petrifying in another sense, giving a reassuring erection.

In his essay "Medusa's Head: Male Hysteria under Political Pressure," Neil Hertz describes the mechanism through which revolutionary threat is associated with the figure of the Medusa. He identifies the English reaction to the French Revolution as an example of a political crisis when Medusa appears as a horrific image of castration. In this context, she embodies the regime's fear of losing its privileges to the fury of women and the unpropertied classes. The scene ultimately confirms Freud's double argument, as Medusa's snaky coiffure also produces the expected apotropaic effect, the hard-on that reassures the establishment of its solid position. Hertz considers scenes of women displaying their genitals in revolutionary France as gestures that concentrate the operation of the revolution: "What the revolution is said to be doing figuratively is precisely what—in a moment—each of the women will be represented as doing literally, suddenly displaying monstrous and unknown forms to a horrified society."[23] What the revolution does is lift its skirt, displaying monstrous Medusaic images to a society that, petrified, looks on in terror of change.

The revolution, we know, is always-already gone, to be construed as revolution only retroactively. It is indeed an opening, but an opening soon closed off by the new law that establishes itself through the revolution.[24] If the figure of Medusa appears in such revolutionary moments, if she is the revolution, she is also soon to be displaced by orderly and classic images of her nemesis: Minerva, Athena's Roman counterpart. Born not from a mother but out of Zeus's head, Minerva promises reconciliation. She substantiates the serenity of the new law, filling the noisy void of the revolution with a new plenitude. This is the mechanism Jack Spector calls "Minervation," whereby the terror produced by revolutionary Medusa is replaced by the deadening tranquility and control of Athena/Minerva.[25] The hairy monster is, with a touch of the brush, replaced by the calmly beautiful, serene Minerva, herald of the tranquility of the new law. In the heat of the moment, it almost seems as if she is what the revolution always wanted, after all.

In the wake of another revolutionary time, responding once again to conservative uses of Medusa as the horror of revolution, Percy Bysshe Shelley wrote his poem "On the Medusa of Leonardo da Vinci in the Florentine Gallery," describing the anonymous *Head of Medusa* in the Uffizi Gallery in Florence, for a long time attributed to Leonardo da Vinci.[26] As a description in poetic form of a visual image, a painting, the poem belongs to the genre of ekphrasis. In fact, W. J. T. Mitchell considers Shelley's "On the Medusa" to be the "primal scene" of ekphrasis.[27] As a genre, ekphrasis attempts to describe the painted image of Medusa, to put the other that Medusa is into words. Starting from Shelley's poem, Mitchell proposes that ekphrasis is at once a minor and obscure genre (through which visual images are rendered verbally) and the principle of poetic art: poetry makes us "see" literary images. Medusa embodies the conflict between a terrified status quo and its revolutionary other, while also pointing to how this tension is dramatized by the desire to capture, freeze, or petrify her image in language.

By the time it reaches Cixous, Medusa comes to perform a relation between a triangular series: female genitals, revolution, and poetic language. Cixous's Medusa puts this triangle in tension, through laughter. Let us look at her, Cixous calls. Not with the gaze of those "trembling Perseuses," all "clad in apotropes" (*bardés d'apotropes*), shielded by a series of mirrors and representations.[28] Let us look straight on (*en face*), without reserve, at our own risk. Let us see her monstrosity. It is a face-to-face interaction that Cixous is after. She will not tell us much about Medusa, she will not give her a physiognomy or describe her ekphrastically, and she will not give her a voice to tell her story. She will just give her laughter: "You only have to look at Medusa straight on to see her. And she's not deadly. She's beautiful and she's laughing (*Il suffit qu'on regarde la méduse en face pour la voir: et elle n'est pas mortelle. Elle est belle et elle rit*)."[29] Cixous retains Medusa's first attribute, her beauty. But she adds sonority to this beauty: "She's beautiful and she's laughing." It is a different way of looking that Cixous challenges her reader to perform, a looking that can see Medusa laughing. Medusa's story is not about Medusa. It is about us, about the "trembling Perseuses" that we are, our faces always turned away from the face-to-face encounter with the other. Always-already petrified in our habitual seriousness, we do not need Perseus's mirror to neutralize Medusa's gaze; it is our gaze that needs work, and Medusa's laughter can help us. For laughter comes as much through the eye as through the ear. "I see with my ears," writes Cixous.[30] From the future perfect the writing "I-now" of "The Laugh of the Medusa" projects, we will have learned to look in this way and see: Medusa's gaze laughs as it does the looking, and does the looking through laughter. Medusa might not be deadly after all; but we will never know unless we dare to look. At our own risk, at the limit of death but—perhaps more challengingly—of life, having fallen into the sound of Medusa's laughter.

In an attempt to put two of his closest intellectual interlocutors in dialog, Derrida would juxtapose Cixous's and Nancy's work on eyes and sight.[31] Nancy writes: "Why is there this thing, sight, rather than sight blended with hearing?"[32] He goes on to further blend sight not only with hearing, but also with touch—in an explicit engagement with the figure of the Medusa. While Nancy seems to reproduce the traditional image of Medusa, he is invested in reconstituting the vision with which she has been associated since Freud: "slits, holes and zones do not present things to be seen, do not reveal anything: vision does not penetrate, but glides along swerves and follows along departures. It is a touching. . . ."[33] Cixous's "operation" on the eye likewise results in hearing: "The joy of the unbridled eye: you can hear better like this"; and a touch: "She had just touched the world with her eye."[34] Importantly, Cixous marks the birth of the new eye with a burst of laughter: "Struck by the apparition she burst out laughing. The laughter of childbirth."[35] Not a grasping or penetration of the seen, at the point of laughter vision is mixed with a hearing and a touching. The encounter with Medusa is reimagined as such a synesthetic experience.

PETRIFICATION   Back to the central scene in Medusa's story: In order to save his mother from the threat of an unwanted marriage, Perseus is challenged to offer his mother's suitor the head of the only mortal Gorgon, Medusa. In narrative terms, Medusa is an obstacle, Perseus is the hero. A terrifying scene unfolds on Perseus's way to the Gorgon hideout: everywhere he looks, he can see men and beasts Medusa has turned to stone. Medusa is asleep when Perseus arrives. Three strategies are available to him: One, Athena can guide his hand and, his face averted, he can strike Medusa. Second, he can attack the sleeping Medusa from behind, avoiding her gaze. Perseus considers the two alternatives, but goes for a third: he uses his shield to reflect the image of an awakening Medusa back upon herself, petrifying her, then decapitates her. Perseus's strategy is to enlist Medusa in her own defeat; he has Medusa medusize herself.

Attention to the temporality of this moment is crucial. For what does Perseus decapitate? Is Medusa at the moment of decapitation flesh or stone? If she is flesh, the mirror trick might not have worked, and Medusa did not turn herself to stone. If she is stone, it is hard to imagine Perseus decapitating a statue. Or is there an intermediary phase, between flesh and stone? Perseus does not linger. He tells us that the three moments—awakening, petrification, and decapitation—are simultaneous. Medusa wakes up; sees herself in the mirror; her power is turned against her; she turns herself to stone; and, in the same instant, she is decapitated. A series of narrative moments is squeezed into this instant.

Where, then, are we to locate Medusa's burst of laughter on this scene? We must assume that Medusa has not seen herself in the mirror before. One glance in one blink-of-the-eye instant is all Medusa has—to see her monstrosity, the snaky coiffure, the petrifying eyes. To see herself seeing herself.

The question is, does Medusa see "her" self? More importantly, whatever it is that Medusa sees, does this someone or something in the mirror have the power to petrify? For if the two Medusas here, the one in front of the mirror and the one in the mirror, are not identical, we become suspicious that Medusa indeed turns herself to stone. The narrative passes over this moment. Told by Perseus to the guests at his wedding, it needs to move on and reconfirm our hero.

What we do know is that Medusa wakes up to her death, which she can see captured, frozen on the screen that the mirror is. At the moment of death, she sees herself become a statue, a figure, a face—to be rhetorically deployed in a long line of figural maneuvers, from Hegel to Nietzsche to Lacan.[36] Burst of laughter. Medusa laughs when she sees herself become the Medusa, when she sees her beauty solidify into the hardness of a statue-figure. But if laughter is an integral part of the event of this transformation, is it possible that one might be able to hear Medusa, as a figure, laugh again? This is Cixous's experiment, belonging to a long tradition in which humans reduced to non-sensing statues perceive, sense, or think.[37]

Once we allow that Medusa turns herself to stone, the question becomes: Do stones laugh? Stones, of course, are dead, silent, and immobile. They are, in fact, the epitome of lifelessness. They are also durable and, in a sense, eternal. In Ovid's narrative, as Perseus is about to kill Phineus by making him look at Medusa's head, he tells him: "I can give you / A great memorial; not by the sword / Are you to die; you shall endure for ages."[38] Turned to stone, Phineus would endure—"caught and fixed forever."[39] And so would Medusa. And yet, can this enduring statue still produce sound? Does it have a voice? It would appear that we could not be farther from such a possibility. In Ovid's narrative, an unfortunate participant in the conflict over Andromeda, Nileus, catches a glimpse of Medusa's head as he is in the middle of producing a sentence: "The last words broke, half spoken; if you saw him, / So, open-mouthed, you might perhaps have wondered / Why the lips made no sound, for all they tried to."[40] Like Phineus, who can perceive his neck becoming hard, Nileus feels his lips freeze. His words remain suspended, half-spoken. Only a deadly silence ensues.

Is it possible, then, to speak of Medusa's laughter after she medusizes herself?

Mladen Dolar traces a philosophical and literary tradition in which, counterintuitive as it might be, stones have a voice.[41] The most important reference point in this tradition is Hegel's invocation of the statue of Memnon in *Phenomenology of Spirit*. The statue is known to have famously produced a sound as the first rays of light touched it in the morning. Hegel uses this example to illustrate the moment within the movement of art when the not-yet-self-conscious spirit emerges from mere matter. Dolar emphasizes that the statue produces a sound only because, as a result of an earthquake, it has been cracked. In other words, the stone is cracked, split, "mere" matter, but also always-already spirit. It is in this crack that the voice of the stone emerges.

We can now propose that Cixous brings laughter to Medusa's story in order to remind us of the crack in the stone. Medusa laughs at the moment when she turns herself to stone, and this laugh leaves a permanent crack in the stone that she becomes. We are asked to listen carefully: perhaps the stone still resonates with laughter. It is an invitation to reconsider Echo's story in the same breath. For, as Dolar reminds us, Echo too is a stone, and the reverberation we call an echo is the voice of a stone. "The Laugh of the Medusa" struggles to hear echoes of Medusa's laughter in the very "crack" Medusa is.

When Teresa de Lauretis reads Cixous's essay, she is skeptical of her invitation to look Medusa *en face*.[42] That is not an easy thing to do, she argues, even if we are in need of utopias. Cixous, however, is a careful reader, and what she is proposing is precisely not a utopia. We can look at Medusa straight on, but only if we see laughter as part of this scene. We will come face to face with Medusa when we have learned to hear echoes of her laughter.

GAPING MOUTHS   In her rewriting of Freud's interpretation of the mythical figure, Cixous gives Medusa laughter because laughter has a special relation not only with the revolution but also with female genitals. Laughter is of the mouth, and the female body does not have only one mouth. Remember Luce Irigaray's play with the two sets of female lips. Avital Ronell also reads the Freudian scenario of the little boy discovering the mother's lack in terms of his discovering another mouth: "For what a child sees, were he to look behind the empirical curtains covering the 'thing' in its not-being-there, comes down to something like an invaginated ear, or lips forming a mouth. Where he was looking for an image of his own penis, he finds that the mother has instead another mouth—a mouthpiece and a receiver that have been kept in reserve, hidden, and virtually silent."[43] The problem for the little boy might be the fact that this mouth is indeed only "virtually silent."

Another female laughing figure helps us here—Sheela. Sheela ("old hag") is the Celtic follower of the Greek Baubo, known for having brought the earth goddess Demeter back to life. Demeter, as the story goes, is searching for her daughter, Persephone, whom Hades has stolen and taken to the underworld. Her distress translates into devastated landscapes. In her attempt to cheer Demeter up, Baubo displays her aged genitals.[44] The sight triggers Demeter's laughter, and she returns to her duties as earth goddess.[45] Spring comes to earth as a consequence.

Like Baubo, Sheela is short and round, a huge maternal body. Her face is calm and silent, smiling. But she uses her hands to pull her vagina wide open, in a gesture of display. Contemporary art has revived Sheela: when feminist artists take on the challenge of representing woman's laughter, it is Sheela's huge vagina that does the laughing. Nancy Spero's painting *Chorus Line* imagines a community starting from a line of dancing Sheelas, their vaginas stylized into wide-open monstrous laughs.[46]

But if female genitals are figured as a mouth, one of the portals through which, as Bakhtin puts it, "the body goes out to meet he world," they are also threatening.[47] The terrifying nature of the mouth is advertised by two rows of teeth: they could close at any time. Female genitals also acquire their threatening dimension through an imagery of teeth. Under "mouth," the OED also lists "the opening between the jaws of a pair of scissors or pincers." The *vagina dentata* is as such a scissors-mouth: it can cut. It thus becomes the example and, as Freud puts it, "the beautiful confirmation" with which he ends his essay on the uncanny: "It often happens that neurotic men declare that they feel there is something uncanny about the female genital organs."[48] Medusa is present on this scene too, as Freud's previous example is that of "dismembered limbs, a severed head, a hand cut off at the wrist . . . especially when, as in the last instance, they prove capable of independent activity in addition."[49] The challenge for Cixous is to rewrite this scene, returning Freud to Freud. In this rewriting, if the female genitals are uncanny it is because they, too, are the scene of the double: the double mouth of the female body, with its doubly double lips touching themselves. What, then, could be more uncanny than the female genitals, laughing, all by themselves?

Cixous's challenge: "Let the priests tremble, we're going to show them our sexts!"[50] What "we" will show, lifting our skirts in a revolutionary gesture in line with the women of the French Revolution, is our sex/text. What will become visible/audible is a monstrosity that goes by the name "sext." This is not a text, textile, or veil that, out of "modesty," covers over what Freud called a defect of the female genital organs. The thing itself is a veil, weaving its texture into a Baubo-inspired laugh.[51] For Cixous defines "text" as "the rhythm that laughs you (*le rythme qui te rit*)."[52] *Écriture féminine*, of which too much and too little has been made, offers the promise of a laughing text. One is asked to read by opening one's ears to its rhythm.

RHETORIC How, then, is one to understand "She who laughs last," the phrase to which Cixous cathects her take on laughter? "She who laughs last" is an attempt to rewrite "he who laughs last," a popular and influential "theory of laughter." With "she who laughs last," Cixous wants to tell us something not only about Medusa but also about laughter and its moment of theory.

Rhetoric has historically had a special investment in laughter. Rhetoric wants to learn from laughter understood in terms of "he who laughs last." He who laughs last laughs best because he wins in public debate. "They laugh that win," goes the popular saying. Hobbes's philosophy is illustrative here.

Hobbes cannot but disapprove of laughter as "sudden glory," but he learns about the rhetorical powers of laughter as understood by the classic rhetoricians. He invests in laughter's mechanism, best described by Quentin Skinner: "For the rhetoricians, the significance of the fact that laughter is an expression of scorn and contempt is essentially forensic in character. If it is true, they argue, that laughter is the outward manifestation of these particular emotions, one can convert it into a uniquely powerful weapon of moral and political debate."[53] While this actual "winning" laughter becomes a *faux pas* in public life, the rhetorical devices inspired by it translate into disarming maneuvers in political debate. Rhetoricians learn from Cicero, who offered detailed advice on the rhetorical power of laughter, which can be used to "break up his [an opponent's] case, to obstruct his arguments, to make light of his cause, to deter him from speaking and to turn aside what he has said."[54] These rhetorical devices are still in use, but the explicit connection between laughter and rhetoric in classical times has slowly been forgotten.

The forensic aspect of "he who laughs last" has tempted feminists. Annie Leclerc, to whose 1974 *Parole de femme* Cixous in many ways responds with "The Laugh of the Medusa," wants to invest laughter with the power of a weapon so that, in her words, one can "deflate his [man's] values with the needle of ridicule."[55] Leclerc extrapolates: "Therefore I say (nothing will stop me): man's value has no value. My best proof: the laughter that takes hold of me when I observe him in those very areas where he wishes to be distinguished. And this is also my best weapon."[56] Let us laugh *at* them, Leclerc invites, at their claims to greatness. Let us use laughter to "break their case." Laughter is a good weapon—a weapon *they* have been using against *us*. Who will have the last laugh now?

This is not Cixous's war. "The Laugh of the Medusa," with its rhetoric of gift and giving, will have nothing to do with laughter understood as a weapon in war. Laughter cannot be a form of investment: "Nor is the point to appropriate their instruments, their concepts, their places, or to begrudge them their position of mastery. Just because there is a risk of identification doesn't mean that we'll succumb. Let's leave it to the worriers, to masculine anxiety and its obsession with how to dominate the way things work—knowing 'how it works' in order to 'make it work.' For us the point is not to take possession in order to internalize and manipulate, but rather to dash through and to 'fly.'"[57] The point will not be to forensically learn how laughter works so that one can make it work in one's favor and have the last laugh. The laugh of "she who laughs last" is not the laugh that stops all laughs; the point for "she who laughs last" is to, like the witch, fly (*voler*: flying and stealing), laughing.[58]

LISTENING/HEARING   Cixous is in an oblique dialog over the uses or non-uses of laughter not only with Leclerc but also with Nathalie Sarraute. 1972 saw the publication of Sarraute's novel *Vous les entendez?* (Do You Hear Them?), arguably one of the most beautiful texts on laughter ever written, and one of the inaugurating texts of another avant-garde movement of the twentieth century, *le nouveau roman*, a twin project to *écriture féminine*. The novel's setting is deceptively simple: A father is having a conversation with a neighbor about a pre-Columbian statue that occupies a place of honor on the family's mantelpiece. He is a former art history professor and an art collector. His children return home from a trip; it is not clear how many they are or how old. In fact, the reader will not know much about them; they are referred to as "they" and "them," as opposed to "us." After a short polite conversation with the two men, the children retire upstairs. Where they laugh—for the rest of the novel. The novel magnifies laughter, it stretches its burst and hyperbolizes its effect. Ellison's "Extravagance of Laughter" suggests that Ellison's burst in the theater reproduces itself—story after story gets told within the framework of Ellison's laughter. When the essay ends, Ellison is still laughing and, as far as the reader of his essay knows, he is laughing right now. *Do You Hear Them?* further pushes the suggestion of an infinite potential for laughter as a framework for narrative.

As always, there is an easy and convenient explanation for "their" laughter: they are young and carefree. We all laugh at this age. The problem is apparently solved and dismissed: "They're light-hearted, eh? They're enjoying themselves. . . . After all, that goes with their age. . . . Both heads are raised, they listen. . . . Yes, young laughter. Fresh laughter. Carefree laughter. Silvery laughter. Tiny bells. Tiny drops. Fountains. Gentle waterfalls. Twittering of birds."[59] Laughter is a depository of childhood happiness. Listening to it, a father cannot but sigh approvingly, if also nostalgically. But this little theory does not really solve the problem. The more one listens, the more one is not so sure. A hermeneutical paranoia develops.[60] A matter of tone. There is something "slightly mischievous [*malicieux*]" (2) about the children's laughter that irritates the father. Irritation is a particular kind of affective quality: the father cannot quite tell what it is that irritates him, his very skin, but he has a "feeling" that his irritation is caused by the laughter upstairs.

The father realizes that he is relieved when the laughter upstairs briefly stops. He tries not to listen, but has no choice: "it comes through the closed door, it insinuates itself. . . . Doesn't it really sound as though someone were prudently drilling [*forer*]?" (4). He is now aware that he wants the laughter to stop. It has slowly become a threat: "the sharp peals of their laughter slip into every coil, permeate every recess" (9). Laughter has a cumulative effect: "Those little titters . . . sharp as needles. . . . But wake up, don't look so vacant. . . . Those titters like the drops of water that are made to drip on the heads of torture victims . . . they drip on us, to make us suffer, to destroy us. . . . Don't you really hear them?" (63) The father's struggle is to block laughter off as white noise. And yet the sound of laughter is insinuating: "just a bit more biting, gently slipping, subtle stinging, caress of needles, a pinch of itching powder . . ." (86). Laughter spreads, it propagates and multiplies. It has by now become the laughter of "the enemy." And yet the situation is profoundly contradictory, since no one can deny that laughter is also joyful, childlike. The father imagines "them" carrying a sign reading "Innocent Laughter." Or is it—he is looking for the right word—"sly [*sournois*]" (128)? "Innocent" and "sly" are captions for the sound of laughter, attempts to translate it into manageable meanings. Do you hear them? The neighbor is not so sure anymore: "This laughter is what you make of it. It'll be what you want" (109). The strategy worked in the past, when fathers made of laughter what they wanted, translating it into their little theories or otherwise dismissing it as noise: "Your laughing? What laughing? I didn't hear anything. I just heard some noise . . ." (104). But not this time. This laughter is exasperating. It has produced a *malaise*.

They want to live *alfresco*—laughing in the open air. They want to live in the present and be in permanent motion: "Their mobile, agile, light minds leap, let themselves be carried along, tossed about, swept along by all that moves, unfurls, comes apart, glides, swirls, disappears, returns . . . hardly perceptible slow apparitions . . . sudden loomings . . . unforeseen shocks, repetitions with infinite shadings . . . reflections . . . iridescences. . . . Nothing revolts them so much as to become motionless, to settle down . . ." (53). While the father fantasizes about verticality, stability, security and values ("we are so sturdy and erect, so well planted" [5]), they float about, distracted. They are ready to sacrifice everything for the sake of movement. The father is afraid that, left to their own devices, they would put a ballerina tutu on the pre-Columbian statue and laugh all the more. They are already using it as a support for their ashtray. There is no doubt about it: they would put a laugh on the Mona Lisa! No more masters, no more devotion: "All equals, all geniuses. . . . You too, you know, are a genius . . . you too, why not? If only you want to be. . . . You too . . ." (115).

There used to be a mother in the picture. She did not understand art either. The father and the mother were "incompatible." When they looked at an art object together, he could sense a "counter-current" coming from her. Did she laugh? Did they learn to laugh from her? "How is it possible to believe—and yet you can see for yourselves—that something so vague, so subtle, lodged in the genes, can be transmitted like a hereditary taint [*tare*] from mother to child?" (47) Yes, they must have got it from her. He had decided that one is alone, we die alone. She, however, left her mark, her taint. Laughter seems to be the mother's "single trait."[61]

Ultimately, all the father wants is to join them. Let me laugh with you. Here, we could laugh at our neighbor. But no, even if they were to allow him in the circle of laughter, which they would, the father cannot laugh. Too much

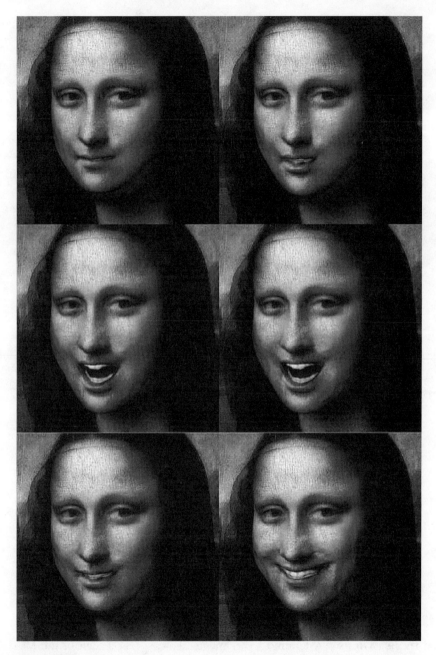

FIGURE 4.1
Mona Lisa Animation, V. Blanz, University of Siegen.

is at stake. Most of all, the father could not entertain the idea that the past, his own life, could have unfolded in different rhythms. The past is an archive of things that could have been, if only he had been able to laugh at the right time. A father's mouth remains closed.

The short sections of *Do You Hear Them?* work as bursts, peals, or ripples of laughter. This is the text one turns to in search of an example of *écriture féminine*—"the rhythm that laughs you." *Do You Hear Them?* actually is a laughing vibration, its movement a nonmusicalized laughing rhythm. Laughter is fluid, it is water-sound; peals of laughter are drops, fountains, and waterfalls; laughter bubbles up, drips, spurts, sprays, and sprinkles.[62] Laughter's tone is a wet tone, a function of its coming from the mouth where, in Adriana Cavarero's words, "wet membranes and taste buds are mixed up with the flavor of the tones."[63] But laughter is also a force, whether stinging or drilling. This piercing quality irritates—for it penetrates the skin, forcing a resistant, impenetrable body to open to the possibility of laughter.

The novel is suspicious of its own translation mechanism: "how could these old sclerotic words retain, enclose the fluid, fluctuating thing that circulates among us, in constant transformation, spreading out in every direction, that no boundary can stop . . ." (136). How can language retain the fluidity of laughter? All language can do is struggle for the perfect adjective: the adjective translates nuances of laughter linguistically, rendering it "innocent" or "sly." The risk is that the adjective could freeze laughter's flow. And yet, beyond the sea of adjectives in which Sarraute's novel swims, laughter insinuates itself. Through the "old sclerotic words," but especially in the spacing between them, laughter makes itself heard.

Listening and hearing have never diverged more.[64] At stake is transforming a mere noise upstairs, something one encounters, "the way we hear the hum of flies, the stridulation of crickets . . ." (4), into a matter of concern. "They" are the new barbarians, laughing and yet polite, sly and yet innocent. We have moved from the struggle to hear Medusa's laughter to "their" laughter. They are, as we say, "our" children. They are young, but youth, as Nietzsche knows well, is a matter not of age but of lightness and the desire to dance and laugh. They come from within, they are our "flesh and blood." And yet they challenge—or is it just an illusion?—what is most dear to us.

Do you hear them?

RESISTANCES   A feminist experiment, Cixous's "The Laugh of the Medusa" appeared at a specific moment in Western intellectual history and in relation to a range of other texts that explored the promise of laughter. The essay offered an answer to the question of how to move from text to life, from *écriture féminine* to laughter, and the other way around. It was profoundly influential in that, on the one hand, it inspired creative thought and, on the other, it served as a starting point for a number of debates. Within these debates, a range of forms of resistance also welcomed Cixous's essay. They, too, are part of the fabric of the laughing feminist century.

One kind of resistance has been what Derrida calls nonreading. "The Laugh of the Medusa" appears on most lists of readings in feminist theory, but there are few actual attempts to read the essay closely, especially if this means listening to it. This state of affairs has been captured by the long insistence on essentialism, the restriction of Cixous's work on the body to the "mere" body, rather than its psychic deployment and reconfiguration. In terms of laughter, this form of resistance has led to the reduction of Cixous's complex and nuanced laughing textual choreography to an argument about the "subversiveness" of women's humor.

A second resistance resounds on the margins of the question whether the appeal to laughter has been a utopia. Every intellectual project has a utopian dimension, an echo of its political engagements.[65] In the particular context of a utopia of laughter, one can hear in this concern resonances of a call for realism and feasibility. The excessiveness of laughter is suspicious, as if philosophical and creative work should be reasonable and temperate. At the end of the day, however, Cixous is not in search of utopia. It is a textual materialism that she is after, one lodged in the sound of laughter.

A third form of resistance hinges upon the celebratory notes of much of the writing in the French feminism of this period. Writing about Luce Irigaray, but making an argument that could be made about Cixous too, Amy Hollywood draws attention to the fact that the celebratory touches in many such texts risk not paying due attention to loss, anguish, and ultimately death.[66] What Cixous's essay brings to this conversation is an acknowledgment that, at the point of laughter, there is both joy and anguish. Despite his antifeminism, Bataille cannot be allowed to leave the stage. Cixous celebrates Medusa's laughter ("She's beautiful and she's laughing"), but also reminds us that she laughs as she sees herself die. This too is a version of "to die laughing." As Hollywood suggests, the point is not to deplore the fact that woman always dies (in fact the laughing woman does not), but to rethink woman's relation to both death and life.[67]

A fourth form of resistance, a variation on the third, rests in the perception of a "pressure to laugh," in Mary Ann Doane's formulation.[68] The feeling that there is a pressure to laugh is the effect of the ubiquitous presence of the figure of "the humorless feminist." The last thing "the feminist" wants is to be humorless.[69] So she needs to laugh. How, then, to respond to this pressure? Moreover, Doane asks, what is a feminist to do when she "finds herself" laughing at a sexist joke? She answers: "Our desire to laugh must not blind us to the still pervasive ideological ordering of the sexual."[70] For Doane, the thing to do is distinguish between the act of reception (which would have us laugh) and the critical act (which would have us resist the laugh at woman's expense). The problem is that the latter is not an easy thing to do. One does not choose to laugh. When we laugh "in response" to a joke, we do not necessarily laugh within its horizon. The methodological shift needed is the one proposed by Samuel Weber: "To comprehend the joke theoretically, therefore, is to address the problem of laughter. . . . [L]aughter imposes itself as the ineluctable problem."[71] We need to start from laughter, rather than from the joke. And then we will be able to see that we do not need to stifle our laughter because the joke is a sexist one.

Finally, there is the warning that laughter is in tension with one's words. In her essay "Our Lips Speak Together," having repeated the question "Doesn't that make you laugh?" Irigaray puts the following sentence in parenthesis: "If you keep laughing that way, we'll never be able to talk to each other. We'll remain absorbed in their words, violated by them. So let's try to take back some part of our mouth to speak with."[72] Cixous, on the other hand, insists that we linger as we laugh, and not turn to speaking too quickly. Most importantly, once we do speak, we can do so with a mouth that does not distinguish between its laughing and speaking parts.

CHAPTER 5

CINEMA, OR THE LAUGHING GAS PARTY

Laughter is shattered articulation.
Walter Benjamin

PHOTOGRAPHIC EXPRESSION We have looked at laughing fragments of
the Western twentieth century: The century of the color line. The century
of the philosophical avant-gardes. The century of feminism. But the twentieth century will also be remembered as the century of cinema.[1] If the century is to be understood as variations on the theme of "the passion for the
real," what is cinema's specificity in the search for the real? The answer to
this question has most often engaged photographic and cinematic claims to
indexicality. A focus on laughter displaces this framework, to explore cinema's
passion for the real as a function of animation and movement. The question
we will ask: Is it possible to tell the story of cinema not, as Giuseppe Torna-
tore's Cinema Paradiso would have it, as a montage of kisses, but as a montage of
laughs? We will begin to sketch this story, arriving at cinema on a continuum
from photography and chronophotography. For if painting found laughter a
challenge, photographic and cinematic technologies presented themselves as
new opportunities to reconsider the possibility of laughter in the visual arts.[2]
Beginning in the second half of the nineteenth century, the new technologies
would be tested for their capacity to "catch" laughter.

Darwin's The Expression of the Emotions in Man and Animals was one of the first
attempts to discern photography's potential as a resource for work on emotion. Darwin confessed that he had looked at painting, hoping to learn about
emotions and their expression. He was familiar with Le Brun's Conférence,
but found painting overall disappointing: "The reason no doubt is, that in
works of art, beauty is the chief object; and strongly contracted facial muscles
destroy beauty."[3] He gave a lot of credit to Charles Bell, whose Anatomy and
Philosophy of Expression he admired because it "includes graphic description of

the various emotions and is admirably illustrated."[4] He found, however, that expression, rather than being a function of superior design, as Bell believed, is a product of evolution. What we call "instincts" are memorized and gradually ritualized habits; they probably started as voluntary actions, but in time became habitual and at last "hereditary." In need of data, Darwin turned to the observation of infants (his own), the insane (who are "liable to the strongest passions, and give uncontrolled vent to them"),[5] "different races of men," and animals.

Among the artifacts he studied, Darwin was fascinated by photographs. Photography, he realized, is capable of offering both material for observation and evidence when it comes to human emotions.[6] Darwin became a collector of photographs. He commissioned yet others, most importantly from the photographer Oscar Rejlander, in the hope that he could illustrate *Expression*. The book belonged to a wave of scientific treatises that began to use photography not only as an "embellishment" (*illustrāre*: to light up, illuminate, embellish) but by way of argumentation. Published in 1872, it became a bestseller and accompanied *On the Origin of Species* in the work of cementing the theory of evolution.

Darwin discussed laughter in a chapter of *Expression* titled "Joy, High Spirits, Love, Tender Feelings, Devotion." He gave a detailed description:

> The sound of laughter is produced by a deep inspiration followed by a short, interrupted, spasmodic contractions of the chest, and especially of the diaphragm. Hence we hear of "laughter holding both sides." From the shaking of the body, the head nods to and fro. The lower jaw often quivers up and down, as is likewise the case with some species of baboons, when they are much pleased. . . . [D]uring excessive laughter the whole body is often thrown backward and shakes, or is almost convulsed; the respiration is much disturbed; the head and face become gorged with blood, with the veins distended; and the orbicular muscles are spasmodically contracted in order to protect the eyes. Tears are freely shed.[7]

Darwin added the production of nonverbal sound to the mix, which he associated with sexual excitement, and the quivering of the jaw. Rather than ask the "why" question in terms of "Why do we laugh?" he wanted to know why a particular affective mix (for Darwin, mostly joy) is linked to a particular expression (and not another). In other words, why the particular symptomatology of laughter? Darwin did not have an answer to this question. Laughter is "hereditary," it is a habit our bodies inherit from our ancestors, but—unlike in the case of the startled reflex, for example, which can be connected to fear—we cannot go back to a given originary moment and find out what triggered the first laugh.[8]

Rejlander agreed to help illustrate *Expression*, confident that photography was suited to the task of representing emotions. He wrote: "photography is eminently fitted to catch and retain transient expressions, which may be caught or induced by the artist, and with all the parts in harmony, a fact which is not certain when painting from nature. The photograph takes the whole at once."[9] Like other photographers of his time, who tested photography's promise to represent expression (Henry Peach Robinson photographed "Fear," H. Cooper photographed "The Sneeze"), Rejlander used his camera to produce photographic images of "Grief," "Appeal," or "Bad Temper."

When it came to laughter, Rejlander offered Darwin two photographs of smiling girls (photographs 1 and 3 in figure 5.1), who can hardly be said to be undergoing the facial and bodily movements in Darwin's description. A few factors converge to produce these smiles. One is the obvious technical challenges posed by lengthy exposure times, which required sitters to be still for minutes on end. The other is the desire for an expressive totality, Rejlander's attempt to "take the whole at once . . . with all the parts in harmony," which had the effect of draining laughter of movement. Yet another is the fact that, in an attempt to establish itself as an art, photography followed the pictorial portraiture tradition and adopted its classic settings, poses, and accessories. Within this tradition, laughter and open mouths more generally remained taboo.

When, in 1891, photographer Henry Peach Robinson wrote *The Studio: And What to Do in It*, he advised trainee photographers to study in the National Portrait Gallery and learn from the great masters of the portraiture tradition. He also drew attention to the lack of variety in pictorial portraiture and, using Rejlander as an example, insisted that photography had a lot to teach painting.[10] The object of portrait photography continued to be "the head," and lighting, the most important technical device available to the photographer, was thought to consist of "the art of setting a head properly on its shoulders."[11] This well-lit head was still an expressive head, displaying, however, a specifically photographic expressivity. The story portrait photography told itself was that of moving from a focus on likeness, which resulted in a flat "map of the face," as Robinson put it, to the facial depth of photographic expression. It simply remained for photography to discover its expressive specificity.

Robinson believed that "The photographer should endeavor to represent his sitters as moderately calm ladies and gentlemen; or, if they are not entitled to the courtesy title, then as decent men and women."[12] It was clear that moderately calm ladies and gentlemen and decent men and women do not express strong emotions, as they have "inherited" a range of honorable facial and bodily poses. When it came to laughter, Robinson wrote: "Some faces are beautiful in repose, hideous in movement. A broad laugh is often beautiful

FIGURE 5.1

Charles Darwin, *The Expression of the Emotions in Man and Animals*, 1872.
Huntington Library.

in nature, because of its evanescence; it becomes intolerable when fixed on paper. But there is a look of animation, far short of a smile, which suits nearly all faces, and which is so permanently beautiful that it deserves to be printed in carbon or enamel."[13] Note that for Robinson laughter can be beautiful in nature; he is concerned only with its reproduction on paper. Since the latter is considered intolerable, photography would search for the expressivity of a subtly animated face. Photography would still movement in order to reach a more complex level of animation. It would largely be the job of the mouth to do the work of animation. The choreography of the photographic mouth would be "far short of a smile," as in early photography the mouth continued to be strictly closed. What mattered was a certain "quality of the smile," and Robinson believed quality smiles were scarce and hard to induce through the range of stratagems available to the photographer.[14]

With the ideal of this subtly animated face on the horizon, Robinson condemned photographers who requested their sitters to smile, "forgetting that many people look idiotic when their simpers and smiles are perpetuated."[15] When the person being photographed tries too hard to be a good sitter, he or she often puts on an "an insufferable smirk."[16] Ladies especially, caught between the desire to show that they have a small mouth and the injunction to smile, end up with a "hysteric grin" on their faces.[17] Robinson had his ways of dealing with open mouths—lowering the face in activities like reading or sewing, gently touching the lower lip of children, etc. He, however, could not but acknowledge that, despite the efforts he described and the endurance of the open-mouth taboo in pictorial and photographic portraiture, in the last decades of the nineteenth century the mouth slowly began to open. So much so that, given the fact that he knew there were few "permanently parted lips, leaving the teeth in full view" in earlier photographs, Robinson suspected a new genetic defect afflicting the British.[18]

Rejlander's use of children, whom Robinson also acknowledged to be good, expressive sitters, as well as his familiarity with a range of expression-inducing stratagems borrowed from the theater, allowed him to experiment with stronger passions and opened the mouth of his sitters a bit more. Rejlander himself appears in many of his photographs, because he often interacted with his sitters in an effort to induce certain expressions. The most successful outcome of his theatrical staging is a photograph in which Rejlander is seen whispering in the ear of a man. Rejlander titled the photograph *Did She?*, suggesting that the sitter's smile is a reaction to a story the photographer is telling him about a shared female acquaintance.[19] The image is reminiscent of an earlier, similar photograph by David Octavius Hill and Robert Adamson, which also seems to be the result of a theatrical arrangement, and in which Hill smiles spontaneously in the company of two friends. But the fact remained that, although it offered useful staging techniques, the theater was of little inspiration when it came to laughter.[20]

FIGURE 5.2

Hill and Adamson, *Edinburgh Ale*, 1843–1847. The J. Paul Getty Museum, Los Angeles.

This is where Guillaume-Benjamin Duchenne de Boulogne's 1862 *The Mechanism of Human Facial Expression* comes in. One of the book's merits is, in Darwin's words, that it is illustrated with "magnificent photographs."[21] Duchenne worked at La Salpêtrière, the hospital for the poor outside of Paris, made famous by Charcot's work with hysterics. His stated goal was to make the muscles of the face speak the language of emotions, to "give voice" to the face.[22] "Expression is to passion what language is to thought," Bell had written.[23] Duchenne set out to decipher the "orthography of the face," the intricacies of the language of passion and emotion.[24]

Duchenne's project involved the use of electricity to galvanize isolated facial muscles to contract into recognizable expressions. By applying a flow of electricity to the face, Duchenne was able to hold the expressions induced long enough for a photograph to be taken. If photography was not developed enough to make instantaneous shots possible, Duchenne devised a mechanism through which the face could freeze its expression to accommodate technological challenges. The photographs—some taken by himself, others by the photographer Adrien Tournachon—were to be "as true as a mirror," and the results of his experimentation were to serve scientists *and* artists.[25] The frontispiece to *The Mechanism of Human Facial Expression* showed Duchenne inducing the laughter of one of his patients.

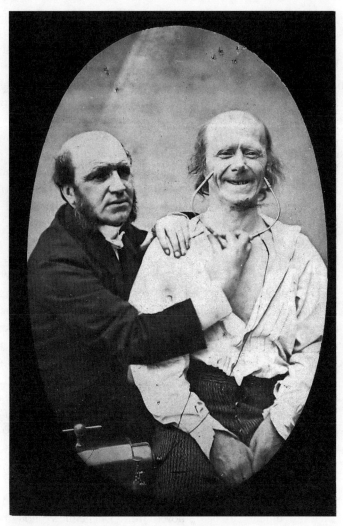

FIGURE 5.3
Guillaume-Benjamin Duchenne, *The Mechanism of Human Facial Expression*, 1862. The J. Paul Getty Museum, Los Angeles.

Duchenne fashioned himself into an art teacher in Le Brun's lineage and, indeed, enlargements of his photographs would be used by students of the École des Beaux-Arts preparing for the annual, otherwise very traditional, *tête d'expression* competition. He would offer new and dependable information for artists attempting to represent human emotions. Painting and sculpture, Duchenne argued, have often erred and created expressions that are incompatible with the actual movement of facial muscles. He famously remodeled *Laocoön*, a favorite model in the artistic training in expression, to show how the sculpture would have looked, had the artist had access to the innovation brought about by the marriage of galvanism and photography. Duchenne also staged a set of photographs for the aesthetic section of his book. Situating his patients (women only in the aesthetic section) within clearly defined narrative and dramatic situations, supported by costumes and gestures, he galvanized their faces, sculpting their muscles into a range of expressions.

Darwin was fascinated and used some of Duchenne's photographs in his book. The three photographs on the right side of the plate in the "Joy, High Spirits, Love" chapter of *Expression* (figure 5.1) show Duchenne's patient, whom he described as "an old toothless man, with a thin face, whose features without being absolutely ugly, approached triviality and whose facial expression was in perfect agreement with his inoffensive character and his restricted intelligence."[26] The patient suffered from an anesthetic condition of the face that made him unable to feel pain. Duchenne could experiment with this patient's face, in his words, "as if I was working with a still irritable cadaver."[27] Photograph 4 shows the patient's "natural expression"; photograph 5, his "natural smile"; photograph 6, his "induced laughter."[28] Duchenne's plate with variations on laughter in *The Mechanism of Human Facial Expression* included a fourth photograph, a "false, incomplete expression of *agreeable surprise, or admiration*."[29] Darwin chose not to include it in *Expression*.

As he prepared his book for publication, Darwin explicitly asked for the galvanizing instruments to be removed from Duchenne's photographs.[30] Some instruments are, however, still visible in the final version of *Expression*. The effect is one of horror, reminiscent of Victor Hugo's *The Man Who Laughs*, whose eponymous character acquires his frozen laughing expression through a medical procedure.[31] This, because Duchenne's patient is indeed a "laughing cadaver."[32] The irony here is a function of photography's close relation to rituals of mourning, death, and cadavers. In its early days, photography was welcomed, among other things, because of its potential to archive images of the dead and preserve them in time. It is not an accident that the postmortem photograph was one of the most popular photographic genres of the nineteenth century. When Robinson reminds us that people from the country put on their best clothes and came to city to have a haircut, go to the dentist, and have their picture taken (Robinson insisted they do the last first), we now

FIGURE 5.4
Guillaume-Benjamin Duchenne, *The Mechanism of Human Facial Expression*, 1862.
The J. Paul Getty Museum, Los Angeles.

know they did so in order to look their best in their photographic afterlife. All photographs have their funereal dimension. We want to look good on our deathbed, and since we will not be there to work on our bodies (a role taken by communal experts, who often sculpt postmortem faces into "peaceful" smiling expressions), we want to play a small role in the composition of our photographs. Duchenne's images are uncanny because they seem to index the laughter of the living dead.

What remains from this history of both magic and horror is the suggestion that photographic technology found itself invested in renewed attempts to "capture" laughter (and its proximity to death), a phenomenon that had intrigued the visual arts for a long time.[33] In the temporal lull required by lengthy exposure times, photography had to stage its freezing operation, through a range of techniques. We now laugh in our photographic portraits, but only if we compose our faces into the "orthography of the face" habit has taught us to associate with a laugh, and freeze the pose for enough time for it to be captured by the camera. Photographic technology would advance, and come closer and closer to the dream of the "instantaneous" shot, but our portraits continue to partake of the photographic operation inaugurated by Duchenne. It is as if we galvanize our faces a little when we laugh in front of the camera. The Nadar brothers photographed this operation in the wake of Duchenne's experiments. *Pierrot Laughing* shows the mime Charles Debureau performing a laugh. It is a convincing laugh.[34] And yet Pierrot is a mime, equipped with makeup, costume and gesture, and we are at no point allowed to forget that this is a performance. What Pierrot performs, however, is Duchenne's patient. His laugh rehearses the photographic operation of laughter.

ANIMATED POTRAITS   One of the fantasies attendant to the birth of cinema was that of the "animated portrait," the cinematic version of the *tête d'expression*. Chronophotography set out to bring movement and time to the art of the "head." It was a dream with a long history in the world of vaudeville, the fairground and its magic lantern shows, a history to which the emergent chronophotographic and cinematic technologies belonged.

One nineteenth-century magic lantern show animated a face by making it laugh: a glass slide was moved across a fixed slide, while black patches on the slipping slide alternately covered and uncovered the two phases of movement. The image had clear affinities with the "grotesques" that magic lantern shows capitalized on, but it also appealed to the desire to animate the human face. As Edward Groom's 1865 *The Art of Transparent Painting on Glass for the Magic Lantern* put it: "by such means the appearance of vitality and movement is given to the eyes and mouth."[35] Animation was to be a function of this mixture of movement and vitality. Importantly, it was agreed that "Nothing could have enlivened the spirit of lantern exhibitions so much as photography," as an 1878 *Magic Lantern Manual* declared.[36]

In the spirit of the magic lantern shows, but having harnessed new technological devices in its service, the magic chronophotography promised was that of our family albums filled with animated, expressive images of our loved ones. As is well known, the story of chronophotography has as its main protagonists Eadweard Muybridge, Étienne-Jules Marey, and Marey's assistant, Georges Demenÿ. Muybridge was a photographer; his use of the camera was very much rooted in the tradition of pictorial representation. Marey, on the other hand, was a physiologist. Marey was interested in physiological functions, most importantly muscle function and respiration. If, as Marta Braun argues, Muybridge's project can be conceived as having as its horizon the pleasure of the eye, Marey's had its education in mind.[37]

Marey set out to study movement. He found himself in need of a method of recording human locomotion, a legible representation of movement in time. His was a modernist project in the service of science. Chronophotography would picture time, spatializing it into a representation of movement. It would thus bring within our visual horizon that which the unaided eye cannot perceive, a more real reality. Describing a chronophotograph of a man shouting, Marey agreed that his facial expression amounted to nothing more than a "grimace." What was peculiar to the new technology, however, was its capacity to catch not the expression proper, but gradual transitions between expressions, which were not visible in any isolated facial expression. Marey went on to say that what appeared as a grimace was the unknown represented

FIGURE 5.6
Laughing Face, hand-colored magic lantern slide. National Media Museum; Science and Society Picture Library.

by such invisible transitions.[38] The new technology promised to touch on this unknown.

In a section of his book titled "Chronophotography of facial expression," having announced that chronophotography was capable of offering images of fleeting changes in facial movement, Marey wrote: "it would be interesting to follow in this way all the transitions between a scarcely perceptible smile and a hearty laugh [*un sourire à peine perceptible et le rire le plus franc*]."[39] For Marey, this possibility remained a question of the merely interesting. His own scientific interests led him to an image of the movement of the jaw in mastication and one of respiration, first attempts to represent the movement of a mouth in time. It was his assistant, Georges Demenÿ, who took on the challenge of capturing the transition between a smile and a laugh, or, as we will see, between a close-mouthed smile and an open-mouthed one.

Although Marey encouraged Demenÿ's efforts, the two parted ways in 1894 on account of the animated portrait fantasy and its commercial implications for the emerging moving picture industry. Demenÿ opened a studio of animated portraits. One of his portraits shows his German sponsor, Ludwig Stollwerk, transitioning from a smile to a laugh.[40] Yet another one is a portrait of a young boy sitting in a chair, laughing. An article in *The New Penny Magazine* in 1901, titled "The Story of a Smile," announced that if "there are fleeting or transitory expressions which the ordinary camera cannot seize," which "are lost even to the eye because it is not quick enough," only what was now called "the cinematograph" could reveal these intermediary states.[41] An illustration accompanied the article, a composite photograph showing "all the varieties of a smile on the face of an old French lady who was photographed unawares by M. Dumeny [sic], the well known student of facial expression."[42]

The art of the animated portrait was short-lived, but a number of artists and scientists whose work was paramount for the emerging cinema were committed to it. Independent of the work of Marey and Demenÿ in France and of Muybridge in the United States, William Friese-Greene dreamed his own dreams about the future of the moving picture in Britain, which also passed through the animated portrait. A chronophotograph of Friese-Greene depicts his face moving from a state of repose to a contortion in a laugh. When Friese-Greene moved to the next step in the history of animation, the experiment would be yet another attempt to animate the human mouth:

> The audience expected slides of pretty scenery or biblical pictures. Instead, a girl's head appeared on the screen. She moved her eyes from side to side and her face broke into a smile. The audience laughed good-naturedly. Someone called: "We know you're there, missy. You can come out now." Friese-Greene lighted a lamp. He explained that it was not a trick. Well, of course, it was in a way, but there was no girl behind the screen. They had seen a moving picture.[43]

LAUGHING GAS   The coming of film was seen as a major promise for laughter. If laughter is movement, film is *moving* picture. If laughter is sound, film had its investment in sound from the very beginning.[44] If laughter is of the face, film has a special relationship with the face.[45] If laughter raises crucial questions related to its temporality, film, its very medium, molds itself on the time of its object. As if coming to test this promise, early film had a lot to say about laughter.

Early motion pictures offered a series of facial close-ups, known as "facial expression films."[46] It was with Edwin Porter's 1907 *Laughing Gas* that laughter took hold of the screen for the first time. The laughing face lingers on the screen—burst after burst after burst. It looks as if an open mouth and teeth

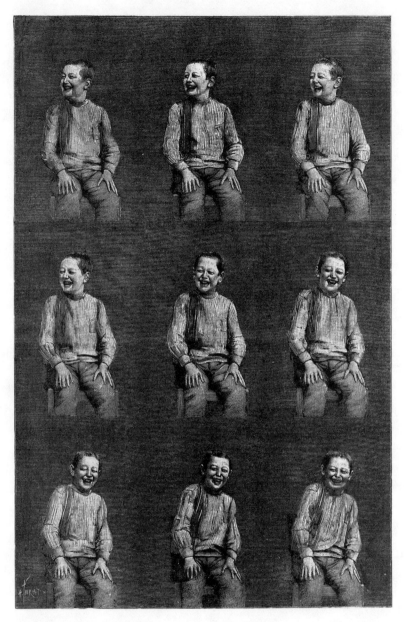

FIGURE 5.7

Georges Demenÿ, illustration in *Scientific American Supplement* (October 1894).
Harvard University Library.

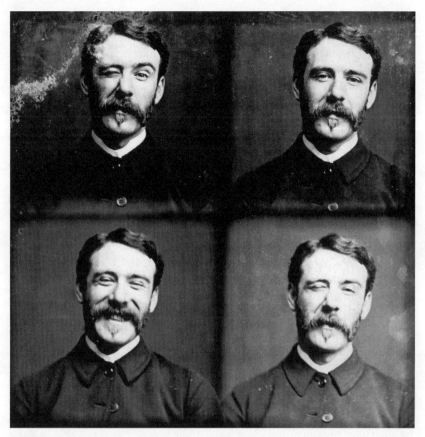

FIGURE 5.8
Portrait of William Friese-Greene, c. 1886. National Media Museum; Science and Society Picture Library.

are welcomed in the realm of the visible. The mouth wide open is an invitation for the viewer to join the laughing gas party cinema promises to be. *Laughing Gas* was itself infectious. Chaplin made his own *Laughing Gas* (1914). And later the film industry would be described in these terms in P. G. Wodehouse's 1936 novel *Laughing Gas*.

Porter's film tells the story of a black woman, Mandy Brown (Bertha Regustus), who has a toothache. She goes to the dentist to have her tooth extracted. The dentist uses nitrous oxide ("laughing gas") as anesthetic. Mandy starts laughing, allowing laughter to run through her whole body, rolling on the floor, hands and feet thrown around. Throughout the film, Mandy goes through a series of locations, all clear landmarks of seriousness, infecting everyone she meets with her unstoppable laugher. In a streetcar divided along class, race, and gender lines, her laughter upsets all rituals. When she is brought to court because of a street disturbance, the judge and the policemen are themselves overwhelmed with laughter, and Mandy dances away. When Mandy, who is a domestic servant, serves dinner to her employers, her contagious laughter makes them turn the exquisite dinner table upside down, and they too join in. When, in a moonlight scene, Mandy runs into a man and he prepares for what appears to be a possible romantic encounter, her laughter ruins any such possibility. In church, Mandy's laughter transforms religious songs into generalized laughter, with the African-American community laughing together as in a choir. The pastor almost has a heart attack.

Mandy can only be a black woman in this context. The dentist and his assistant immobilize her, intoxicate her, and insert their hands in her mouth to extract her tooth. The scene has clear sexual connotations.[47] In the late nineteenth century and early twentieth century, dentists often advertised separately for women patients.[48] As in gynecological practice, privacy was (and remained) an issue for dental practice. In Laughing Gas, if the camera was to peek into this private sanctuary and be a witness to the scene of tooth-pulling, the patient could only have been clearly marked by class, which, in the US cinematic context of the early twentieth century, also meant by race.[49] Even more so if she is to laugh laughs not laughed by respectable people.[50] And yet, when compared to other Edison films in which African-American characters appear, often as minstrel figures, Mandy is clearly not caricaturized. She is beautiful and well dressed. Her only sin—if it still is a sin—is her laughter. The paradox points to Laughing Gas being witness and participant in a transition in visual laughing matters. The film uses Mandy as a black woman, capitalizing on race, but it stops short of reproducing stereotypes of both black laughter and African-American female sexuality. In fact, Mandy just had a tooth pulled and yet she has a perfect laugh. Her face could serve as an advertisement for dentistry, which, in its own attempt to capitalize on race, often used African-American models.[51]

Much as in the case of the "Okeh Laughing Record," the recording industry's attempt to exploit laughter's "contagiousness," the assumption here is that the convulsion on the screen has the potential to trigger an immediate reaction from the viewer. The moving picture can spontaneously move us to laugh. Linda Williams persuasively argues that one of the things the new cinematic technology promised, drawing on photographic representations like those of Charcot's hysterics, was images of women in convulsion.[52] These images would move us—our very bodies. They are the anticipation of pleasures to come, of which pornography is only an accentuation, the point where the industry's promise of immediate pleasure is most visible. Laughing Gas helped advertise the industry's potential to induce the convulsive pleasures of laughter.[53] The film ends with a series of mid-shots of Mandy laughing. Laugh upon laugh upon laugh. It is the cinematic version of a laughing tête d'expression, a burst of laughter unfolding in cinematic time.

Figure 5.9
Edwin Porter (dir.), *Laughing Gas*, 1907.

LIFE UNAWARES   Twenty years after *Laughing Gas*, in the context of revolutionary Soviet Union, Dziga Vertov's *The Man with a Movie Camera* (1928) made it
its task to educate the eye of the cinematic spectator, this time by opening it
to the "tricks" played on it by the camera. Vertov called his film a "theoretical
manifestation on the screen."[54] Interested in cinema's potential to document
the workings of the human face, Vertov dreamed of making "A Gallery of Film
Portraits."[55] To "catch life unawares," the phrase around which he summa-
rized his project, was also to document elusive traces of emotion on the face.

Vertov knew that sitters adjust their faces in the presence of the camera. How, then, to record events as if they were not recorded? A subterfuge
is needed. Rejlander had played with his child sitters, hoping to induce the
expressions he wanted. For the most part, especially when working with
adults, Robinson argued, the result is acting. Vertov works with non-actors:
"Not 'filming life unawares' for the sake of the 'unaware,' but in order to show
people without masks, without make up, to catch them through the eye of the
camera in a movement when they are not acting, to read their thoughts, laid
bare by the camera."[56] The challenge is to catch the face by surprise, unawares,
naked. The project meets with inevitable and predictable obstacles: "Your first
failures. People stare at you, urchins surround you, your subjects peer into
the camera. . . . Girls begin to primp; men make 'Fairbanks' or 'Conrad Veidt'
faces. They all smile affably for the camera."[57] In the presence of a camera,
people pose—poses learned from the theater, the photographic studio, and,
more and more, cinema. And by now posing inevitably involves "smiling affably." The result is that there is no "living person" in front of the camera. We
know that, in his own attempt to catch "life unawares" in a series of "film
portraits," Andy Warhol would film precisely the primping of women and the
Conrad Veidt faces of men, their "star potential," suggesting that, in a postrev-
olutionary twentieth century, the theatrical and the cinematic—the mask Vertov condemned—are in fact the very stuff and life of the face. Vertov's project,
however, belongs to a different era, one still marked by a revolutionary belief
in "the living person" and cinema's epistemological mission of offering a
"FILM-FACTORY OF FACTS."[58] Vertov's horizon: "You gain experience. You
use all sorts of techniques to remain unnoticed."[59]

In the famous magician scene in *Man with a Movie Camera*, the camera is hidden and the children watching the magician are filmed without knowing they
are being filmed. We are presented with the resulting close-ups of a boy and a
girl's laughing faces. We have, in fact, seen the boy's face earlier in the film—
in other words, before the moment of its actual filming—and are now prepared for a lesson in what Vertov calls "the grammar of cinematic means."[60] If
Demenÿ's project is to have his boy's laugh unfold in time, Vertov decomposes
the resulting chronophotograph and takes us back to the still images of the
face. He arrests each shot into a photogram, an image that in fact cannot be

excerpted from the series that constitutes it. Cut to the editing room, where we are shown how cinema makes this laugh "come to life" by creating the illusion of movement. We see the editor at work, stitching "intervals," the raw material of the art of movement, together. This is the dialectical counterpoint to the actual filming of a laugh. The labor of the magician-editor is an inherent part of what Vertov calls the "film-object." If cinematic laughter seems to be a more real laughter (there is movement, animation, "real" time and visual sound here), we are offered a glimpse of the editing scissors that create its reality effects. Experimental photographers of this time entered an explicit dialog with cinematic theoretical statements like Vertov's film. László Moholy-Nagy produced *Double Portrait of Gret Palucca*; Walter Kaminsky made the portrait of Friedrich Köhn. Both are attempts to bring the cinematically inspired combination of movement and animation to photographic expression.

Vertov acknowledged that the "trick" cinema depended on could have important philosophical and ideological consequences for the "dream machine." However, he saw here the potential for a new objectivity. There is a necessary tension between "film fact" and montage, which any film-object should make evident. Vertov concluded that in fact there are no tricks in cinema. He pushes Marey: It is indeed the case that our eye cannot catch certain movements—the elusiveness of a burst of laughter—but Vertov does not believe the human eye (even the eye educated in the school of chronophotography and cinema) can overcome its shortcomings. In order to reach an intensity of perception we are as yet not capable of, we need to deanthropomorphize the eye. The kino-eye, leading to a new "I see," should no longer be a human eye.

The point for Vertov is to acknowledge that the face *is* in motion. There is discontinuity in the continuity of the cinematic image (the photogram in the film strip), but beyond this discontinuity is a deeper continuity, a movement we—as yet—cannot perceive. The art of the close-up revolves around this intuition.[61] In the magician scene, the cinematic burst of laughter is the effect of stitching together a number of photograms of a laughing face; but in fact we know that laughter is movement and the projected image on the screen, while not being its objective representation, strives toward a form of realism that points to a deeper real of movement. Vertov's hope: "My path leads to the creation of a fresh perception of the world. I decipher in a new way a world unknown to you."[62] Only this perception can hope to catch what remains unknown in a burst of laughter.[63]

TEETH A question imposes itself at this point: Where do we draw the line between a smile and a laugh? In the last decades of the nineteenth century, the mouth began to open, and this opening has historically been associated with a laugh. And yet something has happened in the history of the face that

FIGURE 5.10
Dziga Vertov (dir.), *Man with a Movie Camera*, 1928.

FIGURE 5.11
László Moholy-Nagy, *Double Portrait of Gret Palucca*, 1928. The J. Paul Getty Museum, Los Angeles. © Estate of László Moholy-Nagy, Artists Rights Society (ARS), New York.

FIGURE 5.12

Walter Kaminsky, *Friedrich Köhn*, c. 1928. The J. Paul Getty Museum, Los Angeles.

has slightly shifted the tension between smiling and laughing such that it is no longer immediately clear when we are dealing with smiles or laughs. This shift is a function of an important change in our relation to teeth.

In the history of the face, the twentieth century is also the century of the making visible of teeth.[64] Photographic and cinematic technologies played an important role in this process. They can be said to have offered the necessary lighting that would, at least in part, illuminate a mouth historically imagined as a dark cavern. New pleasures would be associated with this mouth (the century that began with Freud was to be a century of renewed orality), which would nonetheless also become a site of discipline and preventive monitoring. Enter dentistry.

The narrative dentistry tells itself is that of the progress of teeth.[65] According to it, following the advent of science and technology, we have moved from a mouth filled with decaying and diseased teeth, rotten gums, and their attendant odors, to one filled with healthy, symmetric, ordered, ever whiter, mint-smelling heralds of modern hygiene. Teeth are little soldiers, marching to the drumbeat of progress, announcing a transition from superstition, charlatanism, and public spectacle (until the nineteenth century, teeth were most often pulled by itinerant practitioners within public theatrical events) to science, reason, and private monitoring (the dentist's office).

What seems more important than this story, however, is that with the coming of teeth, we move from a mouth that was largely outside of the realm of the visible to one that becomes visible as teeth. It is not that the mouth ceases to be a dark abyss (the "mouth of darkness"), but that it stops advertising itself as such and, in an age of bodily management and preventive hygiene, presents its entrance or portal as a site of order. Photography was crucial to this transformation. Indeed, when the mouth begins to open in nineteenth-century photographs, as in the 1870s daguerreotype titled *Man with Open Mouth* (*Homme baillant*), it often seems that it does so in order to advertise its teeth.

Nineteenth-century photography is a gallery of stiff, closed-mouthed, "decent" portraits and *cartes de visite*. Dentistry and the emerging orthodontic industry are quick to understand that, if the mouth is to open and display specimens of newly acquired or newly aestheticized teeth, this open mouth should not be said to be laughing. If dentistry is to become a decent, respectable enterprise, it has to work on the fantasy of a smiling open mouth. The wide toothy smile becomes the object of dentistry, which will from now on capitalize on it. It is the first time in the history of the face that a fully open mouth is said to be smiling, rather than laughing.

Rituals of teeth-baring smiling will soon come to determine social situations. "He who laughs cannot bite," writes Norbert Elias, and indeed, teeth-showing social rituals keep aggressivity at bay.[66] As objects of dentistry and orthodontics, however, teeth lose even more of their threatening qualities. He

FIGURE 5.13
Unknown maker, c. 1852. The J. Paul Getty Museum, Los Angeles.

who smiles can bite even less. Dentistry will work hand in hand with modern surveillance technology (including photography) such that, when it does bite, a dental record helps to identify the culprit mouth. Toothy mouths continue to have their acoustic regimentation, no "noise" will be allowed to come out of them, but their frequent opening and the open mouth's historic association with laughter rather than smiling helps us forget the laughs we do not laugh. The consequence of this change is that the opening of the mouth and the visibility of teeth, as well as the body's receding involvement in laughter, make it ever more difficult to distinguish between a laugh and an open-mouthed toothy smile.

Paolo Mantegazza had pointed to the gendered outcomes of these developments: "ladies laugh little lest they should have precocious wrinkles, while others laugh too much, and on every pretext, that they may show their beautiful teeth."[67] The advantages brought by the display of beautiful teeth would slowly win over the threat of wrinkles, such that by the 1910s, although mainstream portrait photography remains largely conservative in mouth matters, we have fully open, teeth-showing smiles in many photographs. One of August Sanders's portraits seems to capture the timidity with which this happened. Alfred Stieglitz has perhaps immortalized the "new woman" in his photograph of an exuberant Ellen Koeniger. Hannes Meyer's *Lena Lying on the Grass* shows us a woman already comfortably playing with her smile / laugh. By 1937, William Mortensen's *The Model: A Book on the Problems of Posing* would deplore the fact that "we are every day hemmed in, besieged and bombarded by smiles. Acres of gleaming white ivory challenge us from billboards, newspapers, motion picture screens, and commercial portraits, and even pursue us into chaster pictorial precincts."[68]

The toothy smile slowly becomes a brand. The very history of advertising parallels the history of the smile.[69] The face composes its smile for the photographic camera and the new modes of perception photography inaugurates. To be somebody, to be recognized as being somebody, will require a signature smile. Open-mouthed smiling becomes a prerequisite of sociability. You're never fully dressed without a smile. Of course, the smile is class-determined, arguably one of the most visible marks of class. We advertise ourselves and our membership in a group when we smile. Toothy smiles translate into social capital (for individuals, but in the public health movement the assumption often is that in the future the prosperity and "leadership potential" of nations could be ranked according to the quality of their subjects' teeth).[70] In the twentieth century, dentistry would join hands with psychology and, in an effort to increase the motivation of a working class resistant to its pressures, would suggest an implacable link between the toothy smile and individual happiness.[71] Good teeth, allowing for toothy smiles, come to advertise happiness, which, in its turn, cannot do without a smile. You're never fully happy without a smile. More and more, especially on the American scene, there will indeed be a pressure to be happy, which will further cement the need for toothy smiles.

WRONG LAUGHTER Words of caution often come from Adorno's pen. In their now-classic essay "The Culture Industry," Horkheimer and Adorno remind us that the systematic and totalizing form culture takes in modernity, the industry it has become, has co-opted the new cinematic technology to its homogenizing force. Any promise early film might have carried is lost. As part of the culture industry, cinema is in the entertainment business; and entertainment is "the prolongation of work under late capitalism. It is sought by those who want to escape the mechanized labor process so that they can cope

FIGURE 5.14

August Sander, *Portrait of an Unidentified Woman*, 1901–1909. The J. Paul Getty Museum, Los Angeles, © J. Paul Getty Trust.

FIGURE 5.15
Alfred Stieglitz, *Ellen Koeniger*, 1916. The J. Paul Getty Museum, Los Angeles, © J. Paul Getty Trust.

FIGURE 5.16

Hannes Meyer, *Lena Lying on the Grass*, c. 1930–1933. The J. Paul Getty Museum, Los Angeles.

with it again."[72] The leisure time the culture industry fills is a continuation of the never-ending working hours.

The culture industry resonates with laughter. "Wrong [*falsche*] laughter," Horkheimer and Adorno call it.[73] This is not a laughter on the screen, but the generalized laughter of the industry: fun. And it rings false. Adorno and Horkheimer hear rationalizing overtones in the apparently happiness-producing laughter of the culture industry: "Fun is a medicinal bath [*Fun ist ein Stahlbad*] which the entertainment industry never ceases to prescribe. It makes laughter the instrument for cheating happiness."[74] Laughter is "structured amusement," cheating us of the potential for any "real" laughter. We live in a world of "ordained cheerfulness."[75] Hollywood advertised its years of glory in a number of musicals that seemed to unfold under the aegis of *Singing in the Rain*'s "Make Them Laugh."

Horkheimer and Adorno do not discuss laugh tracks, but this is often what seems to be at stake in their formulations. We laugh when we are told to laugh: "the product prescribes each reaction."[76] Laughing with the laugh tracks, we perform an "automated sequence of standardized tasks."[77] We are moved to respond mechanically to stimuli. The irony of this situation should not be lost on us: the culture industry has managed to co-opt *even* laughter. Moreover, it has made laughter an integral part of its mechanism. The culture industry has laughter at its very heart, because laughter carries with it promises of the reconciliation [*Versöhnung*] the culture industry can never offer. The laughter of the culture industry is a parody of laughter. In a parallel argument vis-à-vis contemporary music, Adorno suggests that the very "consciousness of alienation vents itself in laughter . . . involved in this laughter is the decay of the sacral spirit of reconciliation."[78]

Horkheimer and Adorno's discussion of the laughter of the culture industry echoes the debate that accompanied laugh tracks from their introduction in the early 1950s. The laugh track was thought to produce a sense of presence and liveness at a time when television shows were increasingly filmed rather than live productions. Jane Feuer writes: "As television in fact becomes less and less a 'live' medium, in the sense of an equivalence between time of event and time of transmission, the medium in its practices insists more and more on the live, the immediate, the direct, the spontaneous, the real."[79] The laughter of the laugh track was thought to bring something of "the live, the immediate, the spontaneous, the real" to a medium that increasingly did not share these attributes. Laughter, that "property of man," imagined as the most reliable evidence of an immediate, unproblematic presence, could serve this purpose. This is the culture industry exploiting the laughing variation on "the passion for the real."

A second argument in the debate around laugh tracks was that a distant and fragmented television audience could not be counted on to react properly to comedic signals. The audience needed some help. It needed to be told when and how to laugh. The Laff Box was invented, an uncanny machine if ever there was one: "an organlike mechanism with six keys that when played with the left hand, can provide small chuckles, medium chuckles, small laughs, medium laughs, medium heavy laughs, and rollin'-in-the-aisles boffs."[80] Laughter is produced mechanically in a box. The sight and sound of the Laff Box has made many uneasy, which is why it has for a long time been a well-kept secret. Faced with the Laff Box, one had the experience of a laugh dissociated from the body, which appeared to be the effect of ventriloquism. Even more so if one knew that the Laff Box was an archive of old laughs, laughed by people possibly long dead. The Laff Box produced a sense of wonder mixed with a substantial dose of horror. One experiences the same uneasiness today when faced with a large number of laughing toys (at the press of a button, Elmo starts laughing and laughing).

What better way to help people laugh than to give them prerecorded laughter they can emulate? The experience of the "Okeh Laughing Record" showed that laughter's "contagiousness" could be counted on: people responded automatically with laughter. Prepackaged laughter ("canned laughter") produced more laughter. We are told when to spontaneously start laughing. Laugh tracks are the paradigmatic example of what Horkheimer and Adorno describe as the "withering of imagination and spontaneity."[81] Tell us when, where, and how to laugh.

In one of the "Comments" in his *Critique of Judgment*, Kant quotes Voltaire arguing that God gave us hope and sleep to help us through the hardships of life.[82] Kant suggests that Voltaire should have added laughter to the list. God gave us hope, sleep, and laughter. Pushing Kant, Horkheimer and Adorno would say that laughter is hope-giving and a form of sleep. Laughter, understood in a Bergsonian key, is instrumental in the rational standardization and functionalization of culture.[83] Moreover, the culture industry has cleverly devised a mechanism through which it persuades its consumers that all it wants is to meet their spontaneous wishes. The culture industry gives us laugh tracks and convinces us that it is we who want them.[84] Here are Horkheimer and Adorno: "The shamelessness of the rhetorical question 'What do people want?' [*Was wollen die Leute haben?*] lies in the fact that it appeals [*beruft*] to the very people as thinking subjects whose subjectivity it specifically seeks to annul [*entwöhnen*]."[85] The people want what they are offered. They want laughter because laughter is what the menu has to offer ("Make 'em laugh / Make 'em laugh / Don't you know / Everyone wants to laugh"). They are part of the system and not, as the asking of the question would suggest, an excuse for it. Freedom is served to "the people" as a function of choice, but choice is a function of homogeneity.

The culture industry nonetheless also finds itself in the business of staging its own maneuvers every now and then. One film does this work brilliantly: Preston Sturges's *Sullivan's Travels* (Paramount, 1941). On a first reading, *Sullivan's Travels* seems to confirm Horkheimer and Adorno's argument. Its dedication: "To the memory of all those who make us laugh: the motley mountebanks—the clowns, the buffoons, in all times and in all nations, whose efforts have lightened our burden a little, this picture is affectionately dedicated." The film actually asks: "What do the people want?" And "the people," it turns out, are nothing but a movie audience. The question is as problematic as Freud's "What does woman want?" For who can tell? One can always ask "the people." But where are they? How can they be reached? Most importantly, provided one can in one way or another have access to "the people," are they reliable? Can they be trusted to know what they want or what they ought to want? Having asked the question in all its rhetoricity (and shamelessness, as Horkheimer and Adorno emphasize), *Sullivan's Travels* ricochets an answer. We find out that what the people want is laughter.

John L. Sullivan, a successful Hollywood director, having acquired his fame making escapist comedies, takes on the challenge of a social protest film in the tradition of a series of 1930s Popular Front productions.[86] He wants to make "O Brother, Where Art Thou?" and paint a "true canvas of suffering humanity." His next film is to be a document, combining the artistic potential of cinema with its sociological promise. Confronted with the suspicion that he does not know a lot about human suffering, Sullivan goes on the road to familiarize himself with misery. The problem is that the road itself is a cinematic convention. Only the movies can tell us what people want. Sullivan is stuck in Hollywood, and his adventures take the form of short episodes in different cinematic genres (slapstick, screwball comedy, documentary, melodrama). But only up to a point. In his fourth escapade, Sullivan is robbed and eventually finds himself on a southern chain gang. There are no more movies here. Sullivan seems to have encountered "the real world."

In the culminating scene of the film, the prison inmates are taken to a nearby African-American church, where a movie is screened. The pastor announces that the congregation will "share our pleasure with some neighbors less fortunate than ourselves," reminding his parishioners that "we is all equal in the sight of God." On the screen: "Playful Pluto" (Sturges wanted to use a Chaplin clip but did not get permission rights). No sooner does Pluto begin his tricks than both inmates and churchgoers start laughing. And laughing and laughing. Cut to individual faces laughing. Cut to a global image of a group of people laughing. The pleasure to be shared in the church is that of laughter. Sullivan is puzzled. What is going on? He looks around in disbelief. Just when he least expects it, he finds what he has been looking for. Sullivan has unmediated access to "the people." Cautious at first, he gradually joins in. Wave after wave of laughter. Sullivan laughs and laughs while also observing the laughing people. He is, after all, on an anthropological mission, and has unexpectedly discovered his method: he is a participant observer.

Now Sullivan has an answer to his dilemma. The people do not want social protest movies, calls to action. All they want is a little bit of laughter. Back in Hollywood, Sullivan will continue to make comedies: "There is a lot to be said for making people laugh. That's all that some people have." A montage of laughing faces follows. They will get their relief, perhaps, as Sullivan's producers insist, "with a little bit of sex in it." *Sullivan's Travels* tells its own audience what it wants. And what it wants is *Sullivan's Travels*. Horkheimer and Adorno's addendum to Kant: God gave us hope, sleep, laughter—and cinema. That "little bit of laughter" is the new opium of the people, served to them in the new church that the movie theater is. Like the prison inmates in *Sullivan's Travels*, we laugh and forget our chains. Film becomes a drug: in the stupor of intoxication, we watch, waiting for the pleasures of the laughing gas party. After all, what the architecture of the movie theater resembles best is a waiting room.

It is in this sense that laughter is, in Horkheimer and Adorno's words, a "medicinal bath." It is good for us, for our health. We used to go the *Stahlbad*; now we soak ourselves in laughter. We take a serving of laughter and go back to work. No wonder that today it is not only the culture industry that prescribes laughter. We are told to laugh from all directions. There is an industry of laughter. Corporations organize laughing events on the threshold that marks the nondistinction between "working hours" and the rapidly disappearing "leisure time." There are laughter clubs, where one goes to "exercise" for one hour at a time.[87] There are laughter therapists, who preach the benefits of laughter as "stress-reducing."[88] There are medical practices which recommend at least one session of laughter a week. It is Horkheimer and Adorno's worst nightmare: the world is a nightmarish Emerald City, laughing the day—and Horkheimer and Adorno's hopes for our happiness—away.

AM I LAUGHING? While Horkheimer and Adorno's diagnosis of the culture industry is invaluable, Adorno is also one of the most competitive candidates for entry in any gallery of seriousness.[89] In "The Culture Industry," he and Horkheimer conclude: "To moments of happiness laughter is foreign; only operettas, and now films, present sex amid peals of merriment. But Baudelaire is as humorless as Hölderlin. In wrong [falsche] society laughter is a sickness infecting happiness and drawing it into society's worthless totality."[90] Horkheimer and Adorno end up pathologizing laughter once again. They recommend sobriety. ("Joy, however, is austere [Lust jedoch ist streng].")[91] If sex is to bring a moment of happiness, it cannot be imagined among peals of laughter. Happiness itself is a serious affair. Most importantly, art, Horkheimer and Adorno's last bastion of hope when faced with society's totality, is incompatible with laughter. Art is "serious art." Kant thought so too. A certain "dignity" is needed to produce art.[92] One can hear Bataille laughing in response. Baudelaire himself could not resist when faced with the epithet "humorless."

And yet Adorno could not help but admire Chaplin. He met what he calls "the empirical Chaplin" in person. The anecdote he recalls is a challenge to reread Sullivan's Travels and, alongside this reading, to reconsider Horkheimer and Adorno's account of laughter in "The Culture Industry." Adorno and Chaplin are guests at a dinner party in Malibu. Chaplin sits next to Adorno. The very thought is enough to start us laughing. Adorno is introduced to the actor Harold Russell, who lost both arms in World War II and is wearing prostheses. Adorno absentmindedly shakes his "hand" and is startled by the touch: "In a split second I transformed my frightened expression into an obliging grimace that must have been far ghastlier."[93] Next to him, Chaplin is already "playing the scene back." Chaplin is doing Adorno, returning Adorno to Adorno. What does Adorno see when he sees himself in Chaplin's playback, in his "grimace"? The only thing we know is that Adorno thought this story worth recounting.

Chaplin is doing what he does best. He is mimicking Adorno. And Chaplin's mimicry, André Bazin argues, is an allegory of cinema's own mimeticism.[94] What Adorno has in front of him is both the "empirical Chaplin" and the "allegorical Chaplin." Chaplin might have shown Adorno what cinema can be. Did Adorno laugh? If he did, it is a lost laugh for our archive of laughter. But the anecdote (one of Adorno's "vital anecdotes"?) is an impetus to reconsider

Adorno's take on laughter. Notes on another form of laughter, qualitatively different than that of the culture industry, are scattered throughout his work. This is a laughter that can turn the laughter of the culture industry back on itself, and lead to what Adorno calls "a suspension of the law."[95] Laughter has the potential to suspend the culture industry's promise of reconciliation that it initially announces, leading to the possibility of a different kind of reconciliation.

Adorno has Beckett in mind when he elaborates on a "laughter about the absurdity of laughter."[96] For us, the question is, can *Sullivan's Travels* give us a glimpse at this second-order laughter? Let us go back to the scene in the church. On the screen, Pluto is forever caught in flypaper and is struggling to escape. Prison inmates and churchgoers are laughing. Sullivan looks around. Faces contorted by laughter. Row after row of people sitting in the dark laughing. The film briefly freezes the image of a pensive Sullivan when faced with the laughter around him. For a moment, his gaze defamiliarizes laughter. What are the people around him doing? Whatever answer he finds to this question, Sullivan starts laughing. But there is no reason to believe that he simply "joins in" the laughter. His laughter could be a response to the audience's laughter. Perhaps he finds their laughter laughable? Here are "the people," watching a movie to get some relief so that they can go on wearing their chains. Thank God for cinema! The film frames Sullivan's brief moment of suspicion as a close-up of a subtly pensive face about to burst into laughter. The image isolates Sullivan's incipient laugh. It singularizes this laugh, detaching it from the choir of laughs around it, as well as from Sullivan himself, from his face.[97]

"Am I laughing?" is the only line of this scene (it might just as well be a line in Beckett). The film confronts us, the viewers of *Sullivan's Travels*, with ourselves—laughing, chained to our chair or couch, looking for a little bit of relief, some stress reduction. Sullivan's laughter interrupts the circularity of the culture industry, putting pressure on its logic. It is a laughter at the deceiving absurdity of the laughter of "the people," caught in an ideological net that has made laughter complicit with one of its most efficient apparatuses. *Sullivan's Travels* might be a call after all. In Sullivan's brief moment of suspicion, the film self-cancels its message. What do the people want? Apparently, laughter. The laughter that comes as a response can carry many resonances.

EXPERIMENTS Drawing on the promise that laughter brings about a "suspension of the law," experimental film begins its own exploration of laughter. By way of conclusion, we will look here at one feminist experiment: Marleen Gorris's *A Question of Silence* (*De Stilte Rond Christine M.*).[98] The film dramatizes the apparently inexplicable murder of a boutique owner by three women customers. One of the women finds herself shoplifting. Two women in the store join her: they simply and methodically take things they want and put them in

FIGURE 5.17
Preston Sturges (dir.), *Sullivan's Travels*, 1941.

their bags. All, while being watched by four other women, who do not say a word. The Engels-inflected suggestion is that some men in their world—and the shopkeeper stands for all of them—are methodically stealing the product of their work, within legal standards. In what apparently is a paradoxical finale to the flow of events, the last scene of the film, a courtroom scene, offers a communal eruption of laughter, the feminist version of "the laughter of the people." The scene literalizes the suggestion that laughter always bursts at the heart of law.

Christine, the character easily identifiable as "the housewife," remains silent throughout the film. As the Dutch title has it, she dwells in silence. Throughout her life, she has been a taciturn wife, watching television and looking after her kids, following her husband's orders and listening to his complaints, all in silence. "She never talked much. She was the quiet type." Now Christine claims silence as a right; she is weary of language, she wants to be left alone. The boutique scene is quiet too; three women who have never met before kill a man without exchanging a word. The fact that Christine chooses not to talk at all once she is arrested simply draws attention to the silence in which she has been living all along. "Why would she talk? Nobody is listening." But the medical/legal system does not like this silence, which amounts to a bigger crime than the crime itself. There is a need for a caption to Christine's silence: it must be the effect of some sort of womanly illness. A specialist is asked to find a diagnosis for her and her accomplices. "They are completely crazy," the female psychiatrist is informed from the outset, before she even sees her patients. "You can spot women like them miles away."

It is from within this silence that Christine's laughter bursts in the court-room scene. The other two women already seem to know about laughter. They laugh upon being introduced once they are arrested. They laugh throughout their encounters with the psychiatrist. The latter is puzzled. She asks Ann, "the waitress," why she did not remarry. The answer: laughter, laughter, laughter. Why is she laughing? The question seems legitimate. (The alternative to marriage is another marriage.) She asks Andrea, "the secretary," why she does not want to cooperate with her. She might be able to help her in court. Laughter—loud, insolent, suspicious. The psychiatrist replays the tape with these laughs over and over again. ("Don't be afraid of the tape recorder, it's just to help me remember important details.")

Christine finally and publicly breaks her silence in the courtroom. "Don't you see," the psychiatrist argues, "they killed a MAN." The judge cannot hear the emphasis. It does not matter, the case would have been the same if they had killed a woman, comes the judge's answer. Laughter bubbles up in Christine—timidly at first, a whisper of a laugh, as if she is trying it out. Ann, "the waitress," follows suit. One of the four anonymous women who witnessed the crime and, through their silence, participated in it, joins in. Finally, Janine,

FIGURE 5.18
Marleen Gorris (dir.), *A Question of Silence*, 1982. Photofest.

the psychiatrist. The latter gives up her project of "bringing them to reason" and her complicity with the law. She is one of them; had she been there, she too would have killed the shopkeeper. So she laughs.

Soon all the protagonists, spectators to the spectacle of law, are roaring with laughter. Stupor, embarrassment, confusion, disorder in the courtroom. Slowly, laughter dislocates itself from its object, the gender-blind court of law, and, by extension, the law itself. It is a laughter that has its own *raison d'être*, apart from any specific laughable object. And laughter reproduces itself, laughter asks for more laughter. It not only interrupts, but it repeats itself and spreads. In terms of the film's diegesis, the trial will continue in the absence of the three women, who will most probably spend the rest of their lives in prison. But, in the spirit of a revolutionary twentieth century, the burst of laughter at the end of the film suspends the question of what happens next. There is no future, only a now, in which we are all laughing, rendering the law inoperative. Am I laughing?

As Walter Benjamin put it, laughter can be "both the most international and the most revolutionary affect of the masses."[99] This statement, however, needs to be understood from within Benjamin's dialog with Adorno: laughter is potentially revolutionary the moment we know it intervenes within an already laughing Emerald City. Laughter is a second-order burst, suspending a law that is in fact already suspended. What the women at the end of *A Ques-*

tion of *Silence* will do, we do not know. We know only that they laughed, and in the interval that opens the film to their laughter, one hears echoes of what we used to call—not so long ago, still without embarrassment—*hope*. It is never recommended that one start "the people" laughing. Tamed sheep can always become a crowd. Amusement can turn into festival. "The people" are laughing a laughter that is both a medicinal bath they occasionally soak themselves in to help them forget, and the echo of revolutionary noise.

Notes

Introduction

1. Khlebnikov wrote the poem in 1909 and published it in 1910 in Nikolai Kulbin's anthology *The Studio of Impressionists* (St. Petersburg: Butkovskaya, 1910). This translation appears under the title "Invocation of Laughter" in *From Ends to the Beginning: A Bilingual Anthology of Russian Verse*, ed. Ilya Kutik and Andrew Wachtel, Northwestern University (www.russianpoetry.net). Paul Schmidt offers a dramatically different translation:

Hlahla! Ufhlofan, lauflings!
Who lawghen with lafe, who hlaehen lewchly,
Hlahla! Ufhlofan hlouly!
Hlahla! Hloufish lauflings lafe uf beloght lauchalorum!
Hlahla! Loufenish lauflings lafe, hlohan utlaufly!
Lawfen, lawfen,
Hloh, hlouh, hlou! Luifekin, luifekin,
Hlofeningum, hlofeningum,
Hlahla! Uthlofan, lauflings!
Hlahla! Ufhlofan, lauflings!

See Velimir Khlebnikov, *The King of Time*, trans. Paul Schmidt (Cambridge, Mass.: Harvard University Press, 1985).

2. *Zaum* is the "transrational" language Russian futurists opposed to symbolic language. The term was coined by Khlebnikov's futurist friend Alexei Kruchenykh, who used it to talk about linguistic phenomena that included onomatopoeia, children's talk, the language of schizophrenics and mystics, glossolalia, and a range of neologisms. For Khlebnikov, *zaum* was a future language, an alphabet of fantasy one was in touch with intuitively through sound. On *zaum*, see Kruchenykh and Khlebnikov's manifesto "The Word as Such," in *Russian Futurism through Its Manifestos, 1912–1928*, ed. Anna Lawton, trans. Anna Lawton and Herbert Eagle (Ithaca: Cornell University Press, 1988), 55–62. See also Mel Gordon, "Songs from the Museum of the Future: Russian Sound Creation (1910–1930)," in

The Wireless Imagination: Sound, Radio, and the Avant-Garde, ed. Douglas Kahn and Gregory Whitehead (Cambridge, Mass.: MIT Press, 1992); and Marjorie Perloff, *The Futurist Moment: Avant-Garde, Avant-Guerre, and the Language of Rupture* (Chicago: University of Chicago Press, 1986), 33.

3. On laughter and the sacred, see Vladimir Propp, "Ritual Laughter in Folklore: A Propos of the Tale of the Princess Who Would Not Laugh [Nesmejána]," in *Theory and History of Folklore,* trans. Ariadna Y. Martin and Richard P. Martin (Minneapolis: University of Minnesota Press, 1984).

4. Alain Badiou, *The Century,* trans. Alberto Toscano (Cambridge: Polity Press, 2007), 131.

5. For a review of various theories of humor and the comic, usually grouped under three rubrics (the superiority theory, the incongruity theory, the relief theory), see John Morreall, *Taking Laughter Seriously* (Albany: SUNY Press, 1983). The notable exception here is Diane Davis's *Breaking [Up] at Totality: A Rhetoric of Laughter* (Carbondale and Edwardsville: Southern Illinois University Press, 2000).

6. Aristotle, *Rhetoric,* II, 12.

7. Aristotle, *Parts of Animals,* III, 10.

8. Aristotle made man a "laughing animal" strictly by way of emphasizing that animals do not laugh. In modern times, Charles Darwin would insist that some animals, monkeys especially, laugh. See Aristotle, *Parts of Animals,* III, 10; Charles Darwin, *The Expression of the Emotions in Man and Animals* (London: John Murray, 1872), 133.

9. Aristotle believed that children do not laugh a real laugh before their fortieth day (*History of Animals,* 587). Darwin studied his own infant children and decided that they showed signs of smiling around the forty-fifth day of life, while signs of incipient laughter could be observed from day one hundred and thirteen. *The Expression of the Emotions,* 211–212.

10. There is a long theological debate as to whether Christ was a "laughing animal." Baudelaire offered his take on the issue in his essay "On the Essence of Laughter." See Charles Baudelaire, "On the Essence of Laughter," in *The Painter of Modern Life and Other Essays,* trans. Jonathan Mayne (London: Phaidon Press, 1964).

11. Henri Bergson, *Laughter* (Baltimore: Johns Hopkins University Press, 1956), 62.

12. Ibid., 64.

13. Before Bataille, Baudelaire marked a turning point in the tradition of writing on laughter with a decisive statement: "The comic and the capacity for laughter are situated in the laugher and by no means in the object of his mirth." Baudelaire, "On the Essence of Laughter," 154.

14. The term "agelast" was widely used in the early modern period, among others, by Rabelais. See Mikhail Bakhtin, *Rabelais and His World,* trans. Hélène Iswolsky (Bloomington: Indiana University Press, 1984), 267.

15. Georges Bataille, *Visions of Excess: Selected Writings 1927–1939*, trans. Allan Stoekl (Minneapolis: University of Minnesota Press, 1985), 60.

16. This is not a condemnation of all seriousness. Bataille, following Nietzsche, distinguishes between an "earthly seriousness," associated with morality, and the "great seriousness" that often appears "inhuman," associated with "the first, real question mark." Glossing Bakhtin, Julia Kristeva distinguishes between a heavy seriousness, associated with dogmatism, and a light seriousness, which she associates with laughter itself. See Georges Bataille, *Inner Experience*, trans. Leslie A. Boldt (Albany: SUNY Press, 1988), xxxi; Julia Kristeva, "Word, Dialogue and Novel," in *The Kristeva Reader*, ed. Toril Moi (New York: Columbia University Press, 1986), 50.

17. Aristotle's *Rhetoric* emphasized that once one understands the laughter-inducing mechanism, once we know *what* makes us laugh, this knowledge becomes an invaluable weapon in public debate. The orator can learn how to draw a laugh. The laughter of the lowly art of comedy thus acquires an important practical dimension for the art of persuasion. In Aristotle's words, one can "confound the opponents' earnest with jest and their jest with earnest" (*Rhetoric*, III, 18). On the rhetorical uses of laughter in modernity, see Quentin Skinner, "Hobbes and the Classical Theory of Laughter," in *Visions of Politics*, vol. 3 (Cambridge: Cambridge University Press, 2002). See also Antoine de Baecque, *Les éclats du rire: La culture des rieurs au XVIIIe siècle* (Paris: Calmann-Lévy, 2000); Vic Gatrell, *City of Laughter* (London: Atlantic Books, 2006).

18. See Philip Fisher, *The Vehement Passions* (Princeton: Princeton University Press, 2003).

19. Friedrich Nietzsche, *Beyond Good and Evil*, trans. R. J. Hollingdale (Harmondsworth: Penguin, 1990), 218.

20. Norbert Elias, "Essay on Laughter" (unpublished manuscript); unless otherwise noted, all Elias quotes are from this manuscript. See also Michael Schröter, "Wer lacht, kann nicht beissen: Ein unveröffentlichter 'Essay on Laughter' by Norbert Elias," *Merkur* 56 (2002), 860–873.

21. This is an Aristotelian premise: "in man, the portion of the body between the head and the neck is called *Prosōpon* (Face), a name derived, no doubt, from the function it performs. Man, the only animal that stands upright, is the only one that looks straight before him or sends forth his voice straight before him." Aristotle, *Parts of Animals*, III, 1.

22. Gilles Deleuze and Félix Guattari, *A Thousand Plateaus: Capitalism and Schizophrenia*, trans. Brian Massumi (Minneapolis: University of Minnesota Press, 1997), 168.

23. See Georg Simmel, "The Aesthetic Significance of the Face," in *Essays on Sociology, Philosophy and Aesthetics*, trans. Lore Ferguson, ed. Kurt H. Wolff (New York: Harper and Row, 1965); Erving Goffman, "Face-Work," in *The Presentation of Self in Everyday Life* (Garden City, N.Y.: Doubleday, 1959).

24. In the Sixth Meditation, Descartes described the relation between the soul and the body, the *unum quid*, as "quasi-permixed." See Jean-Luc Nancy, *Corpus*, trans. Richard A. Rand (New York: Fordham University Press, 2008).

25. Aristotle, *Parts of Animals*, III, 10.

26. On the mouthlike subject, see Jacques Derrida, *On Touching: Jean-Luc Nancy*, trans. Christine Irizarry (Stanford: Stanford University Press, 2005), 114.

27. The distinction is drawn by Jean-Luc Nancy, *Ego sum* (Paris: Aubier-Flammarion, 1979), 161–162. See also Peggy Kamuf, "Béance," *CR: The New Centennial Review* 2, no. 3 (2002), 37–56; Sara Guyer, "Buccal Reading," *CR: The New Centennial Review* 7, no. 2 (2007), 71–87.

28. Derrida, *On Touching*, 114.

29. This is an argument against Aristotle, who wrote: "the eyelashes are like the palisades which are sometimes put up in front of an enclosure; their purpose is to keep out things that try to get in." Aristotle, *Parts of Animals*, II, 15.

30. Jean-Luc Nancy, "Laughter Presence," in *The Birth to Presence*, trans. Brian Holmes (Stanford: Stanford University Press, 1993), 389–390.

31. On the acousmatic voice, see Michel Chion, *The Voice in Cinema*, trans. Claudia Gorbman (New York: Columbia University Press, 1999), 18.

32. Mladen Dolar, *A Voice and Nothing More* (Cambridge, Mass.: MIT Press, 2006), 70.

33. Jacques Derrida, *Glas*, trans. John P. Leavey and Richard Rand (Lincoln: University of Nebraska Press, 1986), 89–97.

34. Ibid., 93.

35. Alain Badiou, "The Adventure of French Philosophy," *New Left Review* 35 (2005), 67–77. On Badiou's account, the common question was that of the metaphysical subject; the set of common readings was from German philosophy (Hegel, Nietzsche, Husserl, and Heidegger); the writing was a function of a search for a "style" that could put thought in motion; the political moment was that of postwar Europe, which imposed the need for a new relation between philosophy and political intervention.

36. The "writer-combatant" is a figure Badiou invokes to describe a number of poststructuralist philosophers. Badiou, "The Adventure of French Philosophy," 76.

37. Walter Benjamin, "The Author as Producer," in *Understanding Brecht*, trans. Anna Bostock (London: New Left Books, 1973), 101.

38. Ibid., 100. On the exposure of the present, see also Samuel Weber, "Citability—of Gesture," in *Benjamin's -abilities* (Cambridge, Mass.: Harvard University Press, 2008), 105. Weber does not discuss Benjamin's invocation of laughter in this context, but what is at stake for him too is precisely the interrupting function of a "gesture" like laughter and its wonder effects. Weber wrote on the subject in "Laughing in the Meanwhile," *MLN* 102, 1987: 691–706.

39. Benjamin, "The Author as Producer," 101.

40. Ibid.

41. Ibid., 100.

42. Michel Foucault, *The Order of Things: An Archeology of the Human Sciences*, trans. Alan Sheridan (London: Tavistock Publications, 1970), xv.

43. Ibid., xvii.

44. Michel de Certeau, "The Laugh of Michel Foucault," in *Heterologies: Discourse on the Other* (Minneapolis: University of Minnesota Press, 1986), 194.

45. On conceptual neighborhoods, see Gilles Deleuze and Félix Guattari, *What Is Philosophy?*, trans. Hugh Tomlinson and Graham Burchell (New York: Columbia University Press, 1994), 19.

46. The literature on *kairos* is extensive. Walter Benjamin's "Theses on the Philosophy of History" remains the main reference here. For recent contributions, see especially Antonio Negri, "Kairòs, Alma Venus, Multitudo," in *Time for Revolution* (New York: Continuum, 2003); and Giorgio Agamben, *The Time That Remains: A Commentary on the Letter to the Romans*, trans. Patricia Dailey (Stanford: Stanford University Press, 2005). See also Cesare Casarino, "Time Matters: Marx, Negri, Agamben and the Corporeal," *Strategies* 16, no. 2 (2003), 185–206.

47. On *kairos* as the time of laughter, see Davis, *Breaking Up [at] Totality*, 26–27.

48. One of the most suggestive invocations of *kairos* occurs in The Milan Women's Bookstore Collective book *Sexual Difference*, whose last paragraph reads: "There are things which do not come by historical necessity, but because they have been favored. Among these is female freedom. There is an ancient Greek word, *kairos*, which serves to name this favor, this form of necessity which shows itself and can be read, but not actually demonstrated. It means that many disparate things combine together and realize the goal, earlier and better than could those working toward that goal. It is neither pure chance nor iron necessity, but a mixture of both, and better still, something you can enter into, on your part, and the whole will answer you." The Milan Women's Bookstore Collective, *Sexual Difference: A Theory of Social-Symbolic Practice*, trans. Patricia Cigogna and Teresa de Lauretis (Bloomington: Indiana University Press, 1990), 150.

49. Milan Kundera, *The Book of Laughter and Forgetting*, trans. Michael Heim (New York: Penguin, 1986), 224–225.

50. Émile Benveniste, *Problems in General Linguistics*, trans. Mary Elizabeth Meek (Coral Gables: University of Miami Press, 1971), 145.

51. Ibid., 147.

52. Ibid., 149.

53. Echoes of Virgil are present in Kristeva's formulations: *incipe, parve puer, risu cognoscere matrem*—"begin, young child, to recognize your mother by your laughter."

Bataille also quotes the line and is fascinated by the productive ambiguity of the translation, which can read both "Begin, young child, to recognize your mother by your laughter" and/or "by her laughter." See Georges Bataille, "Laughter," in *The Bataille Reader*, ed. Fred Botting and Scott Wilson (Oxford: Blackwell, 1997), 63.

54. Julia Kristeva, "Place Names," in *Desire in Language: A Semiotic Approach to Literature and Art*, trans. Thomas Gora, Alice Jardine, and Leon S. Roudiez (New York: Columbia University Press, 1980), 282. Kristeva's critics have emphasized that she is too quick to identify this space as "prior to the sign." The voice, before it says anything discernable, is already captured in discourse. Even if what the child says is unintelligible, it is *interpreted* as a form of address and appeal, a demand. See Dolar, *A Voice and Nothing More*, 70.

55. Jacques Derrida, "Khōra," in *On the Name*, ed. Thomas Dutoit (Stanford: Stanford University Press, 1993), 111.

56. Ibid., 104.

57. Ibid., 103.

58. Derrida would return to khōra, revisiting the figure/nonfigure of the gaping mouth: "Why? If it is the mother, in any case, who opens the bordering edges as well as the lips of a mouth first described as an opening [*ouverture*], then this happens before any figure—not before any identification, but before any 'identification' with a face [*identification à une figure*]. . . . The mouth is *at the same time* place and nonplace, it is the locus of a dislocation, the gaping place [*le lieu béant*] of the 'quasi-permixtio' between soul and the body, which is to say the incommensurable extension between them and common to both, since the mouth—any mouth, before any orality—opens an opening." Glossing what Nancy had referred to as "a gaping nonplace [*la béance d'un non-lieu*]" without any reference to the mother, Derrida now insists that the mother is present on this scene; the mother *is* this "gaping nonplace." If this space is choral, Derrida proposes, it is not "prior to the sign," but rather "prior to the face." There are already signs here, but they are not "oral." They are, one could say, "buccal," defaced and disfigured. Derrida, *On Touching*, 28–29.

59. Julia Kristeva, *Revolution in Poetic Language*, trans. Margaret Waller (New York: Columbia University Press, 1984), 225.

60. Propp unearths a series of texts describing God or gods creating the world laughing. See Propp, "Ritual Laughter in Folklore," 133–134. Umberto Eco's *The Name of the Rose* cites one such account of the creation of the world: "The moment God laughed seven gods were born who governed the world, the moment he burst out laughing light appeared, at his second laugh appeared water, and on the seventh day of his laughing appeared the soul." Umberto Eco, *The Name of the Rose*, trans. William Weaver (New York: Harvest Books, 1995), 467.

61. Kristeva, *Revolution in Poetic Language*, 223.

62. Louis Althusser, "Lenin and Philosophy," in *Lenin and Philosophy and Other Essays* (New York: Monthly Review Press, 2001).

63. Jacques Derrida, "From Restricted to General Economy: A Hegelianism without Reserve," in *Writing and Difference*, trans. Alan Bass (Chicago: University of Chicago Press, 1978).

64. Jean-François Lyotard, *Libidinal Economy*, trans. Iain Hamilton (Bloomington: Indiana University Press, 1993), 95.

65. Gilles Deleuze and Félix Guattari, *Kafka: Toward a Minor Literature*, trans. Dana Polan (Minneapolis: University of Minnesota Press, 1986). Deleuze speaks of the "coincidence" between poetic and historical events in these terms: "But when the people struggle for their liberation, there is always a coincidence of poetic acts and historical events or political actions, the glorious incarnations of something sublime or untimely. Such great coincidences are Nasser's burst of laughter when he nationalized Suez, or Castro's gestures, and the other burst of laughter, Giap's television interview." Gilles Deleuze, *Desert Island and Other Texts (1953–1974)* (Los Angeles: Semiotext(e), 2004), 130.

66. Jean-Luc Nancy, *The Inoperative Community*, trans. Peter Connor, Lisa Garbus, Michael Holland, and Simona Sawhney (Minneapolis: University of Minnesota Press, 1991); Maurice Blanchot, *The Unavowable Community*, trans. Pierre Joris (Barrytown, N.Y.: Station Hill Press, 1988).

67. Nancy, "Laughter Presence."

68. Jacques Lacan, "L'étourdit," *Scilicet* 4 (1973), 5–52.

69. Hélène Cixous, "Castration or Decapitation?," trans. Annette Kuhn, *Signs* 7, no. 1 (Autumn 1981), 41–55; "The Laugh of the Medusa," trans. Keith Cohen and Paula Cohen, *Signs* 1, no. 4 (Summer 1976), 875–893.

70. All quotes from the Bible are from Jewish Publication Society, *The Jewish Study Bible*, Tanakh translation, ed. Adele Berlin and Marc Zvi Brettler (Oxford: Oxford University Press, 2004).

71. On Sarah's laugh, see Malynne Sternstein, "Laughter, Gesture, and Flesh: Kafka's 'In the Penal Colony,'" *Modernism/Modernity* 8, no. 2 (April 2001), 315–323.

72. On Sarah's incredulity, see M. A. Screech, *Laughter at the Foot of the Cross* (London: Penguin, 1997), xxi.

73. When pushed to talk about the long-postponed question of his Jewishness, Derrida could not but acknowledge that the problematic of the Jew is caught in a discursive network that includes his other preoccupations, including that with khōra: "nothing seems more foreign to the God of the Jews and to the history of the law than everything I interpret, even unto its political future to come, under the Greek name of *khora*, the place, the a-human and a-theological location that opens the place well beyond any negative theology. And yet this manner of interpreting the place can still keep a deep affinity with a certain nomination of the

God of the Jews. He is also The Place." Jacques Derrida, "Abraham the Other," in *Judeities: Questions for Jacques Derrida* (New York: Fordham University Press, 2007), 33.

74. For one response to the image of the feminist as humorless, see Meaghan Morris, "in any event . . .," in *Men in Feminism*, ed. Alice Jardine and Paul Smith (New York: Methuen, 1987), 173–181.

75. Besides what Althusser imagined as the Marxist practice of Lenin's laughter, the counterpoint here is Sergei Eisenstein's "Bolsheviks Do Laugh (Thoughts on Soviet Comedy)," in *S. M. Eisenstein: Selected Writings*, vol. 3, ed. Richard Taylor (London: BFI, 1988), 68–72.

76. Diane Davis's *Breaking Up [at] Totality* was the first to trace the contours of the feminist investment in laughter.

77. Rosi Braidotti, *Embodiment and Sexual Difference in Contemporary Feminist Theory* (New York: Columbia University Press, 1994), 167.

78. Breton famously announced that *Nadja* would indulge in no descriptions. See André Breton, *Nadja*, trans. Richard Howard (New York: Grove Press, 1994).

79. Michel Beaujour, "Some Paradoxes of Description," *Yale French Studies*, no. 61, "Toward a Theory of Description" (1981), 27–59.

80. Nancy, "Laughter Presence," 368.

81. On presence, see Dieter Mensh, "Präsenz und Ethizität der Stimme" [Presence and Ethicity of the Voice], in *Stimme: Interdisziplinäre Annäherungen an ein Phänomen*, ed. Doris Kolesch and Sybille Krämer (Frankfurt am Main: Suhrkamp, 2006), 211–236.

82. Adorno describes his *Notes to Literature* as the site where "the constellation of words and music is preserved, as is the slightly old-fashioned quality of a form whose heyday was the *Jugendstil*." Theodor W. Adorno, *Notes to Literature*, trans. Shierry Weber Nicholsen (New York: Columbia University Press, 1992), 6.

83. On the pedagogical valences of "notes," see Roland Barthes's lecture notes for his courses at the Collège de France, especially *The Neutral*, trans. Rosalind E. Krauss and Denis Hollier (New York: Columbia University Press, 2005). I elaborate on Barthes in "The Professor's Desire: On Roland Barthes's 'The Neutral,'" *Diacritics* 37 (2007), 32–39.

84. Clifford Geertz, *The Interpretation of Cultures* (New York: Basic Books, 1977), 10.

85. Luigi Russolo, "The Art of Noises," in *Modernism and Music: An Anthology of Sources*, ed. Daniel Albright (Chicago: University of Chicago Press, 2004), 180.

86. The whole sentence reads: "We only want Tragedy if it can clench its side-muscles like hands on its belly, and bring to the surface a laugh like a bomb." *Blast* 1, ed. Wyndham Lewis (Santa Barbara: Black Sparrow Press, 1981), 31.

87. T. S. Eliot, "Hysteria," in *The Catholic Anthology, 1914–1915* (London: E. Mathews, 1915), 16.

88. On the anecdote, see Jane Gallop, *Anecdotal Theory* (Durham: Duke University Press, 2002). In *What Is Philosophy?* Deleuze and Guattari suggest that "a few vital anecdotes are sufficient to produce a portrait of philosophy" (72). As one such vital anecdote, Deleuze recounts the story about Spinoza, "the Christ of philosophers," bursting out laughing while watching a battle of spiders he orchestrated. According to Deleuze, the anecdote rehearses in an abbreviated, condensed form the system of the *Ethics*.

CHAPTER 1

1. Samuel Beckett, *En attendant Godot / Waiting for Godot* (New York: Grove Press, 2006), 18–19.

2. In Beckett's *Endgame*, Hamm and Clov also entice each other to laugh and decide not to. ("Hamm: Don't we laugh? Clov *(after reflection)*: I don't feel like it. Hamm *(after reflection)*: Nor I.") In all three cases, the decision is taken after a pause, which the stage directions translate as "*After reflection.*" Samuel Beckett, *Endgame and Act without Words* (New York: Grove Press, 1994), 11, 29, 30.

3. Beckett, *En attendant Godot / Waiting for Godot*, 52–55.

4. Norbert Elias, "Essay on Laughter" (unpublished manuscript); *The Civilizing Process*, trans. Edmund Jephcott (Oxford: Blackwell, 1994). See John F. Kasson, *Rudeness and Civility: Manners in Nineteenth-Century Urban America* (New York: Hill and Wang, 1990), 11–12, for an inventory of possible lines of criticism of Elias's *Civilizing Process*.

5. Elias, "Essay on Laughter."

6. Desiderius Erasmus, *Collected Works of Erasmus*, vol. 25, ed. J. K. Sowards (Toronto: University of Toronto Press, 1985).

7. Antoine de Courtin, whose courtesy book, *The Rules of Civility*, was frequently republished in the seventeenth century, wrote of a *science* of manners. Orest Ranum argues that "Learning this science was the central feature of a humanist education in the entire early modern period." As part of this humanist education, one was repeatedly told that, in Courtin's words, "to be laughing and playing the fool, is [as] bad" (39–40). See Antoine de Courtin, *The Rules of Civility* (London, 1671); Orest Ranum, "Courtesy, Absolutism, and the Rise of the French State, 1630–1660," *Journal of Modern History* 52, no. 3 (1980), 429.

8. Anna Bryson discusses school regulations around 1600 that "enjoin early rising, correct salutations, and due silence, and prohibit loitering, laughter and insolence toward the master." See Anna Bryson, *From Courtesy to Civility: Changing Codes of Conduct in Early Modern England* (New York: Clarendon Press, 1998), 30.

9. Erasmus, *Collected Works of Erasmus*, vol. 25, 275.

10. Ibid., 275–276.

11. There are earlier variations on this theme. See Thérèse Bouché and Hélène Charpentier, *Le rire au Moyen Âge dans la littérature et dans les arts: Actes du colloque international*

des 17, 18 et 19 novembre 1988 (Talence: Presses Universitaires de Bordeaux, 1990); Marjorie O'Rourke Boyle, "Gracious Laughter: Marsilio Ficino's Anthropology," *Renaissance Quarterly* 52, no. 3 (Autumn 1999), 712–741. Closer to Erasmus, Baldassare Castiglione's *Book of the Courtier* (1528) also warned against the temptation of laughter, suggesting that it is not recommended "for a Gentleman to cry and laugh, make noises, and wrestle with himself . . . or putting the Face and Body in strange contortions." Baldassare Castiglione, *Book of the Courtier* (London: Printed for A. Bettesworth, E. Curll, J. Battley, J. Clarke, and T. Payne, 1724), II, 78.

12. See Barbara Correll, *The End of Conduct: Grobianus and the Renaissance Text of the Subject* (Ithaca: Cornell University Press, 1996), 54.

13. Fredericus Dedekindus, *The Schoole of Slovenrie: Or, Cato Turnd Wrong Side Outward* [*Grobianus et Grobiana*], trans. R. F. Gent (London, 1605). The section reads:

> The world affords no better thing, than merry life this day.
> Wherefore be sure that thou of laughter does at all times think,
> Whatever you do, whether you work, play, sit, stand, eat, or drink.
> You so should sometimes laugh, that meat, which in your mouth does lie,
> Might suddenly from out the same into the platter fly. (66)

14. See Daniel Ménager, *La Renaissance et le rire* (Paris: Presses Universitaires de France, 1995), 123–125.

15. For nuances of the Gospels' description of the mocking of Christ, see M. A. Screech, *Laughter at the Foot of the Cross* (London: Penguin, 1997). Screech writes: "After Christians had meditated upon the Crucifixion, never again could laughter be thoughtlessly seen by them—if ever it had been—as a sign of simple joy and buoyant happiness. Laughter is one of the ways in which crowds, thoughtless, cruel or wicked, may react to the sight of suffering" (17). Only one account of this scene potentially makes reference to the actual sound of laughter, Mark's ejaculation "Va!" which Screech translates as "O!" or "Ha!" or "Aha!" In other words, it is unclear if the "mocking" of Christ was accompanied by sonorous laughter. But the tradition did not make the distinction: to mock was to laugh.

16. William Perkins, *A Direction for the Government of the Tongue According to Gods Word* (Printed by Iohn Legatt, 1632), 73–74. On Christian laughter, see also Erica Fudge, "Learning to Laugh," *Textual Practice* 17, no. 2 (2003), 277–294.

17. John Calvin, *Sermon on I Samuel XXX*, in *Corpus Reformatorum*, vol. 58 (*Calvini Opera*, vol. 30), col. 699. See Screech, *Laughter at the Foot of the Cross*, for a discussion of this paradoxical form of Christian laughter.

18. Michel Foucault cautions against a reading of Erasmus's *Praise of Folly* as laughter-friendly. Through the literary device of a personified Folly, Foucault argues, Erasmus distances himself from it and "observes it from the heights of his Olympus, and if he sings its praises, it is because he can laugh at it with the inextinguishable laughter of the Gods." Michel Foucault, *Madness and Civilization: A History of Insanity in the Age of Reason* (New York: Vintage, 1988), 28.

19. Erasmus, *Collected Works of Erasmus*, vol. 27, ed. A. H. T. Levi (1986), 111.

20. Laurent Joubert, *Treatise on Laughter* (Tuscaloosa: University of Alabama Press, 1980), 16. French edition used is Laurent Joubert, *Traité du ris* (Geneva: Slatkine Reprints, 1973).

21. Joubert, *Treatise on Laughter*, 11.

22. Ibid., 72–73.

23. Ibid., 85.

24. Ibid., 28.

25. Ibid., 87.

26. Ibid., 30.

27. Ibid., 73.

28. See Peter Harrison, "Reading the Passions," in *The Soft Underbelly of Reason: The Passions in the Seventeenth Century* (New York: Routledge, 1998), 62–65.

29. Joubert, *Treatise on Laughter*, 33.

30. Ibid., 120.

31. Ibid., 122.

32. On the *savoir-rire*, see also Ménager, *La Renaissance et le rire*, 149–185.

33. Joubert, *Treatise on Laughter*, 88.

34. The impetus for this line of thought is the attribution of a set of apocryphal letters to Hippocrates. See Hippocrates, *Sur le rire et la folie* (Paris: Rivages, 1989).

35. Joubert, *Treatise on Laughter*, 104.

36. René Descartes, *The Passions of the Soul*, trans. Stephen Voss (Indianapolis: Hackett, 1989); parenthetical citations refer to articles in this edition. French edition used is René Descartes, *Les passions de l'âme* (Paris: Chez Iean Gvinard, 1650).

37. For such a revision, see Jean-Luc Nancy, "On the Soul," in *Corpus*, trans. Richard A. Rand (New York: Fordham University Press, 2008).

38. Jennifer Montagu, *The Expression of the Passions: The Origin and Influence of Charles Le Brun's Conférence sur l'expression générale et particulière* (New Haven: Yale University Press, 1994).

39. Le Brun wrote: "there are two movements of the eyebrows which express all the movements of these passions. . . . [T]hat which rises up towards the brain expresses all the gentlest and mildest passions, and that which slopes down towards the heart represents all the wildest and cruelest passions. . . . [I]f the passion is gentle, so is the movement, and, if it is violent, the movement is violent." Montagu, *The Expression of the Passions*, 128.

40. Ibid., 131.

41. Hobbes also discussed laughter in *The Elements of Law, De homine*, and "The Answer of Mr. Hobbes to Sir Will. D'Avenant's Preface before Gondibert." See Quentin Skinner, "Hobbes and the Classical Theory of Laughter," in *Visions of Politics*, vol. 3 (Cambridge: Cambridge University Press, 2002); Skinner, "Hobbes on Laughter," *Philosophical Quarterly* 51, no. 202 (2001), 29–40.

42. See Norberto Bobbio, *Thomas Hobbes and the Natural Law Tradition*, trans. Daniela Bobbio (Chicago: University of Chicago Press, 1993), 40.

43. Thomas Hobbes, *The English Works of Thomas Hobbes of Malmesbury*, ed. Sir William Molesworth (London: John Bohn, 1839), vol. IV, 45.

44. Ibid., vol. III, 19.

45. Ibid., vol. IV, 46. Many responded to what appeared to be Hobbes's reductive definition of laughter. See especially James Arbuckle, *A Collection of Letters and Essays on Several Subjects, Lately Published in the Dublin Journal*, vol. 1 (London, 1729), 77–107.

46. Hobbes, *The English Works of Thomas Hobbes*, vol. III, 46.

47. Marin Cureau de la Chambre's *The Characters of the Passions* included a chapter dedicated to "The Characters of Laughter," which offered an elaborate description of laughter explained as the effect of surprise. See Cureau de la Chambre, *The Characters of the Passions* (London: Printed by Tho. Newcomb for John Holden, 1650).

48. See Philip Fisher, *The Vehement Passions* (Princeton: Princeton University Press, 2003), 79.

49. Hobbes, *The English Works of Thomas Hobbes*, vol. III, 156.

50. Ibid., vol. III, 45.

51. Ibid., vol. IV, 52.

52. Ibid., vol. IV, 53.

53. Malebranche offered a variation on this theme: "Derision or Jeering is a sort of Joy commonly arising at the sight of the Evil that befalls those from whom we are separated." See Father Malebranche, *Treatise Concerning the Search after Truth*, trans. T. Taylor (Oxford: Printed by L. Lichfield, for Thomas Bennett, 1715), vol. II, chapter X, 31.

54. Charles Le Brun, *A Method to Learn to Design the Passions, Proposed in a Conference on Their General and Particular Expression*, trans. John Williams (London: Printed by J. Huggonson, 1734).

55. Leo Strauss writes: "If virtue is identified with peaceableness, vice will become identical with that habit or that passion which is per se incompatible with peace because it essentially is, as it were, of set purpose in offending others; vice becomes identical for all practical purposes with pride or vanity or *amour-propre* rather than with resoluteness or weakness of the soul." Leo Strauss, "On the Spirit

of Hobbes' Political Philosophy," in *Hobbes Studies*, ed. K. C. Brown (Cambridge, Mass.: Harvard University Press, 1965), 18.

56. Hobbes, *The English Works of Thomas Hobbes*, vol. III, 46.

57. Ibid., 47.

58. See Amelie Oksenberg Rorty, "From Passions to Emotions and Sentiments," *Philosophy* 57 (1982), 159–172. On vainglory, see also David Heyd, "The Place of Laughter in Hobbes's Theory of Emotions," *Journal of the History of Ideas* 43 (1982), 285–295.

59. Albert O. Hirshman traces the process through which, as one "remedy" for the passions, one passion is pitched against another in the name of "interest," which acquires political as well as economic overtones. Spinoza explained this mechanism: "An emotion can neither be restrained nor removed except by an emotion which is contrary to and stronger than the one which is to be restrained." Spinoza, *Ethics*, ed. and trans. G. H. R. Parkinson (Oxford: Oxford University Press, 2000), IV, 6–7; Albert O. Hirshman, *The Passions and the Interests* (Princeton: Princeton University Press, 1977).

60. Spinoza's voice is perhaps the most discordant in this choir. He defined his project against those who laugh at the defects of human nature, its passions. In Deleuze's reading, Spinoza reacts to a discourse on the passions within which "morality was founded as an enterprise of domination of the passions by consciousness." See Gilles Deleuze, *Spinoza: Practical Philosophy* (San Francisco: City Lights Books, 1991), 18. Spinoza rejects both the individualism of this discourse (its understanding of the passions in terms of "human nature") and its moralism. There is no "good and evil"; only "good and bad," which are "ways of thinking," a function of what is good or bad for a body encountering other bodies with which it agrees and enters into composition with, leading to an increased power of acting; or disagrees and decomposes, leading to a decrease in the power of acting. What Spinoza calls "virtue" is simply that through which "I" persevere in my being by entering compositions that agree with me and lead to a greater degree of perfection. For Spinoza, the cluster of passions associated with hatred and sadness (*Tristitia*) are bad in this sense; while a cluster of passions associated with pleasure and joy (*Laetitia*) are good. He distinguishes between derision, a sad passion with Hobbesian overtones, not least because it is "unjust in the commonwealth" (IV, 45); and laughter, which is pure pleasure: "I recognize a great difference between derision (which I said in Corollary I to be bad) and laughter. For laughter, like jesting, is pure pleasure, and so, provided that it is not excessive, it is good in itself. Indeed, nothing but gloomy and sad superstition prohibits enjoyment. . . . [T]he more we are affected by pleasure, the greater the perfection to which we pass" (IV, 45). Despite his moderation in advocating a nonexcessive laughter, Spinoza declares: "Joy cannot be excessive, but is always good" (IV, 42). The Scholium that makes the distinction between derision and laughter goes on to advocate a number of other pleasures which the wise man can enjoy; laughter is an umbrella term for such enjoyment.

61. Descartes, *The Passions of the Soul*, a.113.

62. Hobbes, *The English Works of Thomas Hobbes*, vol. III, 85.

63. Philip Dormer Stanhope, Earl of Chesterfield, *Principles of Politeness, and of Knowing the World* (Philadelphia: Printed and sold by Robert Bell, 1778); and *The American Chesterfield, or, Way to wealth, honor and distinction: Being selections from the letters of Lord Chesterfield to his son, and extracts from other eminent authors on the subject of politeness: with alterations and additions suited to the youth of the United States, By a member of the Philadelphia Bar* (Philadelphia: John Grigg, 1827).

64. Philip Dormer Stanhope, Earl of Chesterfield, *Letters of Lord Chesterfield to His Son* (London: J. M. Dent and Sons, 1929), 134.

65. Ibid., 27.

66. Ibid., 10.

67. Ibid., 31.

68. Ibid., 49.

69. Ibid. *Principles of Politeness and of Knowing the World* and *The American Chesterfield* would emphasize a few other touches, to be added to this injunction: "A man may smile, but if he would be thought a gentleman, and a man of sense, he should by no means laugh. . . . [A] loud laughter shows that a man has not the command of himself; every one who would wish to appear sensible, must abhor it. . . . Besides, could the immoderate laugher hear his own noise, or see the faces he makes, he would despise himself, for his folly." Chesterfield, *Principles of Politeness*, 31–32.

70. Thomas Hobbes, "The Answer of Mr. Hobbes to Sir. Will. D'Avenant's Preface before Gondibert," in *Sir William Davenant's Gondibert*, ed. David F. Gladish (Oxford: Clarendon Press, 1971), 53.

71. Ibid.

72. On cheerfulness, see Stuart M. Tave, *The Amiable Humorist* (Chicago: University of Chicago Press, 1960), 37.

73. See David Kunzle, "The Art of Pulling Teeth in the Seventeenth and Nineteenth Centuries: From Public Martyrdom to Private Nightmare and Political Struggle," in *Fragments for a History of the Human Body*, vol. 3, ed. Michel Feher, Ramona Naddaff, and Nadia Tazi (New York: Zone, 1989), 30. Colin Jones draws attention to the fact that the English perceived teeth-showing mouths to be "French," and therefore something to be avoided by proper English gentlemen-to-be like Chesterfield's son. See Colin Jones, "French Dentists and English Teeth in the Long Eighteenth Century," in *Medicine, Madness and Social History: Essays in Honor of Roy Porter*, ed. Roberta Bivins and John V. Pickstone (Houndmills, UK: Palgrave Macmillan, 2007), 81.

74. On noise, see Jacques Attali, *Noise: The Political Economy of Music* (Minneapolis: University of Minnesota Press, 1985); and Douglas Kahn, *Noise, Water, Meat: A History of Sounds in the Arts* (Cambridge, Mass.: MIT Press, 1999).

75. George Savile, Marquis of Halifax, "Advice to a Daughter," in *Halifax: Complete Works* (Baltimore: Penguin Books, 1969), 277.

76. Ibid., 275.

77. Ibid., 273.

78. Ibid., 298. There are earlier variations of the "prohibition" on woman's laughter. Guillaume de Lorris and Jean de Meun's *Roman de la Rose* declared: "Her lips should be kept closed and her teeth covered; a woman should always laugh with her mouth closed, for the sight of a mouth stretched open is not a pretty one." Dante's *Convivio* put it in these terms: "The soul reveals herself in the mouth, almost like a color behind glass. What is laughter if not a coruscation of the soul's delight—that is, a light appearing outwardly just as it is within? It is therefore fitting that in order to show one's soul to be of moderate cheer one should laugh in moderation, with proper reserve and little movement of the lips, so that the lady who reveals herself, as has been said, may appear modest and not wanton. Consequently the 'Book of the Four Cardinal Virtues' charges us: 'Do not let your laughter become strident,' that is, like the cackling of a hen. Ah, wonderful smile of my lady of whom I speak, which has never been perceived except by the eye!" (*Convivio* III, viii, 11–12)

79. See also Jean-Jacques Courtine and Claudine Haroche, *Histoire du visage: Exprimer et taire ses émotions* (Paris: Rivages, 1988), 104.

80. See Linda Walsh, "The Expressive Face: Manifestations of Sensibility in Eighteenth-Century Art," *Art History* 19, no. 4 (1996), 524.

81. Frances Burney, *Evelina, or The History of a Young Lady's Entrance into the World* (New York: Oxford University Press, 2002), 30–31.

82. Ibid., 34.

83. Ibid.

84. Elias writes: "This [embarrassment] is an inseparable counterpart of shame. Just as the latter arises when someone infringes the prohibitions of his own self and of society, the former occurs when something outside the individual impinges on his danger zone, on forms of behavior, objects, inclinations which have early on been invested with fear by his surroundings until this fear—in the manner of a conditioned reflex—is reproduced automatically in him on certain occasions. Embarrassment is displeasure or anxiety which arises when another person threatens to breach, or breaches, society's prohibitions represented by one's own super-ego." Elias, *The Civilizing Process*, 495.

85. Burney, *Evelina*, 34.

86. Hobbes, *The English Works of Thomas Hobbes*, vol. III, 47.

87. Burney, *Evelina*, 32, 30, 43.

88. Frances Burney, *The Early Diary of Frances Burney 1768–1778*, ed. Annie Raine Ellis (London: George Bell and Sons, 1907), 325.

89. Ibid., 325–326. See also Susan Staves, "*Evelina*, or Female Difficulties," *Modern Philology* 73, no. 4 (May 1976), 368–381.

90. Earl of Shaftesbury, *The Life, Unpublished Letters and Philosophical Regimen of Anthony, Earl of Shaftesbury, Author of the "Characteristics,"* ed. Benjamin Rand (London, 1900), 225.

91. Ibid., 225–228.

92. James Beattie, "On Laughter and Ludicrous Composition," in *Essays* (Edinburgh: Printed for William Creech, 1776), 588.

93. Ibid.

94. Ibid., 670.

95. Ibid., 669.

96. Ibid., 670.

97. For an extensive account of such spaces, often exclusively male spaces (London's streets, gentlemanly clubs, taverns, and brothels), see Vic Gatrell, *City of Laughter* (London: Atlantic Books, 2006). It is important to note, however, that the fact that advice is not followed to the letter does not mean it is never followed. It would be interesting to write the nonhistory of laughter, trying to hear the laughs that could have been laughed but, for a range of reasons, were not.

98. Chesterfield, *Letters of Lord Chesterfield to His Son*, 50.

99. Halifax, "Advice to a Daughter," 271–272.

100. Chesterfield, *Letters of Lord Chesterfield to His Son*, 56.

101. Ibid., 30.

102. Ibid., 34.

103. Ibid., 21.

104. Ibid., 31.

105. Michel Foucault, *Discipline and Punish: The Birth of the Prison*, trans. Alan Sheridan (New York: Pantheon Books, 1977).

106. Pierre Bourdieu, *Outline of a Theory of Practice* (Cambridge: Cambridge University Press, 1977), 94.

107. There is an extended literature on the history of physiognomic thought. For an account that specifically places physiognomy within the history of the face, see Jurgis Baltrušaitis, *Aberrations: An Essay on the Legend of Forms* (Cambridge, Mass.: MIT Press, 1989).

108. Johann Caspar Lavater, *Essays on Physiognomy, Designed to Promote the Knowledge and the Love of Mankind*, vol. 1 (London: Printed by T. Bensley, Bolt Court, Fleet Street, for John Stockdale, Piccadilly, 1810), 24.

109. Physiognomy, with its "pseudo-scientific" claims, has not become a respectable discourse and is today easily dismissed as an outdated, prescientific form of divination, alongside chiromancy (the interpretation of handwriting) or metoscopy (the reading of the forehead). This pseudo-science has nonetheless been a constitutive force in the production of perceptive and interpretative practices in modernity, and it is not by any means restricted to the physiognomic treatise and the visual arts. Lavater speaks about it as a science of surfaces and is interested in describing "the physiognomy of things." He imagines physiognomy as the study of the relation between the exterior and the interior; between, as he puts it, "surface and the invisible spirit which it covers—between the animated, perceptible matter, and the imperceptible principle which impresses this character of life upon it" (vol. 1, 20). It is in attempting to describe this very relation that Hegel became interested in physiognomy and phrenology. On Hegel, see Mladen Dolar, "The Phrenology of Spirit," in *Supposing the Subject*, ed. Joan Copjec (London: Verso, 1994), 64–83.

110. An earlier version of this idea appears in Spinoza: "The force of some passion, i.e. of some emotion, can so surpass the other actions, i.e. the power, of a man that the emotion adheres stubbornly to the man." If one such emotion "harasses" the person, in time it stubbornly clings to him or her such that we can recognize a miser or an ambitious person. See Spinoza, *Ethics*, IV, Prop. 6–7.

111. Lavater, *Essays on Physiognomy*, vol. 1, 18.

112. Ibid., vol. 3, 394.

113. Paolo Mantegazza, *Physiognomy and Expression* (London: W. Scott, 1899), 50.

114. Ibid., 48.

115. Ibid., 118.

116. The American physiognomist Samuel R. Wells would also write: "Self-control closes the mouth and draws the lips backward; impulse opens the mouth and protrudes the lips. In the first case there may be passion, but it will be restrained by a stronger will; in the latter, passion is the stronger, and will rule." Samuel R. Wells, *New Physiognomy, or Signs of Character, as Manifested through Temperament and External Forms, and Especially in "The Human Face Divine"* (New York: Fowler and Wells, 1896), 170.

117. Lavater, *Essays on Physiognomy*, vol. 3, 21.

118. Ibid., vol. 1, 152.

119. Sigmund Freud, "Three Essays on the Theory of Sexuality," in *The Standard Edition of the Complete Psychological Works of Sigmund Freud*, ed. James Strachey (London: Hogarth Press and Institute of Psycho-Analysis, 1953–1974), 7: 150.

120. Charles Bell, *The Anatomy and Philosophy of Expression as Connected to the Fine Arts* (London: George Bell and Sons, 1888 edn.), 31.

121. Charles Bell, *Essays on the Anatomy of Expression in Painting* (London, 1806), 127.

122. Giambattista Della Porta, *De humana physiognomonia* (Rothomagi: Sumptibus Ioannis Berthelin, 1650), 179.

123. Lavater, *Essays on Physiognomy*, vol. 3, 47.

124. Ibid., vol. 2, 64.

125. Ibid.

126. Ibid., vol. 1, 159–160.

127. Pierre Gratiolet, *De la physionomie et des mouvements d'expression* (Paris: Bibliothèque d'Éducation et de Récréation, 1865), 123. Gratiolet identifies five categories: 1. the nasal laugh; 2. cachinnation; 3. the convulsive laugh; 4. the excessive laugh; 5. the oral laugh.

128. George Vasey, *The Philosophy of Laughter and Smiling* (London: J. Burns, 1877), 65.

129. Ibid., 66.

130. Ibid., 98.

131. Ibid., 67, 76.

132. Ibid., 109.

133. Ibid., 108.

134. Ibid.

135. For the nineteenth-century debate on laughter, see Robert Bernard Martin, *The Triumph of Wit: A Study of Victorian Comic Theory* (Oxford: Clarendon Press, 1974). While Martin's focus is wit, his discussion often touches on the virtues of laughing. He writes: "The spectre of immoderate laughter was one to which even the supporters of the risible and ludicrous had to give a ritual nod" (8).

136. Mantegazza, *Physiognomy and Expression*, 107.

137. Ibid., 113.

138. Erving Goffman, *Interaction Ritual: Essays on Face-to-Face Behavior* (New York: Pantheon Books, 1967).

139. Ibid., 43.

CHAPTER 2

1. Langston Hughes, *The Collected Poems of Langston Hughes* (New York: Knopf, 1995), 27–28.

2. Langston Hughes, *The Big Sea: An Autobiography* (New York: Knopf, 1940), 239.

3. Langston Hughes and Zora Neale Hurston, *Mule Bone: A Comedy of Negro Life*, ed. George Houston Bass and Henry Louis Gates, Jr. (New York: Harper Perennial, 1991).

4. Ralph Ellison, *Invisible Man* (New York: Vintage, 1995), xvi.

5. Alain Badiou, *The Century*, trans. Alberto Toscano (Cambridge: Polity Press, 2007), 1.

6. Georges Bataille, *The Story of the Eye* (San Francisco: City Lights Books, 1987), 63.

7. There are earlier articulations of the laughing primitivist fantasy in American literature. One important precedent is William Dean Howells's 1871 short story "Mrs. Johnson." The story's title character is set apart by her laughter: "It was only her barbaric laughter and her lawless eye that betrayed how slightly her New England birth and breeding covered her ancestral traits, and bridged the gulf of a thousand years of civilization that lay between her race and ours." William Dean Howells, *Suburban Sketches* (Salem, N.H.: Ayer Company, 1985), 21.

8. Gertrude Stein, *Three Lives* (New York: Modern Library, 1933), 122, 186.

9. Ibid., 63.

10. Ibid., 209. Interestingly, when it came to laughter, the modernist synesthetic mix included taste. Claude McKay's *Home to Harlem* talks about "sugared laughter" (15); "liquor-rich laughter, banana-ripe laughter" (204); "the fruitiness of its [Harlem's] laughter" (267). See Claude McKay, *Home to Harlem* (New York: Harper and Brothers, 1928).

11. Stein, *Three Lives*, 85.

12. Ibid., 85–86.

13. Ibid., 85.

14. Ibid., 92.

15. Ibid., 138.

16. Ibid., 111.

17. Carl Van Vechten, *Nigger Heaven* (New York: Knopf, 1926), 89–90.

18. Ibid., 161.

19. Ibid., 89, 253.

20. Ibid., 222–225.

21. Sherwood Anderson, *Dark Laughter* (New York: Liveright, 1960), 17.

22. Ibid., 18.

23. Ibid., 65.

24. Ibid., 74.

25. Ibid., 79.

26. Ibid., 319.

27. Ibid., 184.

28. Van Vechten, *Nigger Heaven*, 89.

29. Ibid., 14.

30. Baker made a fortune dancing in Paris; as Janet Lyon puts it: "commodifying interracial sociability, she shrewdly appropriated white appropriation." Janet Lyon, "Gender and Sexuality," in *The Cambridge Companion to American Modernism*, ed. Walter Kalaidjian (Cambridge: Cambridge University Press, 2005), 238.

31. On the exemplary figure of dance in the philosophical tradition, see John Mowitt, "Spins," *Postmodern Culture* 18, no. 3 (2008), 1–21.

32. Anderson, *Dark Laughter*, 253.

33. Ibid., 181.

34. Ibid., 176.

35. Ibid., 106.

36. The mixture of these colors is orange, "the color of idleness." See Anson Rabinbach, *The Human Motor: Energy, Fatigue, and the Origins of Modernity* (New York: Basic Books, 1990), 41.

37. Gauguin wrote: "Coming from Europe I was always uncertain of color, unable to see the obvious: yet it was so easy to put a red and a blue on my canvas, naturally. In the streams, golden shapes enchanted me. Why did I hesitate to make all that gold and all that sunny rejoicing flow on my canvas? Probably old habits from Europe, all that timidity of expression of our old degenerate races." Gold is the color of Gauguin's Tahitian wife, "a child of about thirteen." See Paul Gauguin, *The Writings of a Savage*, ed. Daniel Guérin, trans. Eleanor Levieux (New York: Paragon House, 1990), 82.

38. Henri Lefebvre, *The Production of Space*, trans. Donald Nicholson-Smith (Oxford: Blackwell, 1991).

39. Ernest Hemingway, *Torrents of Spring: A Romantic Novel in Honor of the Passing of a Great Race* (New York: Charles Scribner's Sons, 1926), 57.

40. Ibid., 69.

41. Ibid., 74.

42. Ibid., 78.

43. Ibid., 41.

44. Ibid., 64.

45. Ibid., 67.

46. Ibid., 23.

47. The laughter of native peoples is a leitmotiv of colonial writing. Ménager quotes a number of sources that bear witness to the fact that one of the first questions asked in the wake of colonial encounters was whether and how natives laugh, and what word they use for "laughter." See Daniel Ménager, La Renaissance et le rire (Paris: Presses Universitaires de France, 1995), 17.

48. Charles Darwin, The Expression of the Emotions in Man and Animals (London: John Murray, 1872), 16.

49. Ibid., 208–209.

50. Ibid., 209.

51. Mary Douglas, "Do Dogs Laugh?," in Implicit Meanings: Selected Essays in Anthropology (London: Routledge, 2002), 84.

52. Ellison, Invisible Man, 5.

53. Ralph Waldo Emerson, "Manners," in Essays (Boston: Houghton Mifflin, 1883), 115–150. This, it should be noted, is only one of Emerson's faces, seen here through Ellison's work. The two shared a middle name, and Ellison insists on drawing attention to this irony ("my middle name, sadly enough, is Waldo"; Ralph Ellison, "Change the Joke and Slip the Yoke," in Shadow and Act [New York: Random House, 1964], 58).

54. Emerson, "Manners," 120.

55. Ibid., 131.

56. Erving Goffman describes the following social rituals of facial encounters: "It is also possible for one person to treat others as if they were not there at all, as objects not worthy of a glance, let alone close scrutiny. Moreover, it is possible for the individual, by his staring or 'not seeing,' to alter his appearance hardly at all in consequence of the presence of others. Here we have 'nonperson' treatment; it may be seen in our society in the way we sometimes treat children, servants, Negroes, and mental patients." This invisibility is to be contrasted with what Goffman calls "civil inattention," a "directness" of eye expression as acknowledgment of the other's presence accompanied by a withdrawal of attention. The Invisible Man expects the blond man to display "civil inattention," but he gets "nonperson treatment." Erving Goffman, Behavior in Public Places: Notes on the Social Organization of Gatherings (New York: Free Press, 1963), 84. See also Goffman, The Presentation of Self in Everyday Life (Garden City, N.Y.: Doubleday, 1959), 151–153.

57. Emerson, "Manners," 139.

58. Ellison, "Change the Joke and Slip the Yoke," 55.

59. Ellison, Invisible Man, 157.

60. Ibid., 164.

61. "The tooth-brush at Tuskegee is the emblem of civilization," Booker T. Washington wrote. It would be interesting to write the history of the obligatory toothbrush drill, which, as a drill, has as its goal less the cleaning of that most important fragment of the body, the mouth, than its management and preventive monitoring. Washington is a guardian of young African-American mouths, in need of methodical normalization. Booker T. Washington, "Signs of Progress among the Negroes," *Century Magazine* 59 (1900), 473. On oral hygiene as technology of surveillance, see Sarah Nettleton, "Inventing Mouths: Disciplinary Power and Dentistry," in *Reassessing Foucault: Power, Medicine and the Body*, ed. Colin Jones (London: Routledge, 1994), 73–90.

62. Washington, "Signs of Progress among the Negroes," 472.

63. One would need to trace the development of the modern discourse on manners and laughter's place within it as it moves across the Atlantic. George Washington, who, at the age of ten, copied by hand a set of maxims adapted from a French Jesuit manual, *Rules of Civility*, which he promoted, alongside Chesterfield's letters, throughout his life, would be an important figure here. Benjamin Franklin's much-celebrated *Autobiography* helped to disseminate such etiquette strategies, while at the same time injecting them with a dose of a specifically American republican flavor. Such a study would have to account for the historical commercialization of politeness, the sense in which "smiles and manners" became business capital, leading to what Arlie Russell Hochschild calls "the managed heart." On the American civilizing process and its "smiles and manners," see John F. Kasson, *Rudeness and Civility: Manners in Nineteenth-Century Urban America* (New York: Hill and Wang, 1990). See also Arlie Russell Hochschild, *The Managed Heart: Commercialization of Human Feeling* (Berkeley: University of California Press, 1983).

64. Houston Baker tries to reconsider the figure of Booker T. Washington. Reading *Up from Slavery*, Baker discovers redeeming cracks in Washington's mask. He, after all, was doing a job that might have been the only one possible at the time. In doing a lot of long-term harm, Washington did a lot of immediate good. This too might be the work of a trickster. See Houston A. Baker Jr., "Men and Institutions: Booker T. Washington's *Up from Slavery*," in *Long Black Song: Essays in Black American Literature and Culture* (Charlottesville: University Press of Virginia, 1992). Ellison himself, in a 1976 interview, reconsidered Washington along these lines. See Ralph Ellison, "'My Strength Comes from Louis Armstrong': Interview with Robert G. O'Meally," in *Living with Music: Ralph Ellison's Jazz Writings*, ed. Robert G. O'Meally (New York: Modern Library, 2001).

65. W. E. B. Du Bois, *The Souls of Black Folk* (New York: Dover, 1994), 1.

66. Zora Neale Hurston, *Mules and Men* (New York: Negro Universities Press, 1969), 18.

67. Ellison, "My Strength Comes from Louis Armstrong."

68. Johnson's "Laughing Song" was followed by a series of recordings of laughter. The early recording industry, playing with the idea of disembodied voice,

presented its audience with a "talking machine" which could in fact produce a diversity of human sounds. Laughter was to occupy a special place among them, as a test of the machine's "realness." One of the most successful records in this line, which Armstrong probably knew too, was the 1922 "Okeh Laughing Record," a curio of the early recording industry. The record begins as a musical solo. A trumpet is played. Something goes wrong and the laughter of a woman irrupts. The player, a man, struggles to continue his number but soon gives up. His laughter follows. Now both man and woman cannot stop laughing. The man wants to go back to his music, but "the battle" is lost. He abandons himself to laughter. Waves of laughter follow—to be reproduced infinitely in the audience.

69. One might remember here that Frantz Fanon recalls his interpellation into a racist world as a moment of impossible laughter. Fanon writes: "'Look, a Negro!' The circle was drawing a bit tighter. I made no secret of my amusement. 'Mama, see the Negro! I'm frightened!' Frightened! Frightened! Now they were beginning to be afraid of me. I made up my mind to laugh myself to tears, but laughter had become impossible." Frantz Fanon, *Black Skin, White Masks* (New York: Grove Press, 1967), 112. Interestingly, Ellison remembers his own introduction to racial prejudice through the echoes of his mother's laughter when refused entrance into the Oklahoma City zoo. See Lawrence Jackson, *Ralph Ellison: Emergence of Genius* (New York: John Wiley and Sons, 2002).

70. Ellison, *Invisible Man*, 194.

71. Ibid., 265.

72. Ibid., 311.

73. Ibid., 499.

74. Ibid., 534.

75. Ralph Ellison, "An Extravagance of Laughter," in *Going to the Territory* (New York: Vintage, 1995), 192.

76. See Slavoj Žižek, "'I Hear You with My Eyes': or, The Invisible Master," in *Gaze and Voice as Love Objects*, ed. Slavoj Žižek and Renata Salecl (Durham: Duke University Press, 1996).

77. Ellison, "An Extravagance of Laughter," 145.

78. Ibid., 188.

79. The dramatization of *Tobacco Road* was a huge success. It ran for more than seven years (1934–1941), through 3,182 consecutive performances. It was also very controversial, being famously closed down in Chicago in 1934 for its alleged obscenity.

80. Ellison, "An Extravagance of Laughter," 186.

81. Erskine Caldwell, *Tobacco Road* (Athens: University of Georgia Press, 1995), 35.

82. Ellison, "An Extravagance of Laughter," 192.

83. Hughes is an important, if silent, protagonist here. Ellison laughs out loud and sees Hughes's disapproving face. Ellison uses "An Extravagance of Laughter" as an occasion to explain the distance between himself and Hughes. Significantly, Ellison did not make it into *The Book of Negro Humor*, the 1966 collection edited by Hughes. In putting together his collection, Hughes has Ellison laugh in a laughing barrel. But it might be that Ellison has indeed only tangentially touched on "humor" while being preoccupied with "laughter." The two intersect sometimes but they by no means overlap, as Hughes would like them to.

84. Ralph Ellison, "On Initiation Rites and Power," in *Ralph Ellison's Invisible Man*, ed. John F. Callahan (Oxford: Oxford University Press, 2005), 324.

85. Ellison, "An Extravagance of Laughter," 161.

86. Ibid., 187.

87. This lineage goes back to what Frederick Douglass calls "unmeaning jargon." The well-known sentence in Douglass's narrative reads: "The thought that came up, came out—if not in the *word*, in the *sound*;—and as frequently in the one as in the other." Frederick Douglass, *Narrative of the Life of Frederick Douglass* (New York: Dover, 1995), 8.

88. Henri Bergson, *Laughter* (Baltimore: Johns Hopkins University Press, 1956), 86.

89. Ibid., 87.

90. Ellison, "Change the Joke and Slip the Yoke," 53.

91. See Michael Rogin, *Blackface, White Noise* (Berkeley: University of California Press, 1996); Michael North, *The Dialect of Modernism: Race, Language and Twentieth-Century Literature* (New York: Oxford University Press, 1994).

92. Ellison, "Change the Joke and Slip the Yoke," 54.

93. Jessie Faucet, "The Gift of Laughter," in *The New Negro*, ed. Alain Locke (New York: Touchstone, 1997), 161–168.

94. Charles Baudelaire, "On the Essence of Laughter," in *The Painter of Modern Life and Other Essays*, trans. Jonathan Mayne (London: Phaidon Press, 1964), 149.

95. Ibid.

96. Ellison, "An Extravagance of Laughter," 197.

97. Baudelaire, "On the Essence of Laughter," 154.

98. Ibid., 153.

99. Ellison, "An Extravagance of Laughter," 197.

100. Du Bois, *The Souls of Black Folk*, 2.

101. Ellison, *Invisible Man*, 10.

102. Ibid.

103. Ibid., 11.

104. Angela Davis traces a turning point in the history of the blues to the1930s, when women's blues began to be marginalized and men's blues became central to the emerging blues industry. This, in part, had to do with the marginalization of unacceptable sexual content in women's blues, to which the old woman's moan of "I learned to love their father though I hated him too" also belongs. See Angela Davis, *Blues Legacies and Black Feminism* (New York: Pantheon, 1998).

105. See Gayatri Chakravorty Spivak's rewriting of her essay "Can the Subaltern Speak?" in *Critique of Post-Colonial Reason: Toward a History of the Vanishing Present* (Cambridge, Mass.: Harvard University Press, 1999). It would also be productive to pursue this line of inquiry in light of Spivak's reading of *Foe*, J. M. Coetzee's rewriting of Daniel Defoe's *Robinson Crusoe*. In Coetzee's novel, Friday is mutilated, he has had his tongue cut out. When Foe explains the situation to Susan Barton, the novel's female narrator, he has Friday repeat after him, "La La La La," to which Friday responds, "Ha Ha Ha Ha." The challenge, in Spivak's terms, is not to "give voice to Friday," but rather, once we acknowledge that Friday's tongue is irrevocably cut out, to nonetheless learn to listen to the sounds Friday does make. Ha Ha Ha is only a beginning.

106. Barry Shank, "'That Wild Mercury Sound': Bob Dylan and the Illusion of American Culture," *boundary 2* 29, no. 1 (2002), 97–123.

107. See also Ronald Radano, "Denoting Difference: The Writing of the Slave Spirituals," *Critical Inquiry* 22 (1996), 506–544.

108. See, for example, Woody Herman's "Laughing Boy Blues" or Sidney Bechet's "Laughin' in Rhythm."

109. On tone, see Sianne Ngai, *Ugly Feelings* (Cambridge, Mass.: Harvard University Press, 2005); Jean-Luc Nancy, *Listening* (New York: Fordham University Press, 2007).

CHAPTER 3

1. Nancy best expressed the relation the conversation on community had with the work of Bataille: "Not only will this have been written after Bataille, but also to him, just as he wrote to us—because one always writes *to*—communicating to us the anguish of community. . . ." Jean-Luc Nancy, *The Inoperative Community*, trans. Peter Connor, Lisa Garbus, Michael Holland, and Simona Sawhney (Minneapolis: University of Minnesota Press, 1991), 41.

I will discuss Bataille alongside the voices of some of his readers by way of drawing attention to this community. The conversation on community peaked in 1983, which saw the publication of an essay by Jean-Luc Nancy, "La communauté désœuvrée" (The inoperative community), in a special issue of the French journal *Aléa*, edited by Jean-Christophe Bailly. The same year, Maurice Blanchot published a reaction to Nancy's essay, *La communauté inavouable* (Paris: Éditions de

Minuit, 1983); English edition, *The Unavowable Community*, trans. Pierre Joris (Barrytown, N.Y.: Station Hill Press, 1988). Nancy republished his 1983 essay as the first chapter of the book with the same title, *La communauté désœuvrée*, three years later (Paris: Christian Bourgois Éditeur, 1986; English edition cited above). Jacques Derrida joined the conversation in *Politiques de l'amitié* (Paris: Éditions Galilée, 1994); English edition, *The Politics of Friendship* (London: Verso, 2005). Nancy recounted the story of the debate in 2001, when he prefaced an Italian edition of Blanchot's *The Unavowable Community* with a short essay titled *La communauté affrontée* (Paris: Éditions Galilée, 2001). See also Étienne Balibar, "Derrida and the Aporia of Community," *Philosophy Today* (2009).

2. Jacques Derrida, "From Restricted to General Economy: A Hegelianism without Reserve," in *Writing and Difference*, trans. Alan Bass (Chicago: University of Chicago Press, 1978), 251. Bataille's reading of Hegel is mediated by Alexandre Kojève's lectures. See Alexandre Kojève, *Introduction to the Reading of Hegel* (New York: Basic Books, 1969). For an alternative reading of Hegel, see Gérard Lebrun, *La patience du concept: Essai sur le discours hégélien* (Paris: Gallimard, 1972); and Slavoj Žižek's many interventions in this debate.

3. Georges Bataille, "Hegel, Death and Sacrifice," in *The Bataille Reader*, ed. Fred Botting and Scott Wilson (Oxford: Blackwell, 1997), 282.

4. Ibid., 289.

5. Georges Bataille, *Inner Experience*, trans. Leslie Anne Boldt (Albany: SUNY Press, 1988), 47. Unless otherwise noted, all parenthetical references in this chapter are to Bataille's *Inner Experience*. When the French is used, references are to Georges Bataille, *Œuvres complètes* (Paris: Gallimard, 1970–); hereafter cited as OC.

6. Georges Bataille, "Joy in the Face of Death," in *The College of Sociology (1937–39)*, ed. Denis Hollier (Minneapolis: University of Minnesota Press, 1988), 325. Throughout this chapter, parenthetical references to the French edition of the writings of the College are to *Le Collège de sociologie (1937–1939)*, ed. Denis Hollier (Paris: Gallimard, 1979).

7. Derrida, "From Restricted to General Economy," 259.

8. Michel Foucault, "A Preface to Transgression," in *Bataille: A Critical Reader*, ed. Fred Botting and Scott Wilson (Oxford: Wiley-Blackwell, 1991), 24–40.

9. Simon Critchley, "Comedy and Finitude: Displacing the Tragic-Heroic Paradigm in Philosophy and Psychoanalysis," *Constellations* 6, no. 1 (1999), 108–122.

10. In André Masson's famous drawing for the inaugural issue of *Acéphale*, what is left of the head of the sovereign, a skull, is in the place of the sexual organs. The image suggests the rejection of a sovereignty from above, whether religious or secular, and a reorientation to lower, "base," authorities.

11. Bataille's reservation vis-à-vis mysticism is a reservation vis-à-vis the confessional mode: "By *inner experience* I understand that which one usually calls *mystical*

experience: the states of ecstasy, of rapture, at least of meditated emotion. But I am thinking less of *confessional* experience, to which one has had to adhere up to now, than of an experience laid bare, free of ties, even of an origin, of any confession whatever. This is why I don't like the word *mystical*" (3). Bataille is nonetheless inspired by Christian mystics; the very word "experience" in *Inner Experience* resonates with Saint Angela of Foligno's *Livre de l'expérience*. The connection has lead to Sartre's review of *Inner Experience*, suggestively titled "Un nouveau mystique" (*Cahiers du Sud*, 1943). On Bataille's relation to mysticism, as well as the debate with Sartre, see Amy Hollywood, *Sensible Ecstasy: Mysticism, Sexual Difference, and the Demands of History* (Chicago: University of Chicago Press, 2002). Bataille is explicit about the relation between mysticism and laughter: "laughter, considered as I have described it, opens a sort of general experience that, in my opinion, is comparable to what theologians have named 'mystical theology' or 'negative theology.'" See Georges Bataille, "Nonknowledge, Laughter and Tears," in *The Unfinished System of Nonknowledge*, trans. Michelle Kendall and Stuart Kendall (Minneapolis: University of Minnesota Press, 2001), 146.

12. Derrida, "From Restricted to General Economy," 264.

13. Jean Baudrillard, "Death in Bataille," in *Bataille: A Critical Reader*, 140.

14. Bataille, "Hegel, Death and Sacrifice," 286–287 (OC, 12: 336).

15. Ibid., 291 (OC, 12: 336).

16. Ibid. (OC, 12: 341).

17. Ibid., 287 (OC, 12: 337).

18. Nancy, who is otherwise one of Bataille's most generous readers, offers a harsh—if sobering—critique of Bataille's engagement with the notion of sacrifice, tracing a trajectory in his work from his embracing of its potential to a rejection of its ultimate consequences, which Nancy locates in the sacrifice/Holocaust of the European Jews. See Jean-Luc Nancy, "The Unsacrificeable," trans. Richard Livingston, *Yale French Studies*, no. 79, "Literature and the Ethical Question" (1991), 20–38.

19. Bataille, "Joy in the Face of Death," 325.

20. Bataille is fascinated by the anecdote one of Hegel's students tells about having the feeling during Hegel's lectures that death itself speaks from the podium.

21. Georges Bataille, "Preface to Madame Edwarda," in *The Bataille Reader*, 226 (OC, 3: 11).

22. Bataille, "Hegel, Death and Sacrifice," 291 (OC, 12: 342).

23. Ibid., 287. One would have to juxtapose this exclamation to Hegel's own thoughts on comedy, but Bataille does not pursue this connection. On Hegelian comedy, see Alenka Zupančič, *The Odd One In: On Comedy* (Cambridge, Mass.: MIT Press, 2008).

24. Derrida, "From Restricted to General Economy," 256.

25. Roland Barthes, *The Pleasure of the Text*, trans. Richard Miller (New York: Noonday Press, 1973), 55. On Bataille's materialism, see Pierre Macherey, *The Object of Literature*, trans. David Macey (Cambridge: Cambridge University Press, 1995). On Bataille's insistence on experience, see Roberto Esposito, *Communitas: The Origin and Destiny of Community*, trans. Timothy C. Campbell (Stanford: Stanford University Press, 2009).

26. Derrida, "From Restricted to General Economy," 253.

27. Friedrich Nietzsche, *Beyond Good and Evil*, trans. R. J. Hollingdale (Harmondsworth: Penguin, 1990), 219.

28. Bataille, "Nonknowledge, Laughter and Tears," 139.

29. The beginnings of philosophy offered such an occasion in the Thracian maid's burst of laughter in Plato's *Theaetetus*. The anecdote is well known: Wandering one night and studying the stars in the sky, Thales of Miletus, the first philosopher, falls into a well. He starts calling for help. A passerby comes, a young Thracian maid. Hearing his plea, she starts laughing. Thales was preoccupied with things far away in the sky, but has failed to see things in front of his nose. Socrates concludes: "Anyone who gives his life to philosophy is open to such mockery . . . the whole rabble will join the peasant girl in laughing at him." In the twentieth century, the scene was repeated by Martin Heidegger and Hannah Arendt. See Hans Blumenberg, *Das Lachen der Thrakerin* (Frankfurt am Main: Suhrkamp, 1987); Jacques Taminiaux, *The Thracian Maid and the Professional Thinker: Arendt and Heidegger* (Albany: SUNY Press, 1997); and Adriana Cavarero, "The Maidservant from Thrace," in *In Spite of Plato: A Feminist Rewriting of Ancient Philosophy* (New York: Routledge, 1995).

30. The phrase "riant spaciousness" is Julia Kristeva's. See Kristeva, "Place Names," in *Desire in Language: A Semiotic Approach to Literature and Art*, trans. Thomas Gora, Alice Jardine, and Leon S. Roudiez (New York: Columbia University Press, 1980), 283.

31. Bataille on Proust: "the poetic images or the 'impressions' reserve, at the same time as they overflow, a feeling of ownership, the persistence of an 'I' relating everything to itself" (143).

32. The phrase is quoted by Jean Michel Besnier, "Bataille, the Emotive Intellectual," in *Bataille: Writing the Sacred*, ed. Carolyn Bailey Gill (London: Routledge, 1995), 16. Besnier describes Bataille as an *intellectuel pathétique* (emotive intellectual), who "surrenders to events as to a joyful invitation" (17). This, Besnier argues, describes better than the Sartrean *intellectuel engagé* the mode in which some of the best-known figures of twentieth-century literature and philosophy have grabbed hold of the historical events of their time. As Bataille's own life demonstrates, this is not a risk-free adventure. His critics have been quick to note that passionate exultation, enthusiasm, and fervor also characterize frenzied participants in Nazi rallies. Sartre described anti-Semitism as a passion. Ironically, when Simone de Beauvoir imagines a typology of "serious men," the category of "the adven-

turer," a man who likes action for its own sake and is indifferent to the content of his freedom, she seems to be describing Bataille. For his part, Bataille responded by arguing that there is nothing inherently fascist about passion. See Simone de Beauvoir, *The Ethics of Ambiguity*, trans. Bernard Frechtman (New York: Citadel Press, 2000). Bataille addresses the problem briefly in his "Autobiographical Note," where, writing about himself in the third person, he recounts: "Counterattack was dissolved at the end of winter. (The supposed pro-fascist tendency on the part of certain of Bataille's friends, and, to a lesser degree, of Bataille himself.) For an understanding of the element of truth in this paradoxical fascist tendency, despite its radically contrary intention, one should read Elio Vittorini's *The Red Carnation*, together with its strange postface. There is no doubt that the bourgeois world as it exists constitutes a provocation to violence and that, in that world, the exterior forms of violence hold a fascination. Be that as it may, Bataille considers, at least since Counterattack, that this fascination can lead to the worst." Georges Bataille, "Autobiographical Note," in *The Bataille Reader*, 115.

33. Jacques Derrida, "Derrida's Response to Hent de Vries," in *Augustine and Post-modernism: Confessions and Circumfession*, ed. John D. Caputo and Michael J. Scanlon (Bloomington: Indiana University Press, 2005), 89.

34. Hollier, *The College of Sociology*, 13.

35. Jacques Derrida, *The Gift of Death*, trans. David Wills (Chicago: University of Chicago Press, 1995), 24.

36. Bataille writes: "*The entire morality of laughter, of risk, of the exultation of virtues and of strengths is spirit of decision. . . . Without night, no one would have to decide, but in a false light—undergo. Decision is what is born before the worst and rises above. It is the essence of courage, of the heart, of being itself. And it is the inverse of project (it demands that one reject delay, that one decide on the spot, with everything at stake: what follows matters second)*" (25–26).

37. Bataille, whose writing is hardly anecdotal, draws attention to the importance of this anecdote by recounting the story of this encounter on different occasions (see also Bataille, "Nonknowledge, Laughter and Tears," 139).

38. Henri Bergson, *Laughter* (Baltimore: Johns Hopkins University Press, 1956), 71.

39. Ibid., 148.

40. Bataille, "Nonknowledge, Laughter and Tears," 139.

41. Bataille's critique of Bergson's theory of laughter is somewhat reductive. In his desire to criticize mechanized human behavior in the wake of industrialization, Bergson imagined laughter as a tool, to be used toward corrective ends. This, however, is a limited "Bergson." Pierre Macherey draws attention to elements of Bataille's thought that are, in fact, close to other parts of Bergson's work. See Macherey, *The Object of Literature*, 114.

42. Bataille writes: "*The expression of inner experience must in some way respond to its movement—cannot be a dry verbal tradition to be executed on command*" (6). The reference point for philosophy's "dry verbal tradition" is Kant, famously known as the worst

writer in the history of philosophy. Nancy identifies in Kant the very beginning of the modern tension within a philosophy that tries to be schematic and systematic and its desire to be literature. What Nancy calls "the Kantian function in philosophy" is the syncope that reveals the limit of this tension. This syncope is a burst of laughter. Kant wrote on laughter at the end of his meditation on the sublime in the *Critique of Judgment*. See Immanuel Kant, *Critique of Judgment*, trans. Werner S. Pluhar (Indianapolis: Hackett, 1987), 54. According to Nancy, what, in Kant's wake, has been called "the incongruity theory" reveals the inadequacy of the Philosopher, who becomes a literary figure, "Kant," to be caricatured and ridiculed by a literary tradition that begins in his own writing. See Jean-Luc Nancy, *Discourse on the Syncope: Logodaedalus*, trans. Saul Anton (Stanford: Stanford University Press, 2008), 15, 134.

43. Nancy, *The Inoperative Community*, 16.

44. Roger Caillois, "Brotherhoods," in Hollier, *The College of Sociology*, 147. This lecture was given by Bataille, who read and improvised around Caillois's notes.

45. Ibid., 155 (288).

46. Nancy, *The Inoperative Community*, 28, 58.

47. Blanchot, *The Unavowable Community*, 46. Derrida would join this debate on the "elective" side of community. See Derrida, *The Politics of Friendship*, 298. Bataille imagined his relation to Nietzsche as a nonsynchronic friendship: "It is from a feeling of community binding me to Nietzsche that the desire to communicate arises in me, not from an isolated originality" (27). The exigency of this friendship / community is silence and yet, as Nietzsche put it, in the midst of "keeping silent together," there is laughter. On this laugh, see Derrida, *The Politics of Friendship*, 57.

48. Bataille writes: "it would have been necessary to deal not with individuals like those I already know, but only with men (and above all with masses) who are comparatively decomposed, amorphous and even violently expelled from every form." Georges Bataille, "The Use-Value of D. A. F. de Sade (an Open Letter to My Comrades)," in *The Bataille Reader*, 147.

49. See also Giorgio Agamben, *The Coming Community*, trans. Michael Hardt (Minneapolis: University of Minnesota Press, 1993); and Esposito, *Communitas*.

50. Georges Bataille, "Attraction and Repulsion II: Social Structure," in Hollier, *The College of Sociology*, 114 (211).

51. Georges Bataille, "Attraction and Repulsion I: Tropisms, Sexuality, Laughter and Tears," in Hollier, *The College of Sociology*, 108 (198).

52. Ibid., 107 (196).

53. Ibid., 107 (196–197).

54. Blanchot's "infinite conversation" with Bataille elaborates and clarifies the tension between immediacy and mediation: "The immediate excludes everything

immediate: this means all direct relation, all mystical fusion, and all sensible contact, just as it excludes itself—renounces its own immediacy—each time it must submit to the mediation of an intermediary in order to offer access.... 'The immediate excluding everything immediate, as it does every mediation' tells us something about presence itself: immediate presence is presence of what could not be present, presence of the non-accessible, presence excluding or exceeding any present." Blanchot, *The Infinite Conversation*, trans. Susan Hanson (Minneapolis: University of Minnesota Press, 1993), 38.

55. Bataille, "Attraction and Repulsion I," 111 (205).

56. Georges Bataille, "Laughter," in *The Bataille Reader*, 62; OC, 5: 391.

57. Bataille, "Attraction and Repulsion I," 109 (201).

58. Ibid.

59. On inclusion/exclusion, see Étienne Balibar, *We the People of Europe: Reflections on Transnational Citizenship*, trans. James Swenson (Princeton: Princeton University Press, 2003).

60. Bataille draws on the figure of the child to elaborate on this situation. We laugh our "happiest" laugh at a child falling in front of us, because a child is insufficient, joyfully so. In this, of course, we laugh at adult insufficiency which masquerades as sufficiency: "But just as the child grows up, so does laughter. In its innocent form, it takes place in the same sense as does the constitution of society . . . laughter puts those whom it assembles into unanimous convulsions . . . by a necessary reversal, it returns from the child to the father, from the periphery to the center, each time that the father or the center betray, in their turn, their insufficiency" (90).

61. Another way to say this is to say that we laugh because we are not God. Once Nietzsche pronounced the death of God, there was the inevitable thought that "I" might be God. Burst of laughter. "I" cannot be God precisely on account of my insufficiency. Moreover, one discovers that God himself was not God. He too laughed, eventually drowning himself in laughter. It is the Nietzschean story Pierre Klossowski tells: "when a god wanted to be the only God, all of the other gods were seized with uncontrollable laughter, until they laughed to *death*." Quoted by Maurice Blanchot, "The Laughter of the Gods," in *Friendship*, trans. Elizabeth Rotenberg (Stanford: Stanford University Press, 1997), 169–182.

62. Aristotle, *Nicomachean Ethics*, II, 7.

63. For the etymological affinities between laughter and heat and laughter and dance, see Daniel Ménager, *La Renaissance et le rire* (Paris: Presses Universitaires de France, 1995), 11–12.

64. Hollier, *The College of Sociology*, xvii.

65. Nancy, *The Inoperative Community*, 24.

66. Jean-Luc Nancy, "Laughter Presence," in *The Birth to Presence*, trans. Brian Holmes (Stanford: Stanford University Press, 1993), 368; my emphasis.

67. Bataille writes in *Erotism*: "Not every woman is a potential prostitute, but prostitution is the logical consequence of the feminine attitude. In so far as she is attractive, a woman is a prey to men's desire. Unless she refuses completely because she is determined to remain chaste, the question is at what price and under what circumstances she will yield. But if the conditions are fulfilled she always offers herself as an object. Prostitution proper only brings in a commercial element." Georges Bataille, *Erotism: Death and Sensuality*, trans. Mary Dalwood (San Francisco: City Lights Publishers, 1986), 131. Stripped of a few Bataille-specific flavors, this is the "traffic in women" argument Bataille develops in dialog with Marcel Mauss's *The Gift*.

68. Bataille, "Madame Edwarda," in *The Bataille Reader*, 229–230 (OC, 3: 21; translation modified).

69. Jacques Derrida, *On Touching: Jean-Luc Nancy*, trans. Christine Irizarry (Stanford: Stanford University Press, 2005), 307.

70. Bataille, "Madame Edwarda," 229.

71. This kiss is analogous to Angela of Foligno's kissing the wound on Christ's side. "God is a whore," comes Lacan's gloss on Bataille, in the context of his reflections on Seminar III, largely dedicated to Freud's reading of Schreber's diary, itself a fantasy of a sexual encounter with God. Elizabeth Roudinesco calls Lacan's Seminar XX, *Encore*, "an act of homage to the Bataille of *Madame Edwarda*, to the absolute hatred and love of God." Quoted in Hollywood, *Sensible Ecstasy*, 117.

72. Bataille, "Madame Edwarda," 231.

73. Georges Bataille, *The Impossible: A Story of Rats, Followed by Dianus and Oresteia*, trans. Robert Hurley (San Francisco: City Lights Publishers, 1991), 92.

74. This is the anticipated response to what would become Nancy's objection: "In spite of Bataille, and yet with him, we should try to say the following: love does not expose the entire community, it does not capture or effect its essence purely and simply—not even as the impossible itself." Nancy, *The Inoperative Community*, 21, 36.

75. Bataille, "Madame Edwarda," 231.

76. Nancy, *The Inoperative Community*, 31, 76–77.

77. Blanchot's conflict with Nancy over the reading of Bataille also takes the form of different attempts to think about stages in Bataille's thought. Blanchot reminds Nancy of Bataille's infidelity to his own thought. Bataille has not produced a work; being inconsistent and contradictory is consistent with his style ("I slowly became a stranger to the project which I had formulated" [57]). Blanchot's juxtaposing of the two essays that make up *The Unavowable Community* speaks to his refusal to perform a synthesis of Bataille's work. Nancy would return to

this problematic in his essay "Exscription," acknowledging the impossibility of a "commentary on Bataille." See Nancy, "Exscription," in *The Birth to Presence*, 336.

78. Blanchot, *The Unavowable Community*, 41. In order to properly account for the series of "How not to think here of Madame Edwarda?" in this constellation of texts, one would have to include a discussion of Jean-François Lyotard's invocation of Edwarda in his reading of Marx's "libidinal economy." See Jean-François Lyotard, *Libidinal Economy*, trans. Iain Hamilton (Bloomington: Indiana University Press, 1993), 137–143.

79. Blanchot, *The Unavowable Community*, 47–48.

80. Derrida, *On Touching*, 22.

81. Jean-Luc Nancy, "Laughter in the Throat of Death," MLN 102, no. 4 (1987), 719–736; Nancy, "Laughter Presence."

82. Nancy, "Laughter Presence," 369.

83. Ibid., 372. Derrida makes a similar point when he writes: "Everything has doubtless already been said on laughter in Joyce, on parody, satire, derision, humor, irony, raillery. And on his Homeric laughter and his Rabelaisian laughter. It remains perhaps to think of laughter, as, precisely, a remains. What does laughter want to say? What does laughter want? [*Qu'est-ce que ça veut dire, le rire? Qu'est-ce que ça veut rire?*]" Jacques Derrida, "Ulysses Gramophone: Hear Say Yes in Joyce," in *Acts of Literature*, ed. Derek Attridge (New York: Routledge, 1991), 291.

84. Nancy, "Laughter Presence," 378.

85. Ibid., 368. See also the affinities between Nancy's "Laughter Presence" and Derrida's gloss on Mallarmé's *Mimique* in "Double Session," in *Disseminations*, trans. Barbara Johnson (Chicago: University of Chicago Press, 1981).

86. Art history knows of one fatal case of laughter, captured by the famous anecdote: One day an old woman comes to Zeuxis, the ancient Greek portraitist and known master of realistic illusion. She asks him to paint the portrait of Venus. The painter agrees, and the old woman announces that she will sit for the portrait herself. Zeuxis completes the painting and dies laughing looking at it.

87. Nancy borrows from Bataille the vocabulary of touching that Derrida underscores in Nancy's work. Bataille anticipates Derrida's "astonishment" when faced with some of Nancy's formulations of a "touching" which remains too close to the possibility of "attaining" or "reaching" the limit of inner experience. Bataille himself agrees that "I am never sure of having attained it" (42). Or (86), "In truth, we cannot say of the summit that it is situated here or there. (In a certain sense it is never reached.)" See Derrida, *On Touching*, 116.

88. Bataille, "The Use-Value of D. A. F. de Sade," 147. Derrida would intervene in this conversation to show his concern for its urgency as well as to emphasize the risks of thinking community on the model of friendship. Derrida reads Nietzsche against Carl Schmitt, to argue for a mutation in our understanding

of friendship that displaces Schmitt's friend/enemy distinction. This friendship allows us to think a nonsymmetrical, nonreciprocal relation with a new figure, the friend-enemy. Despite the appeal of this promise, Derrida would nonetheless insist that friendship, given the proximity of the figure of the friend to that of the brother, continues to reproduce the old operation of exclusion: "Not a woman in sight. . . . In vain would you look for a figure of a woman, a feminine silhouette, and the slightest allusion to sexual difference" (Derrida, *The Politics of Friendship*, 155–156). The figure Derrida is ultimately interested in, in light of the question of sexual difference in this context, is no longer Edwarda—the lover, the prostitute, the woman under contract. What would it mean to ask the question of sexual difference around the figure of the sister? In his exchanges with Cixous, Derrida gives her the name of "insister"—the sister, the one who insists. See Hélène Cixous, *Insister of Jacques Derrida*, trans. Peggy Kamuf (Edinburgh: Edinburgh University Press, 2007).

89. A dimension of this authorial vanity was Bataille's republication of "Madame Edwarda" under his own name.

90. Maurice Blanchot, "The Main Impropriety," *Yale French Studies*, no. 39, "Literature and Revolution" (1967), 50–63.

91. Blanchot, *The Infinite Conversation*, 331.

92. Bataille and Blanchot seem to be drawing on Wordsworth's line here: "The sea was laughing at a distance." William Wordsworth, *The Five-Book Prelude* (Oxford: Blackwell, 1997), IV, 135.

93. Nancy, "Laughter Presence," 392.

CHAPTER 4

1. Hélène Cixous, "Castration or Decapitation?," trans. Annette Kuhn, *Signs* 7, no. 1 (Autumn 1981), 41–55; first published as "Le sexe ou la tête," in *Les Cahiers du GRIF*, no. 13 (1976), 5–15.

2. Sun-tzu, *The Art of War*, trans. Ralph D. Sawyer (Boulder: Westview Press, 1994). It should be acknowledged that the invocation of the Chinese story by Cixous is a variation on the "Chinese prejudice," an anti-ethnocentrism that cannot escape being ethnocentric. The debate on the "Chinese prejudice" has been prompted by Derrida's use of the phrase in *Of Grammatology*. See Jacques Derrida, *Of Grammatology*, trans. Gayatri Chakravorty Spivak (Baltimore: Johns Hopkins University Press, 1997).

3. Sun-tzu, *The Art of War*, 81.

4. On varieties of silence, see Marnia Lazreg, *The Eloquence of Silence* (New York: Routledge, 1994).

5. Hélène Cixous, "The Laugh of the Medusa," trans. Keith Cohen and Paula Cohen, *Signs* 1, no. 4 (Summer 1976); first published as "Le rire de la Méduse," *L'Arc*

61, special issue, "Simone de Beauvoir et la lutte des femmes" (1975), 39–54. The essay is a classic of "French feminism," despite Cixous's repeatedly expressed reservations vis-à-vis feminism. It has, in fact, become customary to note Cixous's reservations in passing as scholars continue to frame her work in feminist terms. Focusing exclusively on Cixous's fiction, Derrida draws attention to this trend, which he understands as a form of resistance to reading. Derrida speaks of "the feminist institution in all its forms, wherever, in the name of *woman*, a regime [*pouvoir*] sets up its machinery for appropriation, inspection and capitalization. The most blatant figure is this army, the armed woman who, without reading, without translating the enchanting chant of letter and language, finds her paltry stratagem and her allies in the reductive manipulation that consists in classifying the name and the work of Hélène Cixous among the 'great-French-women-theorists-of-the-feminine' (feminine-writing, feminine-sexuality, etc.)." See Jacques Derrida, *H.C. for Life, That Is to Say . . .*, trans. Laurent Milesi and Stefan Herbrechter (Stanford: Stanford University Press, 2006), 140. Derrida's surprisingly harsh words about feminism and feminist practices of nonreading notwithstanding, the goal here is to read patiently, as many other feminist scholars have, and to struggle to hear the laughing resonances of what Derrida calls "the enchanting chant."

6. See Susan Rubin Suleiman, *Subversive Intent: Gender, Politics, and the Avant-garde* (Cambridge, Mass.: Harvard University Press, 1990), 17.

7. Hélène Cixous and Catherine Clément, *The Newly Born Woman*, trans. Betsy Wing (Minneapolis: University of Minnesota Press, 1986), 33.

8. Ibid., 39.

9. Cixous, "Castration or Decapitation?," 49.

10. See Sander Gilman, "The Image of the Hysteric," in *Hysteria beyond Freud*, ed. Sander Gilman et al. (Berkeley: University of California Press, 1993). See also Ilza Veith, *Hysteria: The History of a Disease* (Chicago: University of Chicago Press, 1965). Veith mentions only two instances in the long history of the disease when hysterics are described laughing, in fact alternating fits of laughter and crying.

11. Sigmund Freud, "Fragments of an Analysis of a Case of Hysteria" (1905), in *The Standard Edition of the Complete Psychological Works of Sigmund Freud*, ed. James Strachey (London: Hogarth Press and the Institute of Psycho-Analysis, 1953–1974), 7: 22. The *Standard Edition* is cited hereafter as SE.

12. Georges Didi-Huberman's *Invention of Hysteria* imagines Augustine's attitude along laughter lines: "Surrendered to the mad tremors of the fit, Augustine would laugh. . . . She would cry out and stick out her tongue. Was she mocking the photographer? . . . Augustine would vociferate, laugh and vomit, all at once." Georges Didi-Huberman, *Invention of Hysteria: Charcot and the Photographic Iconography of the Salpêtrière*, trans. Alisa Hartz (Cambridge, Mass.: MIT Press, 2004), 261.

13. Derrida draws attention to the complexity of Cixous's relation to Freud: "And neither psychoanalysis nor Freud and his kinfolk can escape the analytical irony,

which is the very element, the laughter of this often tender, sometime implacable poetics, all the less so since, by a felicitous turn of history, Uncle Freud is part of the family." Derrida, *H.C. for Life*, 31.

14. Hélène Cixous, *Portrait of Dora*, trans. Anita Barrows (London: John Calder, 1977); first published as *Portrait de Dora* (Paris: Des femmes, 1976).

15. Quoted in Susan Sellers, *Hélène Cixous: Authorship, Autobiography and Love* (Cambridge: Polity Press, 1996), 76.

16. Cixous, *Portrait of Dora*, 29.

17. Leonora Carrington, *The Hearing Trumpet* (Boston: Exact Change, 1996), 46.

18. On the affinities between laughing and crying, see Charles Darwin, *The Expression of the Emotions in Man and Animals* (London: John Murray, 1872). Darwin had a photograph of Oscar Rejlander in which Rejlander is sitting next to his famous photograph known as "Ginx's Baby," which depicts a baby crying vehemently. Rejlander had written on the back of the photograph: "There I laughed. Ha! Ha! Ha! Violently—In the other I cried . . . e e e. . . . And yet how similar the expression." Quoted in Christopher Turner, "Tears of Laughter," *Cabinet Magazine* 17 (Spring 2004).

19. On the old hag and the risks of laughing and "making an exhibition of oneself," see Mary Russo, *The Female Grotesque: Risk, Excess, and Modernity* (New York: Routledge, 1994).

20. For Cixous's reading practices, see especially her relation with Clarice Lispector in *Vivre l'orange / To Live the Orange* (Paris: Des femmes, 1979); and *Reading with Clarice Lispector*, trans. Verena Andermatt Conley (Minneapolis: University of Minnesota Press, 1990).

21. Ovid, *The Metamorphoses*, trans. Rolfe Humphries (Bloomington: Indiana University Press, 1955), 103.

22. Sigmund Freud, "Medusa's Head" (1922), SE 18: 274. Freud is referring to the episode in *Gargantua and Pantagruel* in which a devil, who is about to enter a scratching match with a farmer, is scared away by the farmer's wife, who terrifies him with a story: "he [the husband] did but just touch me with his little finger here betwixt the legs, and has spoiled me for ever . . . she uncovered herself up to the chin, after the manner in which the Persian women met their children who fled from the fight, and plainly showed her what do ye call them. The frightened devil, seeing the enormous solution of the continuity in all its dimensions, blessed himself, and cried out, Mahon, Demiourgon, Megaera, Alecto, Persephone! 'slife, catch me here when he comes! I am gone! 'sdeath, what a gash!" François Rabelais, *Gargantua and Pantagruel*, chapter 4.XLVII.

23. Neil Hertz, "Medusa's Head: Male Hysteria under Political Pressure," *Representations* 4 (1983), 29.

24. On the temporality of revolution, see Jacques Derrida, "Force of Law: The 'Mystical Foundation of Authority,'" in *Deconstruction and the Possibility of Justice*, ed. Drucilla Cornel et al. (New York: Routledge, 1992).

25. Jack J. Spector, "Medusa on the Barricades," *American Imago* 53, no. 1 (1996), 28.

26. For a reading of this poem, see Carol Jacobs, "On Looking at Shelley's Medusa," *Yale French Studies*, no. 69, "The Lesson of Paul de Man" (1985), 163–179.

27. W. J. T. Mitchell, *Picture Theory: Essays on Verbal and Visual Representation* (Chicago: University of Chicago Press, 1995).

28. Cixous, "The Laugh of the Medusa," 885.

29. Ibid.

30. Hélène Cixous, "Without End No State of Drawingness or, Rather: The Executioner's Taking off," trans. A. F. MacGillivray, *New Literary History* 24, no. 1, "Culture and Everyday Life" (Winter 1993), 92.

31. This is a response to a series of critiques of the privileging of vision in Western modernity. Both Cixous and Nancy insist that the critique of vision needs to be accompanied by work on the eye.

32. Jean-Luc Nancy, *Corpus*, trans. Richard A. Rand (New York: Fordham University Press, 2008), 31.

33. Ibid., 45.

34. Hélène Cixous and Jacques Derrida, *Veils* (Stanford: Stanford University Press, 2001), 9, 12.

35. Ibid., 9. See also Hélène Cixous, *Insister of Jacques Derrida*, trans. Peggy Kamuf (Edinburgh: Edinburgh University Press, 2007), 183.

36. For the long history of figural uses of the Medusa, see *The Medusa Reader*, ed. Marjorie Garber and Nancy J. Vickers (New York: Routledge, 2003).

37. On statues in the philosophical tradition, see Daniel Heller-Roazen, *The Inner Touch: Archeology of a Sensation* (New York: Zone Books, 2009), 222–236.

38. Ovid, *Metamorphoses*, 114.

39. Ibid.

40. Ibid., 113.

41. I am drawing here on Mladen Dolar's essay "The Voice and the Stone: From Hegel to Beckett" (unpublished manuscript).

42. Teresa de Lauretis, *Alice Doesn't: Feminism, Semiotics, Cinema* (Bloomington: Indiana University Press, 1984), 136.

43. Avital Ronell, *The Telephone Book: Technology, Schizophrenia, Electric Speech* (Lincoln: University of Nebraska Press, 1989), 97.

44. Jean-Pierre Vernant adds an important twist to the story: "What Baubo actually displays to Demeter is her genitals made up as a face, a face in the form of genitals; one might even say, the genitals made into a mask. By its grimace, this

genital face becomes a burst of laughter . . .". Jean-Pierre Vernant, "Death in the Eyes: Gorgo, Figure of the Other," in Garber and Vickers, *The Medusa Reader*, 213.

45. Propp discusses a number of instances in which laughter has "the capacity to evoke vegetable life" through the mediation of a goddess or goddess figure. See Vladimir Propp, "Ritual Laughter in Folklore: A Propos of the Tale of the Princess Who Would Not Laugh [Nesmejána]," in *Theory and History of Folklore*, trans. Ariadna Y. Martin and Richard P. Martin (Minneapolis: University of Minnesota Press, 1984), 137.

46. See Jon Bird, Jo Anna Isaak, and Sylvère Lotringer, *Nancy Spero* (London: Phaidon Press, 1996).

47. Mikhail Bakhtin, *Rabelais and His World*, trans. Hélène Iswolsky (Bloomington: Indiana University Press, 1984), 26. On the threatening dimension of the mouth, see the short fragment titled "Mouth" in Georges Bataille, *Visions of Excess: Selected Writings 1927–1939*, trans. Allan Stoekl (Minneapolis: University of Minnesota Press, 1985), 59.

48. Sigmund Freud, "The 'Uncanny,'" SE 17: 245.

49. Ibid.

50. Cixous, "The Laugh of the Medusa," 885.

51. Glossing the same passages in Freud, Derrida further plays with the homonymy of *le voile* (veil) and *la voile* (sail). The veil that hides is also one that moves along the sea. See Cixous and Derrida, *Veils*, 59.

52. Cixous, "The Laugh of the Medusa," 882.

53. Quentin Skinner, "Hobbes and the Classical Theory of Laughter," in *Visions of Politics*, vol. 3 (Cambridge: Cambridge University Press, 2002), 166. On the uses of laughter in political debate, see also the chapter on the "rire parlementaire" in Antoine de Baecque, *Les éclats du rire: La culture des rieurs au XVIIIe siècle* (Paris: Calmann-Lévy, 2000).

54. Cicero, *De oratore*, I, 372.

55. Annie Leclerc, "Woman's Word," in *New French Feminisms: An Anthology*, ed. Elaine Marks and Isabelle de Courtivron (Amherst: University of Massachusetts Press, 1980), 79. The idea has a longer feminist history, going back at least to Virginia Woolf: "And then I went on warily, on the very tips of my toes (so cowardly am I, so afraid of the lash that was once almost laid on my own shoulders), to murmur that she should also learn to laugh, without bitterness, at the vanities—say rather at the peculiarities, for it is a less offensive word—of the other sex." Virginia Woolf, *A Room of One's Own* (Orlando, Fl.: Harcourt, 1957), 98–99.

56. Leclerc, "Woman's Word," 79.

57. Cixous, "The Laugh of the Medusa," 887.

58. On the textual practice performed by the verb *voler*, see Claudine Hermann, *Tongue Snatchers* [*Les voleuses de langue*], trans. Nancy Kline (Lincoln: University of Nebraska Press, 1991).

59. Nathalie Sarraute, *Do You Hear Them?*, trans. Maria Jolas (Normal, Ill.: Dalkey Archive Press, 2004), 1; first published as *Vous les entendez?* (Paris: Gallimard, 1972). All parenthetical references in this section are to the English edition of Sarraute's novel.

60. It would be productive to draw an analogy between Sarraute's father and the paranoid king in Italo Calvino's "The King Listens." Eve Sedgwick describes paranoid reading in terms of "a distinctively rigid relation to temporality, at once anticipatory and retroactive, averse above all to surprise." In this context, what paranoid reading is averse to is the surprise of a burst of laughter. See Eve Kosofsky Sedgwick, "Paranoid Reading and Reparative Reading; or, You're So Paranoid, You Probably Think This Introduction Is about You," in *Novel Gazing* (Durham: Duke University Press, 1997), 24.

61. On the single trait (*einzigen Zug*), see Sigmund Freud, *Group Psychology and the Analysis of the Ego* (1921), SE 18: 107.

62. On water-sound, see Douglas Kahn, *Noise, Water, Meat: A History of Sounds in the Arts* (Cambridge, Mass.: MIT Press, 1999), 245–259.

63. Adriana Cavarero, *For More than One Voice: Toward a Philosophy of Vocal Expression*, trans. Paul Kottman (Stanford: Stanford University Press, 2004), 134.

64. On the distinction between listening and hearing, see Mladen Dolar, *A Voice and Nothing More* (Cambridge, Mass.: MIT Press, 2006), 148.

65. Deleuze and Guattari write in *What Is Philosophy?*: "Actually, *utopia is what links* philosophy with its own epoch, with European capitalism, but also already with the Greek city. In each case it is with utopia that philosophy becomes political and takes the criticism of its own time to its highest point. Utopia does not split off from the infinite movement: etymologically it stands for absolute deterritorialization but always at the critical point at which it is connected with the present relative milieu, and especially with the forces stifled by this milieu. *Erewhon*, the word used by Samuel Butler, refers not only to no-where but also to now-here." Gilles Deleuze and Félix Guattari, *What Is Philosophy?*, trans. Hugh Tomlinson and Graham Burchell (New York: Columbia University Press, 1994), 99–100.

66. Amy Hollywood, *Sensible Ecstasy: Mysticism, Sexual Difference, and the Demands of History* (Chicago: University of Chicago Press, 2002), 270.

67. Derrida's book on Cixous repeats the old argument: he himself is on the side of death, while Cixous remains on the side of life. Cixous responded to Derrida's book with *Insister*, recognizing herself in it only partially. One possible counterpoint to Derrida's reading is a Bataille-inspired episode Cixous recounts in *Rootprints*. When told about the death of a cousin, "I burst out laughing. Death went through me and I laughed." See Hélène Cixous and Mireille Calle-Gruber,

Rootprints: Memory and Life Writing (New York: Routledge, 1997), 26. On feminism's relation to "to die laughing," see my "To Die Laughing and to Laugh at Dying: Revisiting *The Awakening*," *New Literary History* 36, no. 3 (2005), 477–495.

68. Mary Ann Doane, "Masquerade Reconsidered: Further Thoughts on the Female Spectator," in *Femmes Fatales: Feminism, Film Theory, Psychoanalysis* (New York: Routledge, 1991), 33–43. Sianne Ngai has revisited the issue in "The Zany Science: Post-Fordist Performance and the Problem of Fun" (unpublished manuscript).

69. The humorless feminist is the one who does not get the joke (usually at her own expense). In a different context, Meaghan Morris writes about her: "woman as constitutionally *heavy*—the stolid, earthbound beast, the killjoy, the moral over- seer, the puritanical cleaner of speech, the guardian of social custom (if not symbolic law) . . . that dreaded figure who looms so large in our language that women toil untold hours over their prose to write her off—the humorless femi- nist." See Meaghan Morris, "in any event . . .," in *Men in Feminism*, ed. Alice Jardine and Paul Smith (New York: Methuen, 1987), 176.

70. Doane, "Masquerade Reconsidered," 41.

71. Samuel Weber, "Laughing in the Meanwhile," *MLN* 102, no. 4 (September 1987), 695.

72. Luce Irigaray, *This Sex Which Is Not One*, trans. Catherine Porter and Carolyn Burke (Ithaca: Cornell University Press, 1985), 208.

CHAPTER 5

1. For one account of the century of cinema, see Laura Mulvey's *Death 24x Second*. Mulvey quotes Antoine de Becque: "the cinema has made flesh the history of the century." Laura Mulvey, *Death 24x Second: Stillness and the Moving Image* (London: Reak- tion Books, 2006), 24–25.

2. In addition to the historical arguments about laughter and visual decorum discussed in chapter 1, and the philosophical arguments about laughter and pres- ence developed in chapter 3, one would have to revisit at least two other counts on which one can explain why there are very few laughs in the history of paint- ing. One is the time of laughter. When it attempts to deal with time, painting most often has recourse to narrative; it needs to narrativize time so it can spatial- ize it. Laughter is a challenge to narrative; a burst, it inhabits a dense "now" that resists narrativization and spatialization. Second, and in close relation to this, is the sound of laughter. Part of the challenge laughter poses to painting is that of the need to visualize sound, to make the eye hear. On the possibility of listening to painting, see Jean-Luc Nancy, *Listening* (New York: Fordham University Press, 2007).

3. Charles Darwin, *The Expression of the Emotions in Man and Animals* (London: John Murray, 1872), 15.

4. Ibid., 2.

5. Ibid., 13.

6. Darwin included the following NB with his "List of Illustrations": "Several of the figures in these seven Heliotype Plates have been reproduced from photographs, instead of from the original negatives; and they are in consequence somewhat indistinct. Nevertheless they are faithful copies, and are much superior for my purpose to any drawing, however carefully executed." Ibid., vi.

7. Darwin, The Expression of the Emotions, 202, 208.

8. Others would answer Darwin's question. Anthony Ludovici proposed an evolutionary theory according to which the baring of the teeth in laughter was originally the assertion of one's physical prowess in the face of an enemy. Albert Rapp offered a similar hypothesis, according to which laughter was originally born out of hatred and aggressivity. In Rapp's words, laughter was "basically and categorically savage" (13). Having developed out of "the roar of triumph in an ancient jungle duel" (21), "it was an immediate and vigorous announcement of victory" (23). Anthony Ludovici, The Secret of Laughter (New York: Viking, 1933); Albert Rapp, The Origins of Wit and Humor (New York: E. P. Dutton, 1951).

9. Quoted in Stephanie Spencer, O. G. Rejlander: Photography as Art (Ann Arbor: UMI Research Press, 1981), 114.

10. One of Rejlander's photographs depicted a little cupid (photography) offering a brush to a painter standing by. See Oscar Gustave Rejlander 1813 (?)–1875 (Stockholm: Modern Museum, 1998), 27.

11. Henry Peach Robinson, The Studio: And What to Do in It (New York: Arno Press, 1973), 45.

12. Ibid., 94.

13. Ibid., 95. As an alternative to Robinson's suggestion, an article in The Amateur Photographer titled "In Consequence of a Smile" would later propose that the photographer catch not the smile itself, which could lead to "an expression that is not so very different from the diabolical grin of demoniacal fury," but its aftermath: "let him smile, and then, as the smile is disappearing, not before, make a quick exposure." A. F. Hirshfeld, "In Consequence of a Smile," The Amateur Photographer, February 18, 1908.

14. "A REALLY beautiful smile, natural, without the taint of artifice, is one of the rarest, as well as the most delightful, inventions of nature," Robinson wrote. He followed Darwin in arguing that the smile is the result of evolution, but believed that by the late nineteenth century it had been overdone and was dying out. Robinson, The Studio, 104.

15. Ibid., 94.

16. Ibid., 110.

17. Ibid., 107.

18. Ibid., 108.

19. *The Photographic News*, September 24, 1886. In *The Photography of O. G. Rejlander*, ed. Peter C. Bunnell (New York: Arno Press, 1979).

20. In 1807, Henry Siddons's *Practical Illustrations of Rhetorical Gesture and Action* translated some of the principles of expression developed in painting for the world of the theater. Reissued in 1822, the book was influential throughout the nineteenth century. Siddons imagined its 69 illustrations as a catalog of theatrical facial expression. Two etchings depicted laughter: one is "Vulgar Triumph," an old, toothless witchy woman, cackling; the other is "Mirth," a man sitting in a chair, tranquil, mouth almost closed, apparently singing merrily. Henry Siddons, *Practical Illustrations of Rhetorical Gesture and Action, Adapted to the English Drama, from a Work on the Subject by M. Engel* (London: Sherwood, Neely and Jones, 1822). On the history of theatrical expression, see Joseph Roach, *The Player's Passion: Studies in the Science of Acting* (Ann Arbor: University of Michigan Press, 1993). In order to do justice to the subject, one would have to trace the history of what is called a "theatrical laugh," arguably one of the most immediate signs of theatricality *tout court*, and account for the relation between stage directions like "[laughter]," their frequent transcription as "ha ha ha," and actual laughs laughed by actors on stage.

21. Darwin, *The Expression of the Emotions*, 5.

22. G.-B. Duchenne de Boulogne, *The Mechanism of Human Facial Expression*, trans. R. Andrew Cuthbertson (Cambridge: Cambridge University Press, 1990), 1.

23. Charles Bell, *The Anatomy and Philosophy of Expression as Connected to the Fine Arts* (London: George Bell and Sons, 1888), 197.

24. Duchenne, *The Mechanism of Human Facial Expression*, 34.

25. Ibid., 39.

26. Ibid., 42.

27. Ibid., 43.

28. Darwin's method included showing this last photograph to twenty-four persons, whom he asked to identify what they saw. The result: "three could not in the least tell what it meant, whilst the others, though they perceived that the expression was of the nature of the smile, answered in such words as 'a wicked joke,' 'trying to laugh,' 'grinning laughter,' 'half-amazed laughter.'" The problem, as explained by Duchenne, was that only one muscle was galvanized in this instance: *zygomaticus major* ("the muscle of joy"). Real, natural laughter, however, mobilizes two muscles—*zygomaticus major* and *orbicularis oculi*. The test of real laughter, according to Duchenne, is in the eyes.

29. Duchenne, *The Mechanism of Human Facial Expression*, 69. Darwin's own collection of photographic expression included other photographs—like "Laughing Slightly" or "Laughing Girl"—that also did not make it on the plate in *Expression*.

30. On Darwin's involvement in the manipulation of images in *Expression*, see Jonathan Smith, *Charles Darwin and Victorian Visual Culture* (Cambridge: Cambridge University Press, 2006).

31. Hugo's laughing man was little known as a literary character. Perhaps appropriately, he came to life in Paul Leni's expressionist film *The Man Who Laughs* (1928).

32. Duchenne also experimented with the facial muscles of actual cadavers. See G.-B. Duchenne de Boulogne, *De l'électrisation localisée et de son application à la physiologie, à la pathologie et à la thérapeutique* (Paris: Chez J.-B. Baillière, 1855), 390–391.

33. In painting, laughter's proximity to death led to a number of variations on Zeuxis's laughing death. A brief history of this theme would pass through Rembrandt's *Self-Portrait as Zeuxis* (1662), Arent de Gelder's *Self-Portrait as Zeuxis* (1685), Joseph Ducreux's *Self-Portrait as Mocker* (1770), Jean-Étienne Liotard's *Liotard Laughing* (1770), and Richard Gerstl's *Self-Portrait Laughing* (1908).

34. A contemporary review by Ernest Lacan described the photograph: "Here Pierrot is laughing uncontrollably; his mouth is gaping all the way to his ears, his nose rising all the way to his eyebrows, his tiny black eyes vanishing under the folds of the lids; he is rubbing his hands and arching his back...." Quoted in *Nadar*, ed. Maria Morris Hambourg, Françoise Heilbrun, and Philippe Néagu (New York: Metropolitan Museum of Art, 1995), 41.

35. Edward Groom, *The Art of Transparent Painting on Glass for the Magic Lantern* (Windsor and Newton, c. 1865), 50. In *A History of Pre-cinema*, ed. Stephen Herbert, 2 vols. (London: Routledge, 2000), 2: 290.

36. W. J. Chadwick, *The Magic Lantern Manual* (London: Frederick Warne, 1878), 10. In Herbert, *A History of Pre-cinema*, 2: 307.

37. Marta Braun, *Picturing Time: The Work of Étienne-Jules Marey (1830–1904)* (Chicago: University of Chicago Press, 1992).

38. Étienne-Jules Marey, *Movement* (New York: Arno Press, 1972), 182.

39. Ibid., 180; French edition used is Étienne-Jules Marey, *Le mouvement* (Paris: G. Masson, 1894), 176.

40. See Laurent Mannoni, *Étienne-Jules Marey: La mémoire de l'œil* (Paris: Cinémathèque française, 1999), 292.

41. "The Story of a Smile," *New Penny Magazine*, December 1901. In Herbert, *A History of Pre-cinema*, 1: 109.

42. Ibid.

43. Ray Allister, *Friese-Greene: Close-up of an Inventor* (London: Marsland, 1948), 32.

44. On sound in pre-sound film, see Douglas Kahn, *Noise, Water, Meat: A History of Sounds in the Arts* (Cambridge, Mass.: MIT Press, 1999), 139–156.

45. Mary Ann Doane, "The Close-Up: Scale and Detail in the Cinema," *differences: A Journal of Feminist Cultural Studies* 14, no. 3 (2003), 89–111.

46. Among them, *Fred Ott's Sneeze* and *May Irwin–John Rice Kiss*. See Tom Gunner, "In Your Face: Physiognomy, Photography, and the Gnostic Mission of Early Film," *Modernism/Modernity* 4, no. 1 (1997), 1–29.

47. Erich von Stroheim's *Greed* (1924) would push the implications of this scene.

48. See Michel Dechaume, *Histoire illustrée de l'art dentaire: Stomatologie et odontologie* (Paris: R. Dacosta, 1977), 331.

49. There is a long visual tradition of tooth-pulling, which almost always uses a class-determined patient. See David Kunzle, "The Art of Pulling Teeth in the Seventeenth and Nineteenth Centuries: From Public Martyrdom to Private Nightmare and Political Struggle," in *Fragments for a History of the Human Body*, vol. 3, ed. Michel Feher, Ramona Naddaff, and Nadia Tazi (New York: Zone, 1989), 28–89. Kunzle also draws attention to the fact that toothache has been historically associated with sexual licentiousness and subsequent guilt.

50. There is also an iconography of the laughing gas party, which is often presented as an unleashed orgy. See *The Roots of Dentistry*, ed. Christine Hillam (London: British Dental Association, 1990), 27.

51. See Jan Nederveen Pieterse, *White on Black: Images of Africa and Blacks in Western Popular Culture* (New Haven: Yale University Press, 1995), 206.

52. Linda Williams, *Hard Core: Power, Pleasure, and the "Frenzy of the Visible"* (Berkeley: University of California Press, 1999), 47.

53. James Agee's assessment of early film's investment in laughter is well known, but the orgasmic touches in his description have rarely been noted: "In the language of screen comedians four of the main grades of laugh are the titter, the yowl, the belly laugh and the boffo. The titter is just a titter. The yowl is a runaway titter. Anyone who has had the pleasure knows all about a belly laugh. The boffo is the laugh that kills. An ideally good gag, perfectly constructed and played, would bring the victim up this ladder of laughs by cruelly controlled degrees to the top rung, and would then proceed to wobble, shake, wave and brandish the ladder until he groaned for mercy. Then, after the shortest possible time out for recuperation, he would feel the first wicked tickling of the comedian's whip once more and start up a new ladder." James Agee, "Comedy's Greatest Era," in *Film Theory and Criticism*, ed. Gerald Mast and Marshall Cohen (New York: Oxford University Press, 1985), 482.

54. Dziga Vertov, *Kino-Eye: The Writings of Dziga Vertov*, ed. Annette Michelson, trans. Kevin O'Brien (Berkeley: University of California Press, 1984), 83.

55. Ibid., 316.

56. Ibid., 41.

57. Ibid., 168.

58. Ibid., 59. Vertov called for the elimination of the literary and theatrical representation he saw in American cinema, which he understood in terms of psychologism. He admired Dos Passos: "I am accused of corrupting Dos Passos by having infected him with kino-eye. Otherwise, he might have become a good writer. Others object and say that if it were not for kino-eye, we wouldn't have heard of Dos Passos. Dos Passos' work involves a translation from film-vision into literary language." Ibid., 174.

59. Ibid., 168.

60. Ibid., 155.

61. Vertov admired two things in American cinema: "the rapid shot changes and the close-ups" (Kino-Eye, 6). He shared his fascination with film theorists of his time in bourgeois Europe. Jean Epstein, a believer in cinema as "truth-machine," expressed his own love of close-ups in terms that resonate here: "I will never find a way to say how I love American close-ups. Point blank. A head suddenly appears on the screen and drama, now face to face, seems to address me personally and swells with an extraordinary intensity. I am hypnotized. Now the tragedy is anatomical. The decor of the fifth act is this corner of a cheek torn by a smile. Waiting for the moment when 1,000 meters of intrigue converge in a muscular dénouement satisfies me more than the rest of the film. Muscular preambles ripple beneath the skin. Shadows shift, tremble, hesitate. Something is being decided. A breeze of emotion underlines the mouth with clouds. The orography of the face vacillates. Seismic shocks begin. Capillary wrinkles try to split the fault. A wave carries them away. Crescendo. A muscle bridles. The lip is laced with tics like a theater curtain. Everything is movement, imbalance, crisis. Crack. The mouth gives way, like a ripe fruit splitting open. As if slit by a scalpel, a keyboard-like smile cuts laterally into the corner of the lips. The close-up is the soul of cinema." Jean Epstein, "Magnification and Other Writings," trans. Stuart Liebman, October 3 (Spring 1977): 9. Deleuze is drawing on Kino-Eye when he argues that the close-up is both a face and its effacement: "The close-up is the face, but the face precisely in so far as it has destroyed its triple function [individualization, socialization, communication]—a nudity of the face much greater than that of the body, an inhumanity much greater than that of animals." Gilles Deleuze, Cinema 1: The Movement-Image, trans. Hugh Tomlinson and Barbara Habberjam (Minneapolis: University of Minnesota Press, 1986), 99.

62. Vertov, Kino-Eye, 18.

63. Deleuze admired Vertov for what he perceived was his move away from fluidity, a form of "aquatic lyricism." The alternative to it is a deanthropomorphized "gaseous perception": "for Vertov, the liquid image is still inadequate, failing to reach the particle of matter. Movement must go beyond itself, to its material, energic element. . . . In the final analysis, we would have to speak of a perception which was no longer liquid but gaseous." See Deleuze, Cinema 1, 81, 84.

64. Colin Jones takes this history back to the second part of the eighteenth century, the beginning of dentistry, emerging commercialism, the bourgeois public sphere and its print culture. It is, however, only in the mid-nineteenth century, and in convergence with changes in perception associated with photography, that the mouth truly begins to open. See Colin Jones, "The King's Two Teeth," *History Workshop Journal* 65, no. 1 (2008), 79–95.

65. For a revision of this history, see Sarah Nettleton, *Power, Pain and Dentistry* (Buckingham: Open University Press, 1992).

66. Norbert Elias, "Essay on Laughter" (unpublished manuscript).

67. Paolo Mantegazza, *Physiognomy and Expression* (London: W. Scott, 1899), 113–114.

68. William Mortensen, *The Model: A Book on the Problems of Posing* (San Francisco: Camera Craft Publishing Company, 1937), 38.

69. On the parallel development of dentistry and advertising, see Christine Hillam, *Brass Plate and Brazen Impudence* (Liverpool: Liverpool University Press, 1991), 132–139.

70. See Nettleton, *Power, Pain and Dentistry*.

71. Sarah Nettleton quotes the dentist A. A. Friend: "There should be a correlation between the patient's mouth and her personal happiness." See Nettleton, *Power, Pain and Dentistry*, 48. "Happiness" in this context is also a function of the industry's early advocating of the smile's romantic potential. As early as 1818, an advertisement promised young women that good teeth are guaranteed to win hearts. See Dechaume, *Histoire illustrée de l'art dentaire*, 572.

72. Max Horkheimer and Theodor W. Adorno, "The Culture Industry," in *Dialectic of Enlightenment: Philosophical Fragments*, trans. Edmund Jephcott (Stanford: Stanford University Press, 2002), 109. German edition used is Max Horkheimer and Theodor W. Adorno, *Dialektik der Aufklärung: Philosophische Fragmente* (Frankfurt am Main: S. Fischer Verlag, 1969).

73. Horkheimer and Adorno, "The Culture Industry," 112.

74. Ibid.

75. Theodor W. Adorno, "Is Art Lighthearted?," in *Notes to Literature*, trans. Shierry Weber Nicholsen (New York: Columbia University Press, 1992), 250.

76. Horkheimer and Adorno, "The Culture Industry," 109.

77. Ibid.

78. Theodor W. Adorno, "On the Fetish-Character in Music and the Regression of Listening," in *Essays on Music*, ed. Richard Leppert (Berkeley: University of California Press, 2002).

79. Jane Feuer, "The Concept of Live Television: Ontology as Ideology," in *Regarding Television: Critical Approaches*, ed. E. Ann Kaplan (Frederick, Md.: University Publications of America, 1983), 14.

80. Charley Douglas, "Strictly for Laughs," *Newsweek*, January 10, 1955. Quoted in Jacob Smith, "The Frenzy of the Audible: Pleasure, Authenticity, and Recorded Laughter," *Television New Media* 6, no. 1 (2005), 43.

81. Horkheimer and Adorno, "The Culture Industry," 100.

82. Immanuel Kant, *Critique of Judgment*, trans. Werner S. Pluhar (Indianapolis: Hackett, 1987), 54.

83. Horkheimer and Adorno write: "Laughter about something is always laughter at it [*Verlachen*], and the vital force which, according to Bergson, bursts through rigidity in laughter is, in truth, the irruption of barbarity, the self-assertion which, in convivial settings, dares to celebrate its liberation from scruple." Horkheimer and Adorno, "The Culture Industry," 112.

84. Various attempts to dispense with laugh tracks have proved unsuccessful because they are now recognized as a formal feature of the genre. See Robert Provine, *Laughter: A Scientific Investigation* (New York: Penguin, 2001), 143.

85. Horkheimer and Adorno, "The Culture Industry," 116.

86. See Kathleen Moran and Michael Rogin, "'What's the Matter with Capra?' *Sullivan's Travels* and the Popular Front," *Representations* 71 (Summer 2000), 106–134.

87. See Eric Trump, "Got the Giggles? Join the Club," *New York Times*, July 27, 2002. Another face of the laughter club phenomenon is offered by Mira Nair's documentary *The Laughing Club of India* (2000).

88. This is a trend started by Norman Cousins's 1979 *The Anatomy of an Illness as Perceived by the Patient*, and continued by books like Laurence Peter's 1982 *The Laughter Prescription*. See <http://www.laughtertherapy.com>.

89. Recall the 1968 incident when, in the fervor of the student movement, a few female students in his lecture room exposed their breasts to Professor Adorno. Adorno reacted like a respectable guardian of seriousness. This encounter, Peter Sloterdijk argues, should have been a moment of laughter, but Adorno could not laugh. See Peter Sloterdijk, *Critique of Cynical Reason*, trans. Michael Eldred (Minneapolis: University of Minnesota Press, 1988).

90. Horkheimer and Adorno, "The Culture Industry," 112.

91. Ibid.

92. Kant, *Critique of Judgment*, 54.

93. Theodor W. Adorno, "Chaplin Times Two," trans. John MacKay, *Yale Journal of Criticism* 9, no. 1 (1996), 60.

94. André Bazin, "Charlie Chaplin," in *What Is Cinema?*, vol. 1, trans. Hugh Gray (Berkeley: University of California Press, 2004).

95. Adorno's sentence reads: "Laughter is in league with the guilt of subjectivity, but in the suspension of the law which it announces it also points beyond that complicity. It promises a passage to the homeland." Horkheimer and Adorno,

"Odysseus or Myth and Enlightenment," in *Dialectic of Enlightenment*, 60. Adorno conducted a 1968 seminar on laughter; see "Anmerkungen zum sozialen Konflikt heute: Nach zwei Seminaren," in Theodor W. Adorno, *Soziologische Schriften I* (Frankfurt am Main: Suhrkamp, 1972). See also Shea Coulson, "Funnier than Unhappiness: Adorno and the Art of Laughter," *New German Critique* 34, no. 1 (Winter 2007), 141–163.

96. Adorno, "Is Art Lighthearted?," 253.

97. This is a close-up of an isolated facial trait. Walter Benjamin proposed a new form of physiognomy starting from the reading of such a trait (a grin without the cat). It is a surprising proposal given Benjamin's knowledge of nineteenth-century physiognomy. But Benjamin's vision is of a physiognomy of singularity, which he shared with Béla Balázs. The latter wrote: "In vain does the mouth smile ever so sweetly—the lobe of his ear, the side of a nostril shown in isolated magnification reveal the hidden coarseness and cruelty." If the old, Victorian physiognomy was associated with disciplinary technologies and anthropological classification of urban crowds and exotic peoples, the new physiognomy, Balázs emphasized, would be an art of the people: "The art of reading faces was about to become the very useful property of the masses, thanks to the silent film." If the sweet smile lies, an earlobe, a nostril or, here, a laugh, are entry points into the singular real of a face. See Béla Balázs, *Theory of the Film: Character and Growth of a New Art*, trans. Edith Bone (New York: Dover Publications, 1970), 75. On Benjamin's physiognomy, see Samuel Weber, "Drawing—The Single Trait," *Cahiers Philosophiques de Strasbourg* 27 (forthcoming, 2010).

98. At least one other feminist experimental film could be discussed here: Sally Potter's *Thriller* (1979). See my "'So We Will Go Bad': Cheekiness, Laughter, Film," *Camera Obscura* 21, no. 2/62 (2006), 144–167.

99. Walter Benjamin, "Rückblick auf Chaplin," in *Gesammelte Schriften III* (Frankfurt am Main: Suhrkamp, 1980), 159.

Index